THE
Microsoft® Exchange
GUIDE

THE Microsoft® Exchange GUIDE

Todd Foley
XL Connect Inc.

AP PROFESSIONAL
AP PROFESSIONAL is a division of Academic Press, Inc.

Boston   San Diego   New York
London   Sydney   Tokyo   Toronto

AP PROFESSIONAL
An Imprint of ACADEMIC PRESS, INC.
A Division of HARCOURT BRACE & COMPANY

ORDERS (USA and Canada): 1-800-3131-APP or APP@ACAD.COM
AP Professional Orders: 6277 Sea Harbor Dr., Orlando, FL 32821-9816

Europe/Middle East/Africa: 0-11-44 (0) 181-300-3322
Orders: AP Professional 24–28 Oval Rd., London NW1 7DX

Japan/Korea: 03-3234-3911-5
Orders: Harcourt Brace Japan, Inc., Ichibunan

Australia: 02-517-8999
Orders: Harcourt Brace & Co. Australia, Locked Bag 16, Marrickville, NSW 2204, Australia

Other International: (407) 345-3800
AP Professional Orders: 6277 Sea Harbor Dr., Orlando FL 32821-9816

Editorial: 1300 Boylston St., Chestnut Hill, MA 02167; (617) 232-0500

Web: http://www.apnet.com/

This book is printed on acid-free paper. ∞
Copyright © 1997 by Academic Press, Inc.
All rights reserved.

No part of this publication may be reproduced or transmitted in any form or by any means, electronic or mechanical, including photocopy, recording, or any information storage and retrieval system, without permission in writing from the publisher.

All brand names and product names mentioned in this book are trademarks or registered trademarks of their respective companies.

United Kingdom Edition published by
ACADEMIC PRESS LIMITED
24–28 Oval Road, London NW1 7DX

ISBN 0-12-261915-3

Printed in the United States of America
96 97 98 99 IP 9 8 7 6 5 4 3 2 1

To my wife, Diane

Contents

Introduction   xiii

About This Guide   xv
How Is This Guide Organized?   xv
What Does This Guide Cover?   xvi
Conventions Used in This Guide   xvii
References to Additional Documentation   xviii
From Here   xix

1   What Is Microsoft Exchange?   1

More Than Just "Mail": The Microsoft Exchange Client   2
The Viewer   4
Address Book   7
AutoSignature   8
Mailboxes   9

Public Folders 11
Personal Folders 12
Find 13
Views 14
AutoAssistants 15
Delegate Access 16
Sharing Information 17
Offline Access 18
Getting Started 18
From Here 25

2   Just the Basics   27

New Message Creation 28
Addressing Messages Using the Address Book 32
Sending a Message 34
Opening or Closing a Message 35
Replying to a Message 37
Forwarding a Message 39
Printing and Deleting a Message 40
From Here 41

3   Creating and Sending Mail   43

Formatting Text 44
Finding and Replacing Text within a Message 49
Copying, Moving, or Deleting Information 51
Attaching Files and Embedding Objects 52
Copy To and Blind Copy Addresses 57
Checking Spelling 58
The AutoSignature 60
Saving Incomplete Messages 61
Message Properties 63
From Here 64

Contents ix

4 Addressing and Address Books 65
Using the Global Address List 66
Information about Users: Addressee Properties 70
Using Your Personal Address Book 73
From Here 79

5 Keeping It Under Control: Managing Your Messages 81
Finding Text 82
Filtering Unwanted Messages 85
Sorting Messages 86
Using Views 90
Using Your Assistants 92
Let Someone Else Do It: Secretarial Access 100
From Here 105

6 Customizing the Microsoft Exchange Client 107
Setting Defaults 108
Changing Toolbar Items 115
Hiding Unwanted Screen Elements 119
From Here 120

7 Public and Personal Folders: Sharing and Organizing Information 121
Navigating Public Folders 123
Posting and Replying to Items 125
Using Favorites 129

x   Contents

Creating and Using Shortcuts   131
Folder Properties   133
Folder Design   134
Personal Folders   137
From Here   140

8 The Microsoft Exchange Forms Designer   141

Drag and Drop Programming:
    The Application Design Environment   142
Installing the Microsoft Exchange
    Sample Applications   148
Creating a Microsoft Exchange Application   151
Installing a Form in the Global Forms Registry   153
From Here   155

9 Microsoft Exchange Server Administration   157

Installation and Configuration   158
Setting Up the First Server in a Site   162
Setting Up Additional Servers   187
Setting Up Additional Sites   194
Installing Microsoft Exchange Clients
    from the Network   202
Installing Microsoft Exchange with NetWare   206
Migrating from Other Systems   207
From Here   209

10 Basic Administration   211

Running the Administrator Program   212
DS Site Configuration   215

Contents xi

Information Store Configuration 217
Message Transfer Agent Configuration 221
Setting Up Default Site Addressing 223
Configuring the Public Information Store 226
Setting Mailbox Properties 228
From Here 231

11 Configuring Connectors to Foreign Systems 233

Configuring the X.400 Connector 234
Configuring the Microsoft Mail Connector 236
Hooking Up to the Internet:
   Configuring the Internet Mail Connector 242
From Here 249

12 Administrative Maintenance Tasks 251

Information Store Maintenance 252
Offline IS Maintenance 254
Verifying DS/IS Consistency 257
Configuring Administrative Monitors 259
From Here 264

13 Load Simulator 265

Setting the Test Topology 268
Creating the User Initialization Profile 272
Creating the Public Folder
   Initialization Profile 275
Setting Load Simulation Parameters 276
From Here 281

14 Customizing Microsoft Exchange   283

Modifying Custom Attributes	284
Modifying Details Templates	286
One-Off Address Templates	290
From Here	293

15 Key Management Server: Digital Encryption Security   295

Server Location and Hardware Configuration	297
Server Software Installation	298
Mailbox Security Properties	301
Using the Bulk Security Token Generator	304
From Here	306

16 Windows NT's Interaction with Exchange   307

Services Control Panel	308
Windows NT Backup	310
The User Manager for Domains	312
Windows NT Event Viewer	314
Windows NT Performance Monitor	316
In Conclusion	319

Index   321

Introduction

In just the past few years the entire concept of PC software has changed from one of simple, individual-user applications to one that includes dynamic new platforms for group interaction. This switch from "one-ware" to the concept of "groupware" (software that enables groups of people to interact simultaneously) has revolutionized the way companies manage their essential business needs.

Microsoft Exchange is the hot new entry into the groupware arena. Offering tight interaction with existing Microsoft Office and Microsoft Backoffice products, Exchange allows businesses to leverage their existing desktop and LAN systems to achieve something altogether remarkable—a "virtual workplace" wherein individual employees have instant shared access not only to documents and information but to each other and the global Internet community as well.

xiv Introduction

Other products have claimed the groupware mantle, and software developers have for years been heralding the advent of the paperless office, but Microsoft Exchange represents the first of a new generation of products truly delivering on those early promises. Developed to compete feature by feature with the success of Lotus Notes, and uniquely adapted to extend the functionality of companies' existing desktop software investments, Microsoft Exchange is already the messaging backbone of many Fortune 500 companies.

What does Exchange really do? Almost anything that can be done on a computer—and some things that can be done only on *many* computers. Microsoft Exchange enables the creation of bulletin boards that allow users to discuss common topics and key business challenges and even have quick online meetings. Real-time online conversations can include video, sound, photos, and charts—even up-to-the-second stock quotes and sales figures. Software developers at Exchange sites in Boston and Silicon Valley can review programs as they are being written, modify them together, and send completed modifications to a client in Paris—as quickly as if everyone were in the same room. On a more mundane level, a potluck dinner can be organized in minutes, with all attendees able to discuss and list their contributions so that the potato salad is kept to a minimum and nobody shows up with "zucchini surprise."

If you're wondering "Where's the catch?" then you probably haven't seen the thousands of pages of documentation that Microsoft provides for Microsoft Exchange Server and its associated components. Never fear, however. The basic installation and use of Microsoft Exchange are relatively straightforward. Users of the Exchange Client find a program immediately understandable due to its similarity to other Microsoft Office applications, down to "Cue Cards" and "Wizards" that make even advanced features easy to implement. Administrators find they know a large part of Microsoft Exchange already—since existing Windows NT programs like User Manager, Performance Monitor, and NT Backup are used by Microsoft Exchange. This book provides a much simpler way of getting the information and answers you need about Microsoft Exchange, without memorizing the first 1000 pages of *The Microsoft Exchange Server Administrator's Guide*.

About This Guide

This guide is designed to provide a good, rip-roaring read for the person interested in learning everything about Microsoft Exchange—but its primary use is meant to be as a handy reference guide for both users and administrators. The day will come when, as a user of Microsoft Exchange, you simply must set up a Public Folder to hold all the entries in your company's "Name the Company Mascot" contest. Or perhaps you're a network administrator tasked with hooking your company's e-mail up to the Internet. In either case, this book should provide you with quick, simple answers to your questions—without spending thousands of dollars on a two-week course and twenty pounds of documentation.

How Is This Guide Organized?

This guide is separated into two main sections. The first is dedicated to the Microsoft Exchange Client and is the main section most end users will need to consult. The second is dedicated to Microsoft Exchange Server administration and provides ready answers for those entrusted with installing and maintaining Microsoft Exchange within their organization. Both sections begin with the basics. The Client section starts with simple e-mail use. The Administration section commences with a straightforward single-server installation. Each section then expands on the functionality of Microsoft Exchange in the sequence in which a user would normally learn and use it. This allows you to use this guide as a teaching tool as well as offering intuitive access to information by functionality. Finding out how to best set up your Exchange Server's disk drives is simple with this guide—just look under "Installation—How to Configure Disk Drives." The alternative is to carefully read the dense section on the "I/O Subsystem" in Chapter 5 of the *Microsoft Exchange Server Concepts and Planning Guide.* Who has that kind of time?

What Does This Guide Cover?

This guide endeavors to cover all of the salient points a Microsoft Exchange user or administrator would need to know, including:

- How to just get by
- How to use the Exchange Client
- How to manage messages and documents
- How to use Public Folders
- How to use Exchange from a laptop

- How to use the Microsoft Exchange Forms Designer
- How to set up an Exchange Server
- How to administer Exchange
- How to test and maintain Exchange Server
- How to connect Exchange to the Internet
- How to implement digital security

This guide also includes, in the immortal words of every late-night television advertisement ever made, "Much, much more!"

Conventions Used in This Guide

This guide contains special comments at various key points. These comments might be used to clarify a particularly complicated procedure, offer battle-tested advice or shortcuts, or simply try to scare you silly about areas that offer potential problems. There are three types of comments—Notes, Tips, and Cautions. They will be found positioned beneath the material to which they refer and will be identified by the following icons:

 Important information about a particular topic

 Advice or shortcuts in using Exchange

 Alerts about where special care must be taken

While describing procedures for accomplishing different things within Microsoft Exchange, certain conventions

xviii   Introduction

will be used to indicate required user input. User input will be in boldface, and key names will be named as they appear on the keyboard and displayed as follows: **ESC, CTRL, ALT, DEL, INS, ENTER, NUM LOCK, PRTSC, PGUP**, and so forth.

Simultaneous keypress combinations will be indicated by hyphens (**ALT-C**), while sequences of keypress combinations will be indicated by commas (**ALT-C, B, CTRL-C**).

User menu selections will be in boldface and capitalized (**FILE**), while nested menu selections will be indicated by ellipses (**FILE...OPEN**).

References to Additional Documentation

This guide covers and extends topics covered in the following twenty pounds of documentation:

- *Microsoft Exchange Server Concepts and Planning Guide*
- *Microsoft Exchange Server Installation Guide*
- *Microsoft Exchange Getting Started Guide*
- *Microsoft Exchange Server Application Designer's Guide*
- *Microsoft Exchange Server Administrator's Guide*

From Here

You now ought to be able to say "groupware" with a straight face (or maybe with only a small grimace), as well as have a feel for how this guide is laid out. In the next chapter you'll find out more about what Exchange is and can do and check out its basic components. Right after that comes a crash course in "just getting by"—getting running on how to use Microsoft Exchange for basic e-mail. Ready? Set? Here we go!

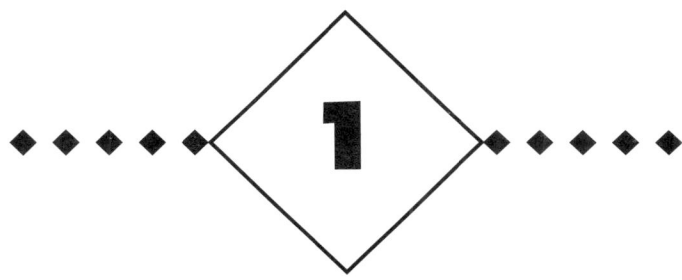

WHAT IS MICROSOFT EXCHANGE?

What is Microsoft Exchange exactly? How do you "start it up" and begin to take advantage of its functionality?

Microsoft Exchange is not just one software application. It is a client/server system with several components. An Exchange Client, an Administration program, the Exchange Forms Designer, the Load Simulator, the Migration Wizard, and other tools together make up Microsoft Exchange. Most users will have hands-on use of only the Exchange Client, the main user interface to the Microsoft Exchange Information Store. The Exchange Client is the only way to directly read mail, post information to Public Folders, run forms applications, etc. It is the key that unlocks the power of Exchange.

2 What Is Microsoft Exchange?

More Than Just "Mail": The Microsoft Exchange Client

Many users will already be familiar with the concept of *e-mail*, text messages sent electronically from computer to computer. The Exchange Client (Figure 1.1) allows you to send e-mail to anyone else connected to your computer—via a network connection at work, a phone line at home, even through the Internet. Unlike some other e-mail systems, Exchange allows you to send more then just text messages. Color graphics, audio and video clips, different fonts and colors for your messages are all supported—allowing you to let others see anything you can create or imagine. With Exchange, you could send your grandmother in Timbuktu a picture of your Memorial Day cookout along with a decorated color birthday card that plays "Yankee Doodle Dandy" when she opens it up—mere seconds after it's sent. This assumes, of course, that your grandmother lives in Timbuktu.

Figure 1.1: The Microsoft Exchange Client

Exchange also goes a step further with e-mail, providing solutions for the unique problems that e-mail creates. It's possible to overload on e-mail, receiving hundreds of messages a day from fellow Exchange users or from automated *mailing lists*, automated mailings sent to large lists of users interested in the same subject. Exchange provides *Filters* to screen out unimportant messages and *Views* to allow you to sort your messages by importance, topic, sender—any combination of criteria you can conceive.

E-mail is only the tip of the iceberg when it comes to the functionality Exchange provides, but it is the basis for them all. Document sharing and management, discussion groups, application development—all the advanced functions Exchange offers use e-mail as a transport, or means of moving information about. This doesn't quite mean that an Exchange program that displays sales totals for the year actually writes a letter to an Exchange server telling it what it's going to do, but it does use the *messaging backbone* (the basic technology that enables e-mail to be sent) Exchange provides to perform any number of advanced operations. It's called a messaging "backbone" because it performs a function similar to the human spine—it provides the framework for all kinds of programs to run, all kinds of group interactivity to occur, without having to worry about individual computer issues or special application training. Once you're using Exchange on your computer, you already have the ability to run everything you might develop—a company Help Desk, a Human Resource Employee Handbook, a system for tracking employee stock purchases—and without having to learn a whole new system.

It's easy to make the mistake of thinking of Exchange as "just e-mail," since that's the most frequently used

4   What Is Microsoft Exchange?

function of Exchange. It's not just e-mail. Basic e-mail is only a small percentage of the total functionality Exchange offers. Before continuing on about all that Exchange can do, however, it makes sense to take a look at what Exchange *is* by introducing you to the component parts of the Exchange Client.

The Viewer

The Microsoft Exchange Client's main window is called the *Viewer*, since it is used to view mail and folder contents (Figure 1.2).

The left side of the Viewer contains a listing of folders, not unlike a directory listing in Windows' File Manager. The right side contains the contents of those folders— again, just like files are displayed in File Manager. Starting

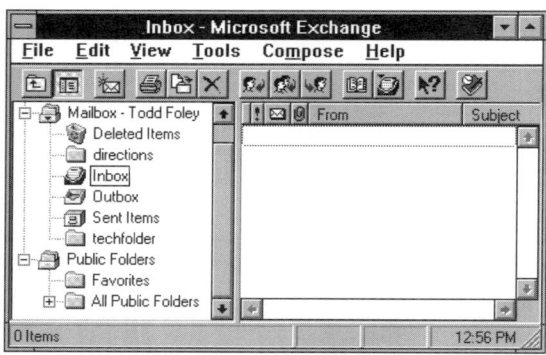

Figure 1.2:   The Exchange Viewer

to see a trend? Right you are! Microsoft intentionally designed the Exchange Viewer to be as similar as possible to File Manager and other Windows programs in order to make using Exchange as simple as possible. As a general rule, if you see something in Exchange that looks like it might work the same way as something in a different Windows program like Microsoft Word or Excel, chances are it does.

To open up a folder and display its contents in the *folder contents list* (the right side of the screen), just click on it with your mouse. You can click on the listed name of the folder or on the folder icon itself. Different icons are used within the Viewer to provide information about folders in the *folder list* (the left side of the window). These icons are as follows:

Closed Folder
This icon represents a closed folder.

Open Folder
This icon represents an opened folder. It is the folder whose contents are currently being displayed in the folder contents list.

Folder Group
This icon represents one of the three main top-level groupings of folders. These are used to distinguish between Public Folders, your Mailbox, and your Personal Folder contents.

A Big Plus Sign
This icon is used to let you know there's more stuff within a folder than is currently being displayed in the Viewer's folder listing. Clicking on this icon will show all of the contents of a folder.

6 What Is Microsoft Exchange?

> **A Big Minus Sign**
> This icon is used to let you know you have already displayed all of the contents of a folder. Clicking on this icon will hide the folder contents from display in the folder listing.

The folder contents list on the right has lots of useful information, too. You can open up and view any item listed in the folder contents list just by double-clicking on it. The listed contents have icons of their own, providing information on the types of items they represent—normal messages, posts to a folder, items with attachments, high-priority messages, etc. The most commonly used icons are as follows:

> **A Normal Message**
> This icon represents a regular Exchange e-mail. If it has other files attached to it, it will also have an attachment icon.

> **An Attachment**
> This icon, always visible directly next to another message icon, indicates that there is another file attached to the message. Opening the message displays the attachment.

> **High Priority**
> This icon, always visible directly next to another message icon, indicates that the sender has designated a particular message as one of high priority.

> **Folder Posting**
> This icon represents a message that someone posted directly to the folder, rather than one that was sent via e-mail. A folder posting is in all other ways just like a regular message.

Application Icon
Items in an Exchange folder can include plain text documents, Microsoft Word documents, Excel spreadsheets—anything that can exist on your computer. Exchange uses the application's normal icon to represent their file type within the folder contents listing.

Address Book

The Address Book (Figure 1.3) contains (you guessed it) all of the predefined e-mail addresses available to you for scheduling and for sending or forwarding e-mail. You automatically open your Address Book whenever you click on the "To" button when creating a new message, or you may call the Address Book directly from the Exchange Client menu **TOOLS...ADDRESS BOOK** option.

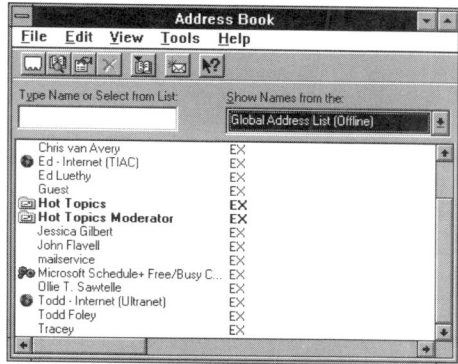

Figure 1.3: The Address Book

8 What Is Microsoft Exchange?

The Address Book also contains detailed information about each individual addressee, available by double-clicking on the addressee's name. This detailed information can include a full street address, phone number, the name of the addressee's secretary, boss, everyone who reports to them, their shoe size, what their favorite color is, etc. The Exchange Address Book can serve as a replacement for printed company directories and provide a wealth of information beyond the address itself.

More than one address listing exists within the Address Book. The *Global Address List* is the default listing and contains all of the addresses of *recipients* (people or groups who can receive e-mail) within your entire organization. Every Exchange user also has a *Personal Address Book* where they can copy their most commonly used addresses from the Global Address List for quick access, as well as store special Internet addresses or even their own distribution lists. If you wanted to create a distribution list that let you mail the "Joke of the Day" to your twenty closest friends with the push of a button, then the Personal Address Book is where you'd do it. You might have other address listings as well, such as a Microsoft Mail post office listing, if your Exchange Server is connected to other systems. For the most part you'll be using the Global Address List—the place where all the addresses you need should be located.

AutoSignature

The Exchange Client allows you to "sign" every message using AutoSignature, a feature allowing predefined standard

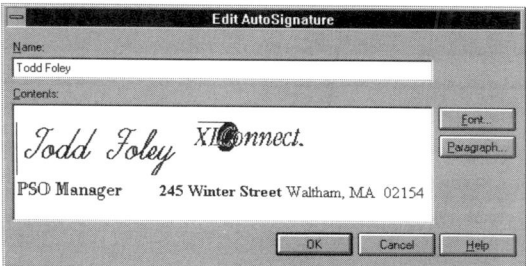

Figure 1.4: Creating an AutoSignature

closings to your messages. Just as within a regular e-mail message, an AutoSignature may include graphics, different fonts and colors for text—even embedded audio clips. Sure beats a rubber stamp! The AutoSignature may be bypassed if desired for a particular message, and more than one AutoSignature may be created in case you'd like to have different signatures for different types of messages. This last feature is particularly useful when your boss doesn't appreciate the "World's Greatest Bowler" signature you've been attaching to all of your e-mail messages. The AutoSignature editing tool (Figure 1.4) is accessible via the **TOOLS...AUTOSIGNATURE** option on the **Viewer** menu.

Mailboxes

Your Mailbox is one of the three main folder groups visible in the folder list (along with Personal Folders and Public Folders). All mail is delivered to your Mailbox, and all

10 What Is Microsoft Exchange?

messages sent, deleted, replied to, or somehow manipulated are found here as well. To organize your messages, the Exchange Mailbox contains, by default, four subfolders that cannot be deleted. You may also create any number of additional subfolders to organize messages to your liking. The four default subfolders and their functions are as follows:

Mailbox Subfolder	Function
Inbox	All your new mail arrives here. Items that you haven't read yet are displayed in bold type.
Outbox	A folder that holds mail that you send until it is delivered. The Outbox is frequently checked for outgoing mail, so messages rarely stay here for more than a few seconds unless you're on a laptop, not connected to the Exchange Server. This folder is used only as a queue by the Exchange Client—if you want to review messages you've sent, look in the Sent Items folder.
Sent Items	This folder stores a copy of each message that you send. You may review any old messages you've sent within it, unless you've deleted them from this folder.
Deleted Items	This folder is the "safety net" for items that you've deleted. If you delete something by accident, you can find it here and move it to another folder. The safety net doesn't hold forever, though—by default, everything in the Deleted Items folder is erased for good when you exit Microsoft Exchange.

Public Folders

Public Folders are one of the three main folder groups visible in the folder list (along with Personal Folders and your Mailbox). Public Folders are similar to your Mailbox Inbox in terms of what they can contain and how their contents are read, but there is a unique distinction—other users can read them also. This ability to have any Exchange user read and post messages to a central, shared location (a Public Folder) is one of the most powerful features of Exchange. A detailed memo no longer needs to be sent out to hundreds of people—it can be posted in a Public Folder for all concerned to view. By displaying responses to the memo in the same folder you can create an instant online discussion group—and use it to resolve issues without face-to-face meetings, phone conferences, or circulation of printed memos. Public Folders can also be convenient repositories of reference information. Why distribute hundreds of copies of an employee manual that will need to be constantly reprinted upon each revision? Just place the manual in a Public Folder and everyone will have instant access to the most up-to-date information. The ability to share information with other users is what groupware is all about, and Public Folders offer that functionality right out of the box.

There are other Exchange features that maximize the usefulness of Public Folders, such as forms and Views, but even without special modifications or development, Exchange Public Folders can offer users a tremendous opportunity to share information and work on projects as a unit rather than as a group of individuals.

12 What Is Microsoft Exchange?

 Public Folders aren't necessarily 100% "public." Access rights to specific Public Folders can be set by the folder creator, so that if you want to share information with only some people, you can restrict access to a Public Folder you've created. This is a handy option when you want only your close friends to read items in the "Why My Boss Is a Jerk" Public Folder. This option also explains why you may not be able to read items in your boss's "Who We'll Fire Next" Public Folder.

Personal Folders

Personal Folders are one of the three main folder groups visible in the folder list. Unlike your Mailbox and Public Folders, however, Personal Folders are an optional service for an Exchange administrator to install and may not be available to all users (so if they're not visible within your Exchange Viewer don't worry, you don't need new glasses!). Personal Folders are exactly like Public Folders in almost every way, except that they are not visible to others (that's why they're *Personal* Folders!). Forms, Views— anything that will work in a Public Folder will work in a Personal Folder. This makes Personal Folders especially useful for prototyping applications or just trying out new things before moving them to a Public Folder. They're also very useful to laptop users, who can copy frequently accessed Public Folders to Personal Folders. Personal Folders are stored locally, on the laptop computer itself— unlike Public Folders, which remain on the main Exchange Server. This means that laptop users can access information in Personal Folders without being connected to a network or a phone line.

Find

Once you've sent out your first few hundred messages, looking up a particular one for reference in your Sent Items folder can get to be a little more difficult. Find to the rescue! The Exchange Client's Find tool, accessible from the **TOOLS...FIND** option on the Exchange Client menu, provides you with the ability to quickly locate a message or folder posting (Figure 1.5). Results of a search using the Find tool are displayed in the Find window itself and may be sorted and opened just as in the regular Viewer window.

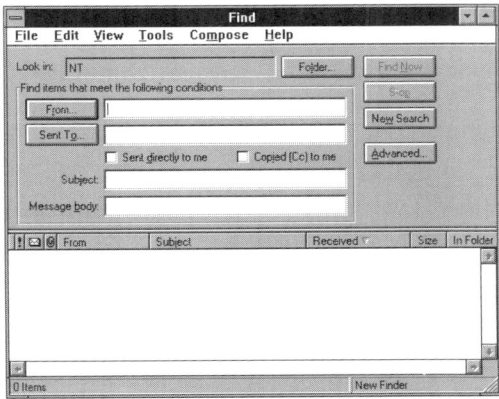

Figure 1.5: Find

14 What Is Microsoft Exchange?

Find allows searches on any word or words contained within a message or posting, as well as on message subject, sender, size, date, importance—almost any criterion. If you are often "copied in" on messages, Find also allows you to limit your searches to messages addressed directly to you—a handy way to get quick results. When searching large amounts of content, the proverbial "needle in a haystack" becomes a little less elusive thanks to Find.

Views

Another key tool in managing information with the Exchange Client gives you the ability to construct special Views, accessible from the **VIEW...DEFINE VIEWS** option on the Exchange Client menu. Views are custom ways of looking at folder content—special ways of grouping and sorting information. The same way you use Find to locate items based on specific search criteria, you can use Views to display information based on special criteria. You can sort all the items in your Inbox by date, or by who sent the e-mail to you, or both. This View can be saved as a *Personal View*, a set of display criteria that only you may invoke, or as a *Folder View*, a set of display criteria that are applicable only within a specific Exchange Folder. If you save a View as a Personal View, you can apply it to *any* folder you wish—Public Folders, Personal Folders—even your Inbox. If you save a View as a Folder View then it can be used only within a specific folder—but if it's a Public Folder then anyone can use your View there! If you are the creator of a Public Folder, you can specify any Folder

View as the default way that everyone sees information in the folder. This is useful if you are using a Public Folder to store something like a status report, which you might want to sort by date, rather than the default View, which sorts items by who sent the report.

AutoAssistants

Microsoft Exchange provides you with two AutoAssistants to help you manage your messages—an Inbox Assistant and an Out of Office Assistant. They both allow you to set up *Rules*, automatically triggered predefined actions, that can be used to sort, move, respond to, forward, or delete your messages—before you've even seen them. AutoAssistants are like electronic secretaries. They screen your messages, alert you to important ones, and let people know if you're unavailable. By providing people who send you messages with a quick reply if you're away from your computer, e-mail becomes as quick and reliable as the phone—no more wondering when someone will read a message you've sent, because you know that if they weren't at their desk an AutoAssistant would have told you so.

The Inbox Assistant manages all messages you receive directly. You can ask it to sort your messages for you by moving messages to special subfolders based on importance, who the message is from, or subject. If you like, you can have it automatically forward any message from your boss and containing the word "Monday" to a coworker, allowing you to take longer weekends (it might work!).

16 What Is Microsoft Exchange?

The Out of Office Assistant, when activated, sends an automated response to anyone who sends you an e-mail. It might say "Out to lunch—back at 1 pm," "On vacation—back on Monday," or simply "Gone fishing." Just as with an AutoSignature, multicolored text, graphics, and audio clips may be used to create your automated reply. While on vacation, you could respond to incoming e-mail messages with an "electronic postcard"—perhaps a graphic image of Disney World that played an audio clip of "It's a Small World." The Out of Office Assistant, like the Inbox Assistant, also allows for intelligent processing of incoming messages. You could use this feature to have your mail forwarded to someone else while you were away.

Delegate Access

If the automatic secretary that Exchange AutoAssistants provide doesn't do everything you need, then it's possible to delegate access to your Exchange Mailbox to a real secretary. You can grant a secretary access to any subfolder, including your Inbox, within your Mailbox. This would allow the secretary to sort messages for you. You may also give "Send on Behalf of" permission to a secretary.

If "Send on Behalf of" permission is granted, then the secretary's name appears after "From" and your name appears after "Sent on Behalf of" in messages that are sent. You can grant this level of access directly in the Microsoft Exchange Client from the Exchange Server tab of the **TOOLS...OPTIONS** window available from the main menu.

Sharing Information

Just as you can give a secretary Delegate Access to one or all of your mailbox folders, you may also grant any Exchange user the ability to share information you have in your Mailbox. To allow others to access one of your Mailbox folders, highlight the folder and use the Permissions tab of the File Properties window available from the main menu. You may select anyone from the Global Address List and grant them any of several levels of access to your folder. You're not done there, however. For someone to access information in the Mailbox folder to which you've given them permission, they must then modify their Viewer options to open your Mailbox as well as theirs. They can do this from the main menu by selecting the **TOOLS...SERVICES** option to bring up the Services window; then they must highlight the Microsoft Exchange Server option, click the **Properties** button, select the Advanced tab, click the **Add** button, and type in your Mailbox name. Sound complicated? It is! Fortunately, Microsoft Exchange provides a much simpler way to routinely share information—the Public Folder. Creating a Public Folder and sharing information between groups of users is simple compared to granting Delegate Access to your Mailbox folders. Simply select the **FILE...NEW FOLDER** option from the main menu, and place any content that needs to be shared within the Public Folder.

Offline Access

You don't need to be connected to your network at work in order to use Microsoft Exchange. Laptop users and home users may connect at scheduled intervals or only when they need to send or receive messages. Personal Folders may be used to copy frequently accessed Public Folders, so that group resources are still available to the disconnected user. Perhaps most important to those pressed for time, Exchange offers the ability to quickly receive just the *header:* the author's name, date received, and subject of the message. The headers that you would like to read can then be marked and *downloaded* (transferred from work to a laptop over a phone line). This allows remote users to receive only messages they want to read, without having to wait for "junk mail" to be downloaded over a slow telephone connection.

Getting Started

Once you're familiar with the basic components of the Microsoft Exchange Client and have a good start on understanding the capabilities that Microsoft Exchange has, it might make sense to learn how to start the whole thing up in the first place. You'd think it would be pretty straightforward since it is a Windows-based program—just click on the Exchange icon, right? Well—yes. But since Microsoft Exchange is more than just a single software program (groupware, remember?) it requires a few preliminary steps. Before you can start Exchange, you must first be connected to the network, and you must have configured Exchange to open *your* Mailbox on startup.

How to Log on to the Network

In order to connect to the Microsoft Exchange Server and send and receive mail, you must log on to the network that the Exchange Server is on (Figure 1.6). Chances are you are already logging on to the network for other purposes. If you are, then there is no need to do anything differently. If not, however, you will have to enter your username and password prior to running Exchange. Once you've entered your information, hit the **OK** button and go on to start Exchange.

The Microsoft Exchange User Profile

Prior to the first time you use Microsoft Exchange, you must set up your Microsoft Exchange user profile, accessible

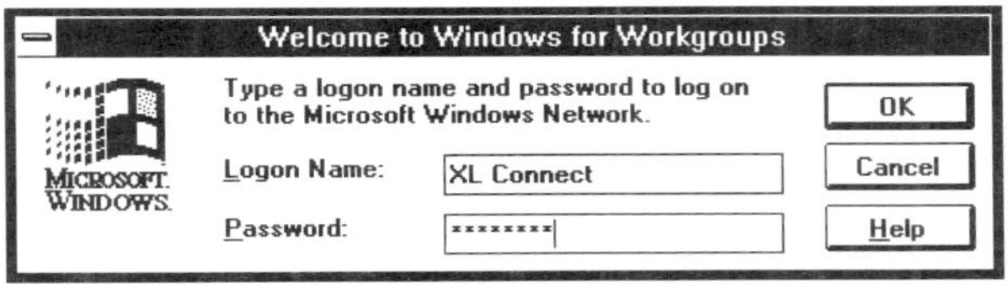

Figure 1.6: A Logon Prompt

20 What Is Microsoft Exchange?

from the Mail and Fax icon in your Windows control panel. To do so, simply click on the **Add** button in the Mail and Fax window (Figure 1.7). This will launch the Microsoft Exchange Setup Wizard, which will prompt you for the name of your Exchange Server as well as your Mailbox name. This information should be provided to you by your Exchange administrator. Once you've typed in the requested information, click on the **Next** and **Finish** buttons to finalize your new profile. That's it! This process need only be done once—provided you continue to use the same machine. If you often use several different machines, you can create a profile for yourself on each machine or ask for your Exchange administrator's help in creating a network-based profile.

If you wish to access your Exchange Mailbox from another computer on the network that someone else is using to access Exchange, you will have to go through this

Figure 1.7: The Mail and Fax Window

Getting Started 21

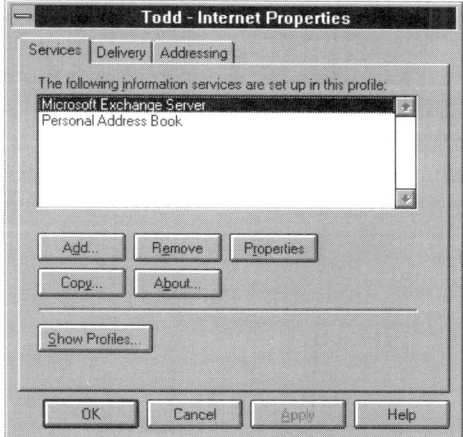

Figure 1.8: An Existing User Profile

process again. The process to do so is the same as the one above—with one important difference. If a user profile already exists on the computer you are using, the Mail and Fax window will initially display the old User Profile and have a **Show Profiles** button visible. Click on this button to show the normal profile creation window, and walk through the setup process discussed earlier. Once completed, change the default startup profile in the main Mail and Fax window to be the one you've just created, and go on to start Microsoft Exchange.

How to Start Microsoft Exchange

To start Exchange, just double-click the Microsoft Exchange icon found in the Microsoft Exchange program group. If that makes sense to you, go ahead and skip the rest of this chapter, dedicated to a review of Windows

22 What Is Microsoft Exchange?

basics. You're ready for a crash course on "just getting by" with Microsoft Exchange. If you're not sure what a program group is, or you'd just like a refresher course on Windows features such as online help, menus, HotKeys, and dialog boxes—stay tuned.

The Microsoft Exchange Icon

Quick Review: The Microsoft Windows Graphical Environment

Most people don't think of Microsoft Windows as a DOS-based application that allows multiple application instances to coexist through frequent switching of processor utilization between applications. What everyone thinks of as Microsoft Windows is actually a separate program called Program Manager. Program Manager is the "main window" that organizes all the different applica-

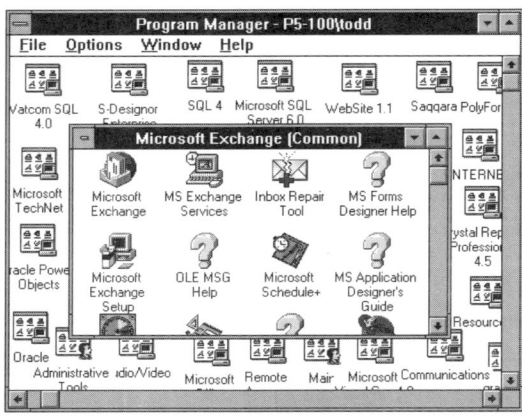

Figure 1.9: The Microsoft Exchange Program Group

tions (represented by small pictures, or *icons*) available to a user into different, smaller windows called *program groups*. Clicking twice on an application icon will start the application. Clicking twice on a program group icon will open the program group window, allowing access to the application icons held within. The program group "window" in Program Manager that Microsoft Exchange creates when installed is labeled, aptly enough, "Microsoft Exchange." The application icon that starts Microsoft Exchange is also labeled "Microsoft Exchange," as shown in Figure 1.9.

Windows, Menus, HotKeys, and Dialog Boxes

In order to navigate successfully within Windows applications, some basic familiarity with common Windows objects is required. The most basic Windows object is—surprise!—the window itself. A *window* is actually an on-screen "box" within which a program runs. There are always three gray buttons on the top of a window—one on the left corner, containing a dash, and two on the right corner, containing up and down arrows. Clicking on the dash button reveals a menu of window manipulation options, including options to close the window, move it, resize it, minimize or maximize it. Clicking on the up arrow button in the top right corner of a window will also maximize it, while the down arrow will minimize it. To minimize a window is to reduce it to icon size. To maximize a window is to make it fill the screen. Once maximized, a window displays a "restore" button containing both an up and a down arrow, which when clicked will return the window to its sizing just prior to having been maximized.

24 What Is Microsoft Exchange?

Menus in windows, such as the one in the Program Manager window, are text options listed on a white horizontal bar just beneath the window's title bar. Clicking on one of these options (FILE, EDIT, VIEW, HELP, etc.) will reveal a list of other nested options that may call other windows or perform specific tasks—such as the **FILE...PRINT** option, which prints selected documents in many programs.

HotKeys are single keystrokes or simultaneous keystroke combinations that trigger menu options without having to select them from the menu. HotKeys, if they exist for a particular function, are usually visible next to the menu option. For instance, if you click on the **EDIT** menu option in most programs, the **COPY** option has a HotKey, **F8**, listed next to it. Hitting the **F8** key within that program is just the same as selecting **EDIT...COPY** from the main menu.

Dialog boxes are special windows that "pop up" in response to some action or event within a program. Typically they require some sort of input before they go away, sometimes something as simple as clicking on an **OK** button. Dialog boxes are windows within windows—used by most programs to ask you a few questions before going on.

The Online Help System in Microsoft Exchange

Help is never far away within Microsoft Exchange. The Exchange Viewer has a **HELP** menu option that will offer access to all of the Microsoft Exchange help topics, complete with a table of contents and full index searching. Exchange also offers "context-sensitive" help, meaning that if you use the **F1** HotKey while using the Viewer,

Exchange looks at what you're in the middle of doing and displays a help topic related to it. Think of **F1** as a panic button—when you need help, it's there. Exchange also offers "point-and-click" help by using a special help icon on the Viewer toolbar. This icon, which looks like a question mark with a mouse pointer next to it, offers a unique aid to identifying items within the Viewer window. Click on the icon, then on any item you're not sure of—another icon, a menu item, whatever. A help screen will then pop up describing the object you clicked on. You can never have too much help—especially when just starting out!

From Here

Got all of that? Don't worry if you don't! This was more of a "30,000 foot overview" of the components and features of the Exchange Client, meant to give you a feel for what could be done with Exchange. You've already seen all of the main pieces of the Exchange Client, and as long as you can now start Exchange up, you're ready for the next chapter's crash course in "just getting by"—how to use Exchange for basic e-mail functions. After that, you'll get a chance to be a real e-mail pro with all of the advanced functions Exchange offers for creating and sending mail.

JUST THE BASICS

You want to stop mucking around and start using Exchange right away, huh? No problem. Using Exchange for basic e-mail functions is as simple as using Windows itself. Learn a few basic functions and you'll be able to do all of the basic things e-mail allows—creating and sending messages, addressing e-mail, reading your e-mail, forwarding, replying, printing, and deleting. If you're willing to settle for "just getting by" with Microsoft Exchange, then these basics will be all you'll need to be a Microsoft Exchange user. If not, then these functions will be the building blocks for all kinds of advanced functions and wizardly tricks. Get ready, it's crash course time!

New Message Creation

If you're going to use e-mail, you've first got to know how to create a new message (if you used only old messages, then the fun would go out of "Watson, come here—I need you" pretty quickly). To begin, start Microsoft Exchange and open up the Viewer. Remember, the Viewer is the main window of the Microsoft Exchange Client. If your profile was set up correctly, all you should need to do to start Exchange and open the Viewer is to double-click on the Microsoft Exchange icon. If it wasn't that easy (Murphy's law strikes again!), then take another look at the "Getting Started" section in the previous chapter.

Once Exchange is up and running, you can begin creating a new message by clicking on the envelope icon on the

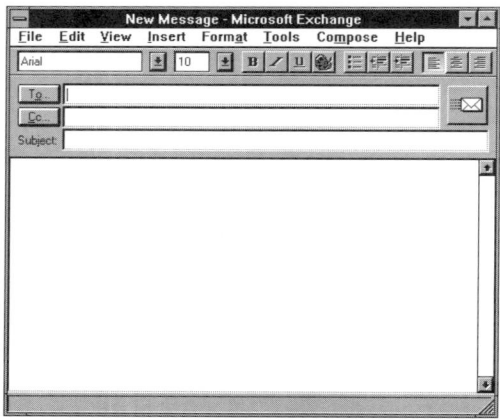

Figure 2.1: The New Message Window

New Message Creation 29

toolbar (a gray bar right under the menu that holds icons that perform frequently used functions). This opens the New Message window (Figure 2.1). You could also open the New Message window by using the **CTRL-N** HotKey or by selecting the **COMPOSE...NEW MESSAGE** menu option. If you find all the options confusing, don't worry—there's no wrong way to begin creating a new message. Most of the important functions in Exchange have three different ways to be executed, just like the function to open the New Message window. You can use whichever you find easiest—or mix and match as the mood strikes you. The three common methods of doing things in the Viewer and the way they are used to begin creating a new message are:

1. **The toolbar:** Click on the envelope icon.
2. **HotKeys:** Hit the **CTRL** button and the letter **N** on the keyboard at the same time.
3. **The menu:** Select the **NEW MESSAGE** option found beneath the **COMPOSE** menu item.

The Compose New Message Icon on the Viewer Toolbar

The New Message window is actually an Exchange *form*, a specially designed window used for entering or viewing specific types of information. Exchange forms are just like paper forms—they make it easier to enter information (unless it has something to do with health insurance and a visit to your doctor). In this case, the New Message form is set up to make it easy for you to create a new message. All you have to do is "fill in the blanks" and enter information into the form *fields*, boxes for typing in information on a form. The four default fields on the New Message form are as follows:

- **To:** Type the e-mail address of the person to whom you wish to send the message into this field.
- **CC:** "CC" stands for "carbon copy." Type the e-mail address of someone you wish to receive a copy of the message into this field.
- **Subject:** Type the subject of the message into this field.
- **Unlabeled big white box:** Type the actual message into this field.

To begin, place the *cursor*, the blinking placeholder that marks where your typing is entered, into the **To:** field. You can move the cursor by clicking on a box with your mouse or by tapping the **TAB** key. Type the e-mail address of the person to whom you wish to send the message into the field.

Exchange gives you three options for entering an address (more choices again!). You can:

1. Type the e-mail address itself.
2. Type the person's name.
3. Click on the **To:** button and choose from the Address Book.

We'll look at using the Address Book in just a second, and it's probably the easiest way to address a message. This is because the first two options, typing a name or an address directly into the field, require that you type the name or address exactly as it's listed with Exchange, without any spelling errors. If you do decide to type a name or address, then you can use the **Check Names** feature of Exchange to verify what you've typed. You can select the **TOOLS...CHECK NAMES** option from the menu or use the **CTRL-K** HotKey to have Exchange examine all names and addresses in the **To:** and **CC:** fields. If the names and addresses in those fields are correct, then they will be underlined. If incorrect, you will be prompted to either choose from the Address Book or create a new address.

You may enter two or more addresses in the **To:** field by separating them with semicolons. Why, then, is there a **CC:** field? What's the difference between entering two names in the **To:** field or one in the **To:** field and one in the **CC:** field? Well, whether you enter an address in the **To:** or the **CC:** field, the person will still receive the message. You should use the **To:** field, however, for the person or persons for whom the message is directly written, and the **CC:** field for "FYI" recipients whom you wish to receive a copy but who do not necessarily need to read the message immediately. This allows you (and all other users) to use Exchange's Views and Filters to manage your messages by reading the messages addressed directly to you first and messages that you are "copied in on" second.

Be sure to enter a description of the message in the **Subject:** field. Recipients will see this description in the message header, before opening the message for reading. Laptop users often decide which messages to download based on the subject and other header information. A good **Subject:** description allows recipients to quickly ascertain the contents of the message, as well as letting them sort, find, and filter messages with greater ease.

The bottom half of the New Message form is an unlabeled text entry field that you should type or paste your message into. The field will allow multiple lines to be entered, and it scrolls to allow you to place extremely large messages in the small visible window.

Addressing Messages Using the Address Book

The easiest way to address messages is to click on the **To:** button on the New Message form and choose a name from the Address Book (Figure 2.2). The Address Book is actually a collection of address books—the Global Address List, a Personal Address Book, and possibly a Post Office Address Book (if Exchange is connecting to a Microsoft Mail system). The default Address Book is the Global Address List, and it contains the names of all of the recipients within a Microsoft Exchange organization in alphabetical order.

When called from the New Message form's **To:** button, the Address Book offers an additional "recipients" window

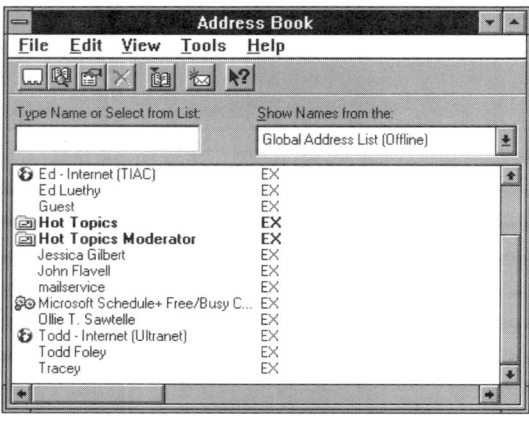

Figure 2.2: The Address Book

Addressing Messages Using the Address Book 33

containing the addresses selected as recipients for the current message. Selecting any name in the Address Book and then clicking on the **To** or **CC** button in this window will place the name in the appropriate field in the New Message form—no typing or spelling check required! Just click on the **OK** button when all recipients have been selected and your message is addressed.

To find a name in the Address Book, you can scroll through the list or use one of the Address Book search features. Simplest to use is the "smart" **Type Name** field (the Address Book has entry fields—it is an Exchange form just like the New Message form) in the top left-hand corner of the Address Book. Just start typing the name for which you're searching into this field, and the list will automatically scroll to the name closest to matching what you've typed. The more letters you type, the more exact the match. This feature can be used instead of or in conjunction with the **Find** button, which brings up a dialog box with a **Find Names Beginning With** field. Entering a letter or letters into this field and selecting **OK** will filter the names visible in the Address Book, limiting them to just names beginning with the entered letter(s). When used together, these search features allow even the largest listing of names to be navigated quickly.

Not sure to which "John Smith" you wish to send an e-mail message? Try selecting the name in the Address Book and clicking on the **Properties** button. Doing so will pop up detailed information about the addressee, including job title, phone number, department, and manager.

Remember to click on the **OK** button once all recipients have been selected or the **Cancel** button to discard selected names.

Sending a Message

Now that you've created your message, what are you going to do with it? If your goal is to send it immediately, then you have three options (choices again!). There's a big, friendly flying envelope icon in the top right-hand corner of the New Message form. Clicking on that icon with your mouse will speed your message on its way. If you have manually typed addresses or names into the **To:** or **CC:** field, they are automatically checked just before sending your message. Just as if you had used the **Check Names** option, errors in addressing will bring up a window allowing you to choose from names similar to the one(s) in error or to create a new address.

Don't like the flying envelope? You also have a HotKey and a menu option to choose from. To send a message from the New Message form immediately, choose any of the following:

Sending a Message from the New Message Form

Method	Option
Toolbar	Not really on a toolbar—click on the flying envelope icon in top right corner of the form
HotKey	**CTRL-ENTER**
Menu item	**FILE...SEND**

If you don't wish to send a message immediately, you also have the option of saving it for later. To save the unsent message in your Exchange Inbox, use the **FILE...SAVE** option on your New Message form. You can open the message later, edit it if desired, and then send it.

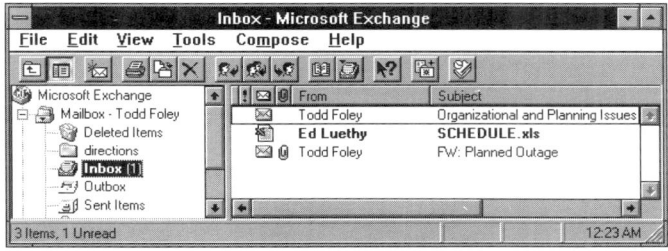

Figure 2.3: Message Listings in the Exchange Viewer

You may also save the message outside Exchange using the **FILE...SAVE AS** option to save the unsent message to a local or network drive. You'll learn more about saving messages in the next chapter.

Opening or Closing a Message

Now that you've sent a message, you probably want to be able to read messages, too. Or maybe you've just saved a message and you want to open it up again to edit and send it. Opening messages in Microsoft Exchange is easy. Just click on the folder (the Inbox if you've just saved or received a message) in the Viewer, and then double-click on any part of the message header in the folder contents listing (Figure 2.3). You could also click on the header once and then hit **ENTER**, or use the **FILE...OPEN** menu option—but I'll go out on a limb on this one and recommend double-clicking as the easiest way to go. Once open, you'll notice that the message looks different than it would in a New Message form. Exchange uses a special

Read Message form when you open messages. The Read Message form has a toolbar and displays who the message was from and when it was sent—otherwise it's pretty much like the New Message form.

Exchange opens a new window for each open message, so it's important to close messages once you've read them (or else you'll end up with a whole lot of open windows, which can slow down your system). One way to avoid opening simultaneous message windows is to use the Previous and Next icons on the toolbar of the Read Message form, represented by an up arrow icon and a down arrow icon, respectively. Clicking on the Previous icon will close the current message and open the message immediately prior to the current one in the folder contents listing. Clicking on the Next icon will (you guessed it!) close the current message and open the message immediately after the current one in the folder contents listing. The various methods of using the Previous and Next functions are as follows:

Scanning Messages with the Read Message Form

Method	Previous	Next
Toolbar	Up arrow icon	Down arrow icon
HotKey	**CTRL-<**	**CTRL->**
Menu item	View...Previous	View...Next

If you aren't scanning through messages, or if you simply want to close a single message, then the methods used to close any Windows window can be used. You can double-click on the dash icon in the top left corner of the window or use the **FILE...CLOSE** menu option or the **ALT-F4** HotKey. Don't worry about exiting too soon—closing a message window won't close out Exchange altogether.

Replying to a Message

You've got creating and sending a message down now, and you can open up and read your mail. But what do you do when you want to reply to a message? You could just create a new message to the person who sent you the original message, but it's much easier to use the **Reply** functions of the Read Message form to do all the hard work of addressing and including text from the original message for you. It's simple—just select the **COMPOSE** menu item and then the **Reply to Sender, Reply to All,** or **Post Reply in this Folder** option. What? Too many Reply options? Well, **Reply to Sender** is probably the Reply option you want. Selecting it will open up a New Message form with the **To:** field already filled with the name of the person who sent you the message and the **Subject:** field filled out with "RE:" followed by the original message subject. Also, the full header and body of the original message will be indented and listed in the New Message Form's main message text field (in case the sender forgot what was said in the original message).

The **Reply to All** option will do the same things as the **Reply to Sender** option, with one exception. All original recipients will receive replies. This means that if someone else received the same original message you did, they will receive a copy of your reply as well. This is a handy feature if you have to keep everybody "in the loop," but it can create a lot of unnecessary mail messages if used indiscriminately. It's best to get in the practice of using the **Reply to Sender** option in order to avoid creating "junk mail" for everybody on the original mailing list.

38 Just the Basics

The **Post Reply in this Folder** option is like the **Reply to Sender** option, except that it doesn't really reply at all. Rather than send your reply to the original sender, it *posts* it (saves the message within a folder) instead. This option is useful only if the original message is located in a Public Folder, where others can see the original message and your posted response. If the original message was sent directly to you, then using this option will just post your reply into your Inbox, where only you could read it. No point in talking to yourself any more than you already do.

The various methods of using the Reply functions are as follows:

Method	Reply to Sender	Reply to All	Post Reply in This Folder
Toolbar	Icon of an arrow pointing toward a person's head	Icon of an arrow pointing toward two peoples' heads	By default, no toolbar icon displayed
HotKey	**CTRL-R**	**CTRL-SHIFT-R**	No HotKey
Menu item	**Compose... Reply to Sender**	**Compose... Reply to All**	**Compose... Post Reply in This Folder**

Apparently, the **Post Reply in This Folder** option isn't as popular as the others, since Microsoft didn't feel it was worth giving it a HotKey or default toolbar icon. There is, however, a toolbar icon available for the option, and you can add it to your toolbar using the **TOOLS...CUSTOMIZE TOOLBAR** menu option if you use it frequently.

Forwarding a Message

Suppose you get a message that is just so fantastic you have to share it with someone else. Perhaps your boss wrote you a great performance review, or you just received the secret recipe to your Aunt Myrtle's world-famous cole slaw. You need to send that message off to at least a dozen people right away! To do so, just open the message or highlight it in the folder contents listing and then use the **COMPOSE...FORWARD** menu option (or the **CTRL-F** HotKey) to open the Forward Message form.

Once opened, the Forward Message form (Figure 2.4) looks quite a bit like a message reply. The text and header information of the original message is indented and placed at the bottom of the form's main message entry field. The

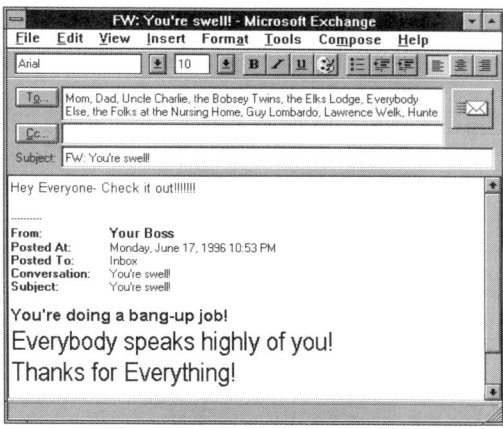

Figure 2.4: Forwarding a Message

Subject: field is prepopulated with the subject of the original message, prefaced by "FW:". All you need to do is address the message, add any additional comments, and send it on its way with a click of the flying envelope.

Printing and Deleting a Message

You ought to be able to send messages whizzing all over the place by now. You can create, send, read, forward, and reply to messages—enough to take care of all the chain letters you'll ever receive. Let's finish up our crash course by figuring out how to "spit 'em out and throw 'em out" or how to print and delete your messages.

Printing messages within Exchange is very similar to printing files using Notepad, Microsoft Word, or any other Windows program. Just use the **FILE...PRINT** menu option or the **CTRL-P** HotKey to print the message you're currently viewing. Exchange will print out the message's header information—who sent it, to whom it was sent, and the subject, as well as the message text. Any attachments to the message will not be printed this way. To print attachments, the attachment must be opened up separately and printed. Exchange will also not completely print out the message form. You'll print the message header and text, but the field boxes, the flying envelope icon, even the **To:** button are unrendered on your printer. Not exactly *WYSI-WYG* (what you see is what you get), but it will properly print out font sizes and even colors and images. Who needs a flying envelope printed out, anyhow!

Deleting messages within Exchange is easy to do as well—just use the **FILE...DELETE** menu option or the **CTRL-D** HotKey. Deleted something by accident? No problem—just look in your Deleted Items folder. By default, any message you delete is saved in this folder until you exit Exchange.

From Here

Congratulations—you've just graduated from the Microsoft Exchange E-Mail Basics Crash Course. You now ought to be able to use the Microsoft Exchange Client for basic e-mail functions—everything you need to just get by. In the next chapter you'll learn how to use all kinds of advanced functions while creating and sending mail—including changing colors and fonts, attaching files, checking your spelling, and jazzing up your messages with photos, audio clips—even movies! After that, you'll get a chance to address e-mail over the Internet and create your own personal mailing lists of hundreds of your closest friends. It's time to become an Exchange wizard!

Creating and Sending Mail

OK! You've gone through the crash course on e-mail use and you're ready to take advantage of the advanced features Exchange has to offer. You're in for a treat—Exchange will allow you to get as creative as you like with your messages. Styles, colors, movies, sounds, the sheet music for the "Star Spangled Banner"—all can be included in your daily e-mail. You can have "secret recipients" whom you can copy in on messages without others knowing. You can end each message with a custom footer, message, or "signature"—automatically. You can create templates or forms for frequent types of correspondence and make certain that "supercalifragilistic" gets spelled correctly every time. Along the way, you'll also find out how to make the features of Exchange work for *you*—allowing you to communicate quickly, effectively, and with style.

Formatting Text

One of the simplest, yet most dramatic, ways to alter the appearance of an e-mail message in Exchange is to alter the formatting of the text. Microsoft Exchange utilizes the *Rich Text Format* (a standard file format allowing extensive formatting information to be embedded along with plain text) to permit different fonts, alignment, text colors, and other formatting features normally found only within advanced word processors such as Microsoft Word. Exchange supports varied typesets—almost any font installed on the client machine.

Changing the Font

How do you do it? To change the font while using the New Message form, place the cursor in the main message text entry window, and use the **FORMAT...FONT** menu option to select from all of the available fonts installed on the client machine. Alternately, highlight the text whose font you wish to alter, and select a new font from the dropdown font list available in the upper left corner of the toolbar. There is an additional dropdown list allowing selection of various font sizes immediately to the right of the font selection dropdown list on the toolbar. Go ahead and get someone's attention by starting your message out with "HEY!" written in giant 48-point Haettenschweiler font. Chances are it's a message that will be read!

Bold, Italics, and Underlining

Perhaps just making the text huge and using a different font isn't enough. If you want to make text stand out in a

Formatting Text 45

normal word processing document, you change the text to be bold, italicized, or underlined. The same may be done simply within Microsoft Exchange. Just as in Microsoft Word, the three most frequently used formatting functions are represented on the New Message form toolbar with **B**, *I*, and U buttons. Highlighting a word and clicking on one of these buttons renders the appropriate formatting upon the highlighted word. You may also use the same **FORMAT...FONT** menu option used to choose font types and sizes to add the appropriate bold, italics, or underline formatting to your message.

Centering and Alignment

Perhaps you wish to entitle your message with a centered header (Figure 3.1). You type your title "My Message" on the first line, then change the font size from the default 10-point to a robust 20-point. You also change the font from Times New Roman to Arial, and underline the entire title.

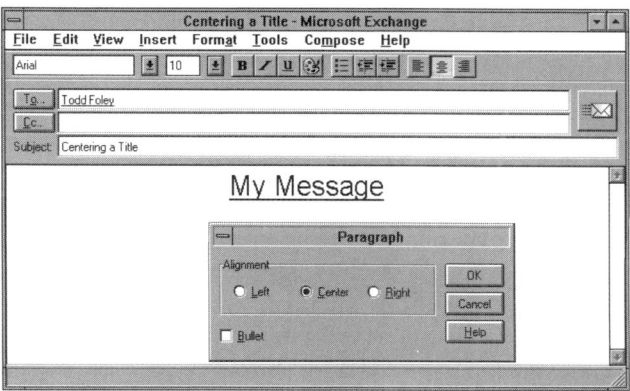

Figure 3.1: Centering a Title

How do you center the title so that it appears in the middle of the message window, regardless of how it is sized? Just use the **FORMAT...PARAGRAPH** menu option to change the paragraph in which the cursor is located to be left aligned, right aligned, or centered. You may also use the alignment icons on the toolbar to accomplish the same thing. Using the **ALT-A, P** keystroke combination will bring up the Paragraph Formatting window, allowing alignment changes to be made. You can also use the following HotKeys to make formatting changes:

Formatting Function	HotKey
Format Bold	**CTRL-B**
Italicize	**CTRL-I**
Underline	**CTRL-U**
Center Text	**CTRL-E**
Left-align Text	**CTRL-L**
Right-align Text	**CTRL-G**
Increase Indentation	**CTRL-T**
Decrease Indentation	**CTRL-SHIFT-T**
Toggle Bullets On/Off	**CTRL-SHIFT-L**

Indenting and Bullets

Both indenting and bulleted list creation are available as toolbar options on the New Message form Formatting toolbar. If for some reason these buttons are not visible, check the **VIEW...FORMATTING TOOLBAR** menu option to make sure it is checked. Oddly, only the creation of bulleted lists is available as a menu option: use the **FORMAT...PARAGRAPH** option to display a "Bullet" checkbox, which, when checked, converts selected text to a bulleted list. When converted to bulleted list format, text will display a round bullet immediately to the left of each item but will not indent text beyond the graphic.

Indenting may be accomplished with the toolbar command simply by placing the cursor on the desired line or by selecting a block of text with the mouse. When the Indent Left or Indent Right icon is selected from the toolbar, all selected text (or all text on the line the cursor is on) is moved appropriately. Text may be indented more than one tab stop through repeated use of the indent icons on the toolbar, applied to the same text.

Changing the Color of Text

One of the most dramatic ways to enhance your messages is to use Exchange's text color options. Clicking on the palette icon on the Formatting toolbar or using the **FORMAT...FONT** menu option will allow you to alter your text color to any color you choose. Tired of plain old black and white e-mail? How about maroon, teal, lime, fuchsia, or aqua? Judicious application of different colors can give selected text greater emphasis, make comments stand apart from plain text, even allow simple revisions to be passed along between coauthors—all within a normal piece of e-mail!

The background color for the New Message form, as well as the Read Message form, is white by default. Changing your text color to yellow may make the text difficult to read. Changing the text color to white makes it invisible! You can use this feature to send "secret messages" within your e-mail. Just convert the text you wish to "hide" to the color white. At first glance, the text doesn't exist. When

48 Creating and Sending Mail

printed or unformatted, however, the text is visible in black and white! To "decode" such a hidden message, or simply to unformat messages back to plain text, there is a special "Clear All Formatting" HotKey, **CTRL-SPACEBAR**. This HotKey will clear all color, font, and font size formatting from selected text. It will not clear alignment, indentation, or bulleting information, however. Also, since it clears only selected text, to remove all formatting from a message it must be used in conjunction with the "Select All," **CTRL-A**, HotKey.

Changing System Defaults

Although we'll get into more detail on customizing the Exchange Client's appearance and functionality later on, it's worth noting here how to alter the default message font and formatting information. Selecting the **TOOLS...OPTIONS** menu option opens up the System Options window, with many variable settings. Selecting the Send tab will allow you to modify the default options of the New Message form. While on this tab, clicking on the **FONT** button will bring up a font/formatting window identical to that opened using the **FORMAT...FONT** menu option on the New Message form. Changes in font size, style, color, etc., made in this window, once saved, will alter the way text is formatted by default on the New Message form. This can be quite a time-saver if you are always changing the font size or color of your message text. If your boss is nearsighted, just increase the default font size from 10 point to 20 point, and you'll never see him squint at your e-mail again!

Finding and Replacing Text within a Message

Just as in more advanced stand-alone word processing programs, Microsoft Exchange offers the ability to search through a message's text for a particular word or phrase. It also offers the ability to replace occurrences of such words or phrases with new text, handy for correcting misspelled names or incorrect terminology.

To find a particular word or phrase within the body of an Exchange message, first place the cursor into the main text entry box by clicking on it with your mouse. If the cursor is not located within the main text entry box, the function cannot be performed and the menu options for finding and replacing text will be grayed out and unusable. Once the cursor is properly located, the menu option to open the Find dialog box from the New Message form is **EDIT...FIND**. You can also use the **CTRL-SHIFT-F** HotKey. Once opened, the Find dialog box contains a Find What: text entry field, where the text you wish to search for must be typed. Two options are also presented as checkboxes: Match Whole Word Only and Match Case. If checked, the Match Whole Word Only option will find a match only if the words you type in the Find What: box match up with stand-alone words in the message text. For instance, if you typed the word "car" into the Find What: box, and checked the Match Whole Word Only option, then you would find the word car only if used as a separate word (e.g., "I drove my car") rather than part of another word (e.g., "I parked in

50 Creating and Sending Mail

the carport"). If the Match Whole Word Only option were not checked, than both occurrences would be found.

If the Match Case option is checked, then Find will find a match only if the message text matches the text in the Find What: box exactly—both uppercase and lowercase characters must be identical in both. If it is unchecked, then the search is case insensitive.

Clicking on the **Find Next** button begins the search from the cursor to the end of the message. Once a match is found, clicking on the **Find Next** button again will jump to the next match in the message.

Replacing text is similar to finding text. In fact, the Replace window has exactly the same options (Find What:, Match Whole Word Only, Match Case, a **Find Next** button) as the Find window, with a few additions. Also included are a "Replace With:" text entry box, where the new text you wish to replace the found text with is entered, and two buttons—**Replace** and **Replace All**.

The Replace window is opened by using the **EDIT...REPLACE** menu option or the **CTRL-H** Hot-Key. Usage is similar to that for the Find function, with the text to be replaced entered into the Find What: box and the **Find Next** button triggering the search. Once a match is found, clicking on the **Replace** button replaces the matched text with the text in the Replace With: box. Alternately, clicking the **Find Next** button again skips replacement of the match and jumps to the next one. You do not need, however, to go through every match to replace text. If you are confident that every occurrence of the searched for text needs to be replaced, then you could simply click on the **Replace All** button to do so automatically. This is a very handy feature for quickly replacing references to "The Bozo in Charge" with "Our Esteemed Leader" when the need suddenly arises.

Copying, Moving, or Deleting Information

Exchange supports all of the normal Windows Clipboard functions, such as copying, cutting, and pasting text or other information. It also follows the normal conventions for these functions. All are options available beneath the New Message form's **EDIT** menu option. All also use the normal Windows HotKeys for execution, as displayed below:

Function	HotKey	Menu Item	Toolbar
Copy Text	**CTRL-C**	EDIT…COPY	Icon of two documents
Cut Text	**CTRL-X**	EDIT…CUT	Scissors icon
Paste Text	**CTRL-V**	EDIT…PASTE	Clipboard icon

To move text or other information in one step (as opposed to cutting and pasting), a "drag and drop" method must be used. First, the text is selected using the mouse. Next, the selected text is clicked on with the mouse and *without releasing the mouse button* is "dragged" or moved to the cursor location desired. Once the mouse button is released, the operation is completed and the text is "dropped" into place. This method is exclusively mouse driven, although the same function can be accomplished

52 Creating and Sending Mail

using HotKeys or menu items in two steps by first cutting the text and then pasting it to the desired location.

To delete text, the **DEL** key can be used character by character or on large blocks of selected text. Simply highlight any text to be deleted and hit the **DEL** key. If it's the entire message that you'd rather do without, then you can delete the whole thing by using the **FILE...DELETE** menu option or the **CTRL-D** HotKey. Don't mix up the two—once the file has been deleted, no **UNDO** function will bring it back!

 Whoops! Didn't mean to delete that text? Maybe you wanted the one paragraph that's left deleted, not the twenty pages that just got blown away? Never fear! UNDO is here! Use the EDIT...UNDO menu option, or the CTRL-Z HotKey to jump back one step and remove the effects of your last edit or typing sequence. Don't be too overconfident, though. UNDO, unlike the similar function in Microsoft Word, will go back only one step. If you delete important text, then type some more, then use UNDO, only your typing will be removed—the important text will be gone.

Attaching Files and Embedding Objects

Want to jazz up your messages with a little real jazz? Miles Davis, Duke Ellington, Count Basie, Toots Thielman—that kind of jazz? All you need to do is embed an audio file into your message. Want to punctuate an important memo

Attaching Files and Embedding Objects   53

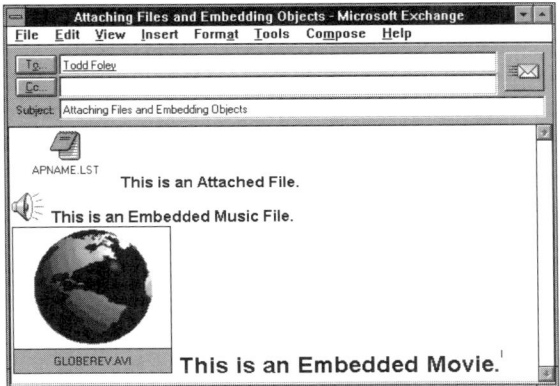

Figure 3.2: Attaching Files and Embedding Objects

with a three-second film clip from Jurassic Park? Just embed the video file into your message. Want to send your colleague in Madrid a copy of *War and Peace* in electronic format? Just attach the document to your message. Nothing makes e-mail messages sing quite like actual singing, and Exchange allows you to attach and embed all kinds of multimedia files in your messages (Figure 3.2).

What's the difference between attaching a file and embedding an object? Basically, an embedded file is an integral part of the message, and an attached file is "attached"—just along for the ride. If you attach a file, the recipient will see an icon representing that file displayed in the message. The icon will be the same as the application icon for the application used to create the attached file, e.g., a Microsoft Word icon if the attached file is a Microsoft Word document. When someone reads the message containing the attachment, they can click on the attachment icon, which will separately launch the program in which the attachment was created, in order to view the attachment. To carry our Microsoft Word attachment example further, if you click on the icon for a Microsoft Word attachment within an Exchange message, Microsoft Word will be started up (outside Exchange, on its own) and the document attached viewed within Word.

If that same Microsoft Word document were embedded within the Exchange message, then it would become part of the Exchange message; that is, the text, any associated graphics or charts, etc., comprising the entire Word document would be visible as part of the message text, not as a separate icon. There would be no need to launch Microsoft Word to view the document; it would already be visible. Similarly, if an audio file or movie clip were embedded in the Exchange message, then the file would play back within the message, not from an external program.

Why attach files at all? Why not just embed everything into the Exchange message? Well, not every file type can be embedded into Exchange. The application associated with a particular file type must be properly installed and "registered" on your machine before appearing as an option for embedding. Any file type at all may be attached to an Exchange message—even if the application it was created in is not installed on your machine. Also, remember that anything embedded in an Exchange message becomes part of the message. Frequently (especially with documents and spreadsheets) you'll want the recipient to have a copy of the file separate from your message. In such a case, attaching the file becomes the best solution.

So how do you do this stuff, anyhow? To attach a file to a message, use the **INSERT...FILE** menu option on the New Message form. Select the file and click on the **OK**

Attaching Files and Embedding Objects 55

button. You'll see a new icon representing the attached file appear within your message. Nothing to it, huh? Well, you can certainly get more complicated while attaching files. What if you want to attach another Exchange message, rather than a file?

To attach another Exchange message to your e-mail, use the **INSERT...MESSAGE** menu option to bring up a listing of all your Exchange folders. Choose the message you wish to attach, and hit the **OK** button. An icon representing the attached message will appear in your e-mail.

While inserting files or other Exchange messages into your message, you have the option of doing so as an attachment (the methods we've already reviewed), as text, or as a link. If you try to insert a file or message as text, then Exchange will attempt to convert the file to plain-vanilla text and place it into the message body. This is different from embedding, where the original formatting of the file (if it is a document) is maintained. Trying to insert a non-text file (such as an audio clip) as text will result in a whole lot of gobbledygook being pasted into your message, but when used properly, inserting as text can serve as a quick way to include pure text files in your message without having to cut and paste from another application.

Inserting a file as a "link" doesn't attach the file at all, even though an icon representing the file does appear in the message. What is sent with the message is a reference to the actual file that you "inserted"—a pointer to where it is. For this to work, it requires that both you and the recipient of your message have direct access to this file, perhaps in a shared directory on a network file server. When the recipient of the message clicks on the "linked" icon, the application associated with the file is launched, and the file is read, not from Exchange but at its original

56 Creating and Sending Mail

location. Using links is a handy way to provide reference to a file, perhaps a spreadsheet containing changing sales data, that is updated frequently by several people. Rather then sending an "old" copy of the information, you can send a link to the information so that your recipient can read it "live" and get up-to-the-second sales (or other) information.

What about embedding? To begin, use the **INSERT...OBJECT** menu option in the New Message form. You can select either the Create New or Create from File option. If you select Create New then you can choose from any of the listed *Object Types,* applications installed and properly registered on your machine for object linking and embedding. Once you've selected an Object Type, clicking on the **OK** button will launch the application, allowing you to create and save a new file within that application just for your message. Once completed, use the **FILE...UPDATE** menu option within the application to complete the embedding of your new file into the Exchange message.

If you choose the Create from File option while embedding, Exchange will allow you to browse and select any existing file for embedding. This is the easiest way to embed any of the thousands of audio and movie clips available on CD-ROM or from the Internet. Make certain, however, if you embed an existing file that it is a file format of one of the registered Object Types. Exchange will allow you to embed any file, but when you or your recipient clicks on the icon and doesn't have the appropriate software, an error message saying "No Application is Associated with this File" will appear. If you're uncertain about the file type or about what software your recipient might have, it's safer to attach the file.

Copy To and Blind Copy Addresses

What if you want to send a copy of a message to someone, but you don't want everyone else to know about it? How do you keep their names off the list of addressees? Is there a way to have such a "secret recipient"? The **BCC:** field makes these things possible.

If you wish for someone to receive a copy of the message you are sending, then you add their name to the **CC:** (for "carbon copy") field on the New Message form. More than one person may be "copied in" on a message, simply by adding multiple names to the **CC:** field. Upon receipt of a direct message or of a carbon copy message, the message displays in its header a list of all the people to whom that message was addressed. If you use the Reply to All function while reading the message, all recipients, both primary recipients and carbon copy recipients, receive a copy of your reply.

The **BCC:** (for "blind carbon copy") field is identical to the **CC:** field with one exception—no one but the sender can see who is included in the **BCC:** field. The message is forwarded to a **BCC:** recipient just like a **CC:** recipient, but no header information is provided on the **BCC:** addressee. Even the Reply to All function works with **BCC:** recipients, in which case the person using the Reply to All function never knows that they are sending a message to the **BCC:** addressee. Sound pretty sneaky? Well—it is. Still, there are times when it is certainly useful to include someone in a message without going to the trouble of forwarding messages separately to them, and **BCC:** inclusion is a way to do that. What if you were planning a surprise party for someone and you wanted to take them "out to lunch" so that people could set up the party and surprise the guest of honor upon your return? You could send the person an e-mail asking them to lunch and **BCC:** the entire guest list so that they know what's going on. Sound like I'm reaching for a nonsneaky use of **BCC:**? Maybe that's why the **BCC:** field is not displayed by default on the New Message form. To use the **BCC:** field you must first use the **VIEW...BCC BOX** menu item to display the **BCC:** field on your form. After that, you may copy in secret recipients to your heart's content!

Checking Spelling

Have you ever sent an important letter, only to find out after it was in the mailbox that you'd spelled something important, maybe even someone's name, wrong? Word processors have spell checkers that help alleviate this problem, but most e-mail packages do not. Exchange is a happy exception. No longer do you need to worry about "I" before "E" or even C-A-T. Exchange will check the spelling of all your messages, either automatically or on demand.

To manually check the spelling within a message, use the **TOOLS...SPELLING** menu option on the New Message form. You may also use the **F7** HotKey. Selecting this option will either return a "Spelling Check Complete" dialog box if all is well or return a more detailed Spelling window if an item not in your dictionary is discovered. As with the Microsoft Word spell checker, the Spelling window offers suggestions for proper spellings of the offending word and the opportunity to use the **Change** or **Change All** button to correct the misspelling. If the spelling is correct, but simply not in the electronic dictionary, then you may use the **Ignore** or **Ignore All** button to bypass checking on the offending word, or the **Add** button to add the word, as spelled, to your dictionary. This feature makes the spell checker intelligent, able to learn new words, acronyms, and names from you as you write. All you need do to prevent misspelling a difficult name is to enter it correctly once and add it to your dictionary. The Exchange spell checker will remember the name and correct you if you ever misspell it!

The **Options** button in the Spelling window opens a window allowing you to customize (and automate) spell checking on your messages. You may automate spell checking by selecting the "Always check spelling before sending" option. You can gain the able assistance of the spell checker by selecting the "Always suggest replacements for misspelled words" option, which will provide you with close matches to the misspelled word from its dictionary. You can even reduce the number of "misspellings" the spell checker detects by using the "Skip words in uppercase" option to avoid spell checking on proper names and titles. Words with numbers can also be bypassed, as can the original text in a reply or forward (why check someone else's message?).

As long as the Exchange spell checker is used, e-mail can be as accurate and professional as all other business correspondence.

The AutoSignature

Ever get tired of writing "Sincerely Yours" on the bottom of every letter? Maybe you even went out and had a rubber stamp made to make signing papers a little easier. Exchange provides you with a tool to automatically sign each and every e-mail exactly the way you want—without even having to think about it. Just use the **TOOLS...AUTOSIGNATURE** menu option in the New Message form to open the AutoSignature window, and then click on the **NEW** button to create your first AutoSignature.

The New AutoSignature window has two text entry boxes, a Name: box and a Contents: box. Despite what you might think, the Name: box isn't for your name but rather for a label (or "name") for the AutoSignature you're creating. Nobody but you will ever see what's typed into the Name: box; it serves simply as a way for you to tell multiple AutoSignatures (why create just one?) apart. The Contents: box is the whole shooting match—everything typed into this box is your AutoSignature and can be added to the end of every message. A **Font** and **Paragraph** button are available, mirroring the **FORMAT...FONT** and **FORMAT...PARAGRAPH** options on the New Message form, allowing multicolor fonts, different styles (try using the Script font for a real "handwritten" signature), different alignment and bulleting, etc.

Although no **Insert** button exists in the New AutoSignature window, you can still embed audio and video clips (or almost anything else) into your AutoSignature, simply by cutting and pasting them in. The normal cut and paste HotKeys (**CTRL-X** and **CTRL-V**, respectively) work just fine in the AutoSignature window, so go ahead and paste that clip of "Auld Lang Syne" into your AutoSignature.

All done creating your AutoSignature masterpiece? Just click on the **OK** button, and you'll be back in the AutoSignature window with the "name" of your new AutoSignature now listed in the AutoSignature Selections: box. Highlight the "name" and click on the **Default** button to set this new AutoSignature as the normal one to be used. Be sure to check the "Add the default selection to the end of outgoing messages" box, or no one will get to see your new AutoSignature.

When all looks OK, click on the **Close** button to return to the message. If you didn't want to include this message automatically, you could deselect the "Add the default selection to the end of outgoing messages" box and use the **Insert** button to place the AutoSignature manually. Either way, you've just created an electronic rubber stamp!

Saving Incomplete Messages

What if you start something that you can't finish? If you've started an Exchange message but aren't quite ready to send it, you have the option of saving the message to a file or to an Exchange folder.

To save a message to a file, use the **FILE...SAVE AS** menu option to open up the Save As form. You can assign the message a file name, place it in any directory, and choose to save it as one of the following three formats:

1. **Text:** Readable by any application, but will not preserve formatting, font, color information, or maintain attachments.
2. **RTF:** Maintains most if not all formatting and attachment information, compatible with many applications.
3. **MSG:** Exchange message format, viewable only with Exchange, will preserve all formatting and attachments exactly.

What format should you use? As a general rule, save incomplete messages in a folder rather than to a file. If for some reason you want to use a file instead (perhaps to give to someone who doesn't have Exchange), then use the format that maintains the most formatting information while remaining compatible. Generally, this will be RTF format. RTF files are usable by most word processing applications, and the format will keep most of your font formatting information.

To save a message to an Exchange folder, simply use the **FILE...SAVE** menu option to save the message to the folder it was created in (wherever you were when you selected the **COMPOSE...NEW MESSAGE** option). If you wish to save the file to a different folder, use the **FILE...MOVE** option to move the message. Doing so will automatically save it.

Creating Message Templates

By saving messages, you can create form letters, standard responses, workflow forms, message templates, etc., quickly and easily. Create your message, leaving *all pertinent fields blank (e.g., if creating a name and address form, create the NAME: field, just don't type your name after it). Then save the message to a special template folder or to a *.MSG file. Whenever you need to fill out another form, open up your template and complete it. Why type any more than you have to?*

Message Properties

Do you want to mark a message as "Urgent"? Would you like to receive a receipt when someone actually reads your message? These options can be set using the **FILE...PROPERTIES** menu option on the New Message form. Selecting this option brings up a window allowing you to set the message "Importance" to High, Medium (the default), or Low, as well as setting the sensitivity of the message to Normal, Personal, Private, or Confidential. These properties are visible in the folder contents listing and are criteria used in Views and Rules to screen messages. Changing an Urgent message's priority to High ensures quick review. Changing the message sensitivity when appropriate lets the recipient know when your e-mail should not be forwarded.

The New Message Properties window also allows you to set both delivery and read receipts for your message. When selected, a delivery receipt will send you a confirmation e-mail the minute it arrives in a recipient's mailbox. A read receipt will generate a confirmation message to you once the recipient has opened your message.

From Here

You should now have all the tools you need to be an e-mail wizard with Microsoft Exchange. Special formatting, audio and video clips, AutoSignatures, and spell checking, even message templates and "secret" **BCC:** messages—all will enhance your e-mail usage and allow you greater flexibility in communicating with others.

In the next chapter, we'll learn some tricks and tips on using Exchange's different address books, including how to address e-mail to the Internet and how to mail a single message to two or three hundred of your closest friends—instantly. After that we'll find out how to unlock the organizational power of Exchange using Views, Filters, and Rules. We'll even find out how to let everyone instantly know when you're out to lunch! (Though they probably know already... .)

ADDRESSING AND ADDRESS BOOKS

You've finally mastered the art of e-mail! You've seen in the previous chapter video clips, automatic signatures, secret recipients—all the wizardly tricks an e-mail guru needs to know. Now to whom do you send these electronic masterpieces? To a coworker sitting next to you? To an Internet "pen pal" halfway across the globe? Perhaps to two or three hundred of your closest friends? This is where Exchange's advanced addressing capabilities come into play. You'll find that Exchange offers tremendous flexibility in how you organize and use lists of other Exchange users. You can create new Internet addresses, build distribution lists of hundreds of users (to whom you can send messages with the push of a button), even correspond with groups via Public Folder addressing, rather than direct mail. You'll also learn how to find out detailed information about other users—from their phone number to who their supervisor is—instantly using the Address Book.

Using the Global Address List

Every Exchange user in an organization has a *user mailbox*, an account with Microsoft Exchange that allows them to receive and send mail. Unless an administrator has hidden a user mailbox from the list, all users are listed by full name in the Global Address List, a comprehensive database of Exchange users, distribution lists, and other recipients and resources (Figure 4.1). The Global Address List is the default listing displayed in the Address Book, accessible from the **TOOLS...ADDRESS BOOK** menu option or by using the **CTRL-SHIFT-B** HotKey.

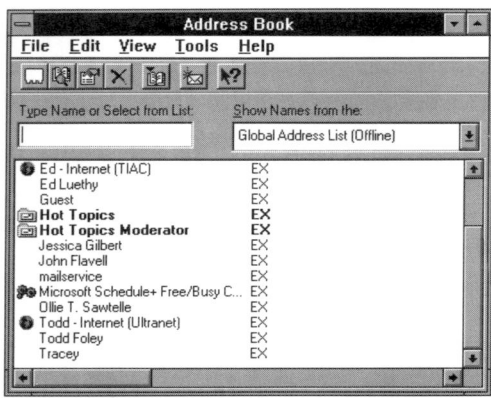

Figure 4.1: The Global Address List

Searching the Address List

The Global Address List contains the names of all Exchange users, in alphabetical order. In a large organization with thousands of users, finding a particular user can become difficult—especially if you know only their first name! The Address Book offers two search tools to help you with locating someone in a hurry—the "Type Name or Select from List" box and the **Find** function.

The Type Name box, in the top left corner of the Address Book, is a dynamic search field. To quickly find the Address Book listing for a particular user, simply start typing that user's name into the Type Name field, and, as each letter is typed, the list will scroll to the first name matching the typed characters. For example, if you were searching for the name "John Q. Smith", you might start typing the name into the Type Name box. The minute you typed the letter "J," the Address Book would change its display of the Global Address List so that the first name beginning with a J (e.g., "Jay Thomas") was at the top of the list. Next, if you typed the letter "o" to bring the entered text in the Type Name field to "Jo," the Address Book would change its display of the list so that the first name beginning with Jo was displayed (e.g., "John Johnson").

In this manner, it is possible to quickly find desired addressees with a minimum of scrolling and typing—the minute a desired addressee is visible in the display window, you can click on the envelope icon to create a new message, preaddressed to the selected user.

The Address Book's **Find** function is available through use of the **TOOLS...FIND** menu option or through use of the **CTRL-SHIFT-F** HotKey. There is little to choose from in the Address Book's Find window (Figure 4.2). All

68 Addressing and Address Books

you have to play with are a "Find Names Beginning With" text box, where you enter as much of the person's first name as you need to locate them, and an **OK** and a **Cancel** button. After typing in someone's first name, hitting the **OK** button will return you to the main Address Book window. The Address Book will display a new Address List, consisting of only those listings which match exactly the name you typed into the "Find Names Beginning With" text box.

Since it eliminates all nonmatching names from the Address Book's Address List display, the **Find** feature is most useful when you are searching for a "needle in a haystack"—perhaps when you know only the first letter of someone's name within a large organization. The "Type Name or Select from List" search, since it directly scrolls the Address List for you and is immediately usable without opening another window, will probably allow you to find a desired mailbox quicker and with less fuss during a normal search. Of course, it is in alphabetical order, and you

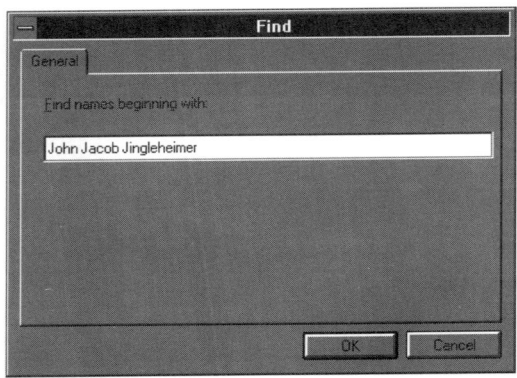

Figure 4.2: The Find Window

Using the Global Address List 69

could just scroll through the list yourself (but what a waste of perfectly good technology that would be!).

Contents of the Address List

So far, we've mentioned user mailboxes only as items listed in the Global Address List—but there are other types of listings as well. The Address List also includes *distribution lists* (one address that triggers messages to a large group of users), *Custom Recipients* (special non-Exchange mailboxes, probably for users external to your organization but accessible over the Internet or some other means) and Public Folders (you can send mail directly to a folder, just like a regular Exchange user—if an administrator has configured it to do so). Except for the user mailbox, which has no icon, each different type of recipient is represented by a different icon in the Address List, as follows:

A Distribution List Icon
Distribution lists can contain hundreds, even thousands of individual Exchange user mailboxes, Custom Recipients, and Public Folders. A distribution list could even contain other distribution lists! Sending a message to a distribution list triggers sending a copy of that message to everyone (and everything) that's part of that list.

A Custom Recipient Icon
Custom Recipients are like regular user mailboxes—they're just not part of your Exchange organization. Custom Recipients are usually created by an administrator to give Address Book listings for people in other companies that have frequent interaction with your own.

70 Addressing and Address Books

 When sending a message to a Custom Recipient, remember that if the Custom Recipient doesn't have Exchange, they probably won't be able to appreciate Rich Text Formatting like colored fonts, embedded graphics, and audio which you use when communicating with other Exchange users (although they should get attached files), so you may wish to "tone down" messages to Custom Recipients.

 A Public Folder Icon
Sending an e-mail to a Public Folder is just like a normal "post" to that folder. Administrators sometimes (but not always) enter Public Folders in the Global Address List to make frequent posts to that folder easier and to allow Public Folders to receive messages as part of distribution lists.

Information about Users: Addressee Properties

The Global Address List contains far more than just users' names. There are pages of "Properties" for each user, containing detailed information about the user's physical location, title and standing within the organization, contact information, e-mail addresses, and distribution list membership. The amount of detail available for each user is dependent on how much data your Exchange administrator maintains, but at a minimum, the Global Address List can serve as an excellent online replacement for your organization's phone directories. Using

Information about Users 71

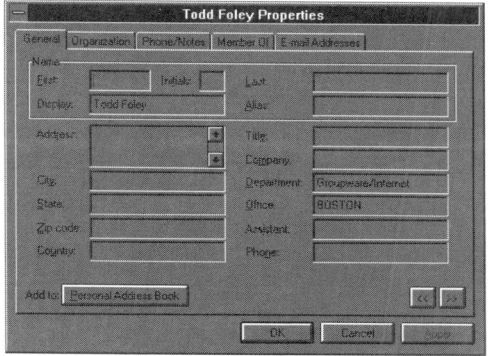

Figure 4.3: Address Book Properties

Exchange to maintain listings of company employees' department affiliations and telephone extensions allows you to revise the directory in one central place, with the new information available to all users instantly—no more distribution of paper, bound directories, etc.

To access the wealth of user information found in the Global Address List's user Properties, you might use the **FILE...PROPERTIES** menu option or click on the Properties icon (a picture of a hand holding a piece of paper) on the Address Book toolbar. The easiest way to bring up user properties, however, is to double-click on the user's name in the Address List.

Once opened, the Properties window (Figure 4.3) will always display five "tabs," or pages, of information. The five pages of information displayed are:

1. **General**—Basic information about the user: name, address, phone, etc.
2. **Organization**—Who the user's manager is, who reports directly to the user.

3. **Phone/Notes**—Extended contact information and general notes about the user.
4. **Member of**—All the distribution lists to which the user belongs.
5. **E-Mail Addresses**—Special Internet, Microsoft Mail, and X.400 addresses for the user.

In addition to listing all of the above information, administrators have the option of adding "Custom Properties" as well. It's entirely possible that you might double-click on a user's name in the Address List and be able to read what that user's shoe size is, learn their favorite color, even find out what their nickname was in grade school (if you have an especially mean Exchange administrator!). The Properties feature of the Address List can be configured to fit almost any business need—and, as a result, prove to be an especially valuable resource.

Navigating the Properties Window

To change from "page" to "page" in the Properties window, simply click on one of the tabs visible at the top of the window. There are five tabs, designed to look like manila file folder tabs. Each tab is labeled with the name of one of the five pages available in the Properties window. Clicking on a particular tab displays the appropriate page in the window.

In addition to changing from page to page, the Properties window offers the option of adding an individual user directly to your Personal Address Book, simply by hitting the "Add to:" **Personal Address Book** button visible at the bottom left corner of the window. You may also view properties of different users by using the "<<" and ">>" buttons found in the bottom right corner of the window.

These buttons will change the selected user to the user listed directly prior to the current one in the Global Address List (if the << button is used) or to the user listed directly after (the >> button). These tools make it easy to view the properties of multiple users quickly, as well as offer you the ability to save important users in your Personal Address Book.

Using Your Personal Address Book

Exchange gives every user the ability to maintain a Personal Address Book (Figure 4.4), containing frequently used items from the Global Address List. The Personal Address Book also gives you the ability to create custom addresses, build Internet addresses, even create your own

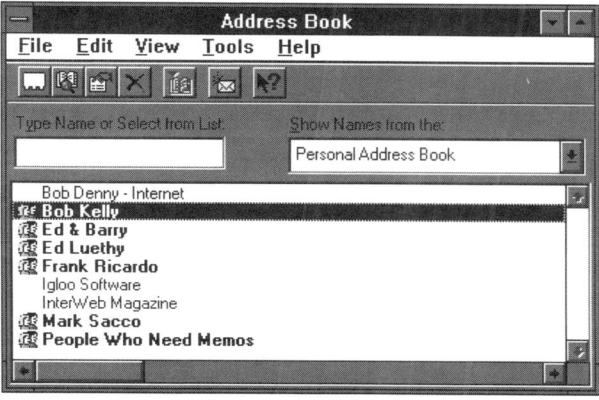

Figure 4.4: The Personal Address Book

distribution lists with hundreds of users! With just a few mouse clicks, the Personal Address Book can become your "little black book" of special Internet addresses, powerful distribution lists, and friends' user mailboxes. Opening up this special functionality is as simple as opening the Address Book and then changing the selection in the "Show Names from The:" box (in the top left corner) from "Global Address List" to "Personal Address Book."

Copying Names from the Global Address List

The most common entry in your Personal Address Book will probably be frequently used user mailboxes, distribution lists, Custom Recipients, or Public Folders already listed in the Global Address List. Copying these items into your Personal Address Book helps eliminate the need to search through the much larger Global Address List and puts your common addressees at your fingertips. Strangely, Exchange does not allow you to copy an item from the Global Address List while you have the Personal Address Book open! In order to copy a name from the Global Address List, you must have the Global Address List open, rather than the Personal Address Book. Once the Global Address Book is open, select the name you wish to copy to your Personal Address Book and use the **FILE...ADD TO PERSONAL ADDRESS BOOK** menu option or the **Add to Personal Address Book** icon on the toolbar. The name you've selected will automatically be added, and you may then open the Personal Address Book to review the new entry. Also, as we saw earlier, you may copy a user to the Personal Address Book from the Properties window by using the "Add to:" **Personal Address Book** button.

Creating a Custom Address

When you have the Personal Address Book opened, you have the option of creating a custom address, one not found in the Global Address List. To do so, use the **FILE...NEW ENTRY** menu option or the **New Entry** icon on the toolbar (an image of a card file card). The New Entry window will appear (Figure 4.5). This window will allow you to select any of the following custom address types to create a custom address in your Personal Address Book:

1. **Microsoft Mail Address**—For Microsoft Mail users connected to your Exchange Server but not using Exchange.
2. **MacMail Address**—For Macintosh users who are on a Microsoft Mail for Appletalk Networks system connected to your Exchange Server.
3. **Internet Address**—For anyone on the Internet!

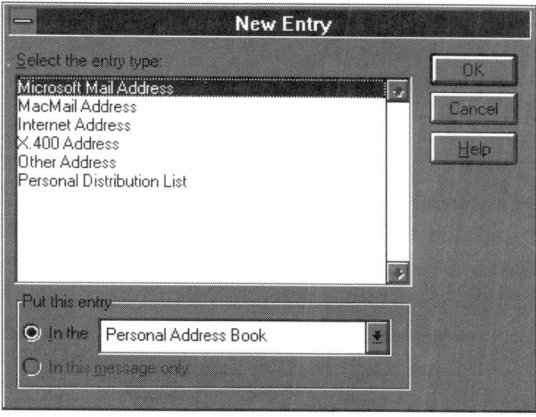

Figure 4.5: Creating a Custom Address

76 Addressing and Address Books

4. **X.400 Address**—For users in other companies connected to your Exchange Server using the X.400 protocol.
5. **Other Address**—(not usually useful) Allows you to enter *any* type of e-mail address, provided the e-mail type is recognized by your Exchange Server and the recipient is actually connected somehow to your system. Unless you know exactly what to enter here, and your administrator has configured a special e-mail type not listed in the Entry Types box, selecting this type will result in an unusable address.
6. **Personal Distribution List**—This type will allow you to build a distribution list of hundreds of your closest friends, permitting you to send a single message to all of them at once.

Not all of the above entry types may be listed for you, depending on the connectors and gateways that your Exchange administrator has installed. If your system is hooked up to the Internet, however, then Internet Address will be an option! Also, you should always have the ability to create a Personal Distribution List.

Addressing E-mail over the Internet

To create a custom Internet address, one you can use over and over again to send e-mail to someone on the Internet, select the Internet Address option from the New Entry window. The New Internet Address window will appear (Figure 4.6). You'll notice four tabs are available, with the SMTP-General tab being displayed initially. The four tabs available are as follows:

1. **SMTP-General**: This is where you enter the actual Internet e-mail address.

Using Your Personal Address Book 77

2. **Business**: This is exactly like a normal user mailbox Properties page. If desired, enter in detailed information about the addressee for later reference—name, address, phone, etc.
3. **Phone Numbers**: Another Properties page—enter detailed contact information here.
4. **Notes**: An open page for entering detailed notes about an addressee.

You can enter as much or as little information on the Properties tabs as you like, but you must complete the SMTP-General tab to create a valid Internet address. The SMTP-General tab has a Display Name text box where you must enter a name for your new address, as you would like it displayed in your Personal Address Book. After doing so, you must enter the actual Internet address in the E-mail Address text box. Unlike the way other mail systems work, there is no need to use any special syntax in entering the Internet e-mail address. If the recipient's Internet address is *tfoley@xlconnect.com*, then that's exactly what you should type into the box—nothing else.

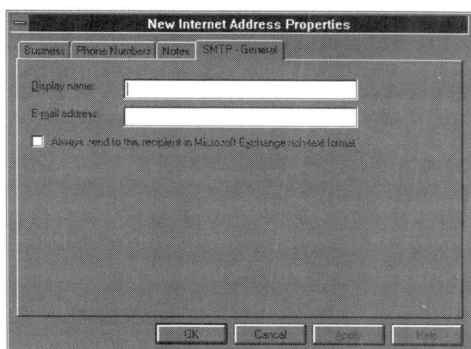

Figure 4.6: New Internet Address

78 Addressing and Address Books

The only other entry on the SMTP-General page is a checkbox labeled "Always Send to this Recipient in Microsoft Exchange Rich-Text Format." Check this box only if you are certain that the recipient is using Exchange or an Internet e-mail reader that supports colored fonts, embedded images, and elaborate formatting information. If you're not sure, leave the box unchecked, and bear in mind that the messages this recipient receives might not look as fancy as they do to you in your Exchange Viewer.

Once the SMTP-General page has been filled out and you've entered as much detail as you wish on the other tabs, click on the **OK** button to create your Internet address. You may now use this entry in your Personal Address Book to send e-mail messages over the Internet!

You've learned how to create a custom Internet address in your Personal Address Book that can be used over and over again. But what if you only wanted to send an Internet e-mail to an address you wouldn't need again? As long as your Administrator has set up Internet connectivity, you can enter any Internet e-mail address directly in the "TO:" field of the New Message form! Just type in the address in the TO: field the same way you would in the E-mail Address text box on the SMTP-General tab of the New Entry window in your Personal Address Book. When you send the message, it will go directly out over the Internet! Of course, if you plan to reuse an Internet address, it will be more convenient to have it in your Personal Address Book.

Creating Your Own Personal Distribution List

To create your own Personal Distribution List, allowing you to instantly send a single message to large groups of users with the push of a button, select the Personal Distribution List Entry Type in the New Entry window. This will open the Personal Distribution List Properties window, containing a Name: field, a large text box (initially empty) containing a list of all the members of the list, and an **Add/Remove Members** button. Type a name for your distribution list, as you would like it displayed in your Personal Address Book, into the Name: field. Next, click on the **Add/Remove Members** button. Doing so will open the Edit New Personal Distribution List Members window, allowing you to choose from any existing member of the Global Address List or your Personal Address List. You may even select other distribution lists! Once you have added all desired members to your list, click on the **OK** button to return to the Personal Distribution List Properties window. All of the members you've selected should now be visible. Click on the **OK** button to store the new distribution list into your Personal Address Book. When you select the new distribution list as a recipient for a new message, every single member of the distribution list will receive a copy!

From Here

You now should be able to send e-mail messages using Microsoft Exchange to anyone—anywhere. You've seen how to build distribution lists that can make the process of sending out memos, updates, and notices to hundreds of users quick and painless. You've learned how to use Exchange to review detailed information about individual users, as well as how to use the Internet to contact anyone around the world.

In the next chapter, we'll find out how to unlock the organizational power of Exchange using Views, Filters, and Rules. We'll also see how to use the Out of Office Assistant to let people know exactly when you're available (or just "gone fishing"!). Later, we'll see how to customize the Exchange Client to maximize its usefulness and "tweak" it to conform to your specific needs. We'll also look at how to share documents, messages, and other information with all Exchange users—instantly!

Keeping It Under Control: Managing Your Messages

Now that you have messages zinging their way across the known universe (or at least from desk to desk), you will soon find that one of the greatest advantages of electronic mail is also one of its worst problems. Exchange makes sending e-mail to hundreds of users instantly simple and efficient—which means that you can end up with dozens, even hundreds of messages a day! Some of these messages will be about important work issues, others just friendly chatter, still others just low-priority "general information memos" or even outright "junk mail." How are you going to read and respond to all of these messages in a timely manner? How do you separate the wheat from the chaff, sift the gold from the sand, do something else during your day other than stare at a computer screen? The answer resides with some of the most powerful capabilities of Exchange—Text searching, Filters, sorting, Views, and Rules.

Finding Text

Once you have a mailbox or folder full of messages and documents, finding a particular important message can be like finding a needle in a haystack. Fortunately, Exchange gives you the ability to perform text searching on all of the messages in your Inbox or in any other folder. To activate this feature, use the **TOOLS...FIND** menu option or the **CTRL-SHIFT-F** HotKey to open the Find window (Figure 5.1).

Find will search the current folder you are in by default, but clicking on the **Folder** button will open a Find Items

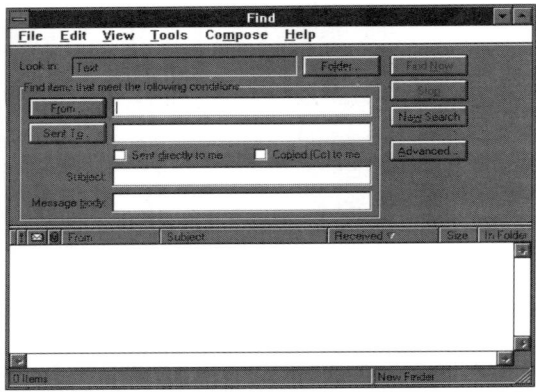

Figure 5.1: The Find Window

in Folder window allowing any mailbox, Public, or Personal Folder to be singled out for searching. Checking the Include All Subfolders box at the bottom of this window will tell Exchange to look in all folders beneath the one selected as well. Once selected, the target folder is listed in the "Look in:" text box at the top of the Find window.

Once you've specified where to look, Exchange gives you substantial options as to what to look for. The basic search options available are as follows:

Search Option	Finds Matching Text Within:
From	The name of the person who sent a message
Sent To	The names of recipients of a message
Sent Directly to Me	Messages where your name was listed in the To: field
Copied (CC) to Me	Messages where your name was listed in the Cc: field
Subject:	Text in the Subject: field of a message
Message Body:	Any text found within the main text box of a message

Once search criteria have been filled out, clicking on the **Find Now** button will select all matching messages and display them in the bottom of the Find window just as in a normal folder contents list display. All of the features available in a normal folder contents listing are available, including Views, sorting, and Filters (more on that stuff soon!). Double-clicking on any listed message will open it up for your review—and you've found your needle in a haystack!

The Find window also has an **Advanced** button, which triggers sophisticated *Rules*-based searching. Exchange

84 Keeping It Under Control

Rules are special conditions that trigger specific actions—a fancy way of saying that "When *this* condition happens, then do *this* action." The action triggered by the Rule created in the Advanced Find window is (no surprise) a search of messages in the selected folders. The conditions, however, are completely configurable. The advanced search conditions you can specify include:

- The size (or range of sizes) of messages
- Whether or not a message has been read
- How important a message was
- When the message was received

You can also use as conditions any fields or properties of a form or document, such as:

- The name of the application used to create a document
- The author's name, company, or manager
- The document's title, keywords, or revision number
- The number of pages or lines in a document
- Special comments or categorization information

So you want to find all messages in the "Junk Mail" Folder that were written by Crazy Edward in December 1996 and are under 2000 bytes in size? Then click on the **Advanced** button in the Find window and let Rules-based searching do the work for you! Finally, and perhaps the most impressive of all the conditions you can set, you can check the "Only items that do not match these conditions" box and immediately find all the messages that do *not* match all of your other conditions. This is especially useful for quick double-checking of the searching rules you're creating when first getting the hang of things.

Filtering Unwanted Messages

The easiest way to find messages you want to read isn't to use the Find window to search for them. The easiest way to find messages you want to read is to remove all the messages you *don't* want to read. How do you pull off this neat trick? Exchange allows you to create *Filters,* conditions for displaying messages in the folder contents list that allow you to display only messages you want to see. Use the **VIEW...FILTER** menu option to create a Filter for any folder you have opened (Figure 5.2).

Filters are rules based, just like searching. You specify conditions that have to be met to display an item (or not display an item if you check the "Only items that do not match these conditions" box), and, once you click on the **OK** button, only those messages appear in your Viewer window. The basic and advanced Filter options are identical to the basic and advanced search options: who a message is from, who a message was sent to, the subject of a message, etc. You can also specify that only messages sent

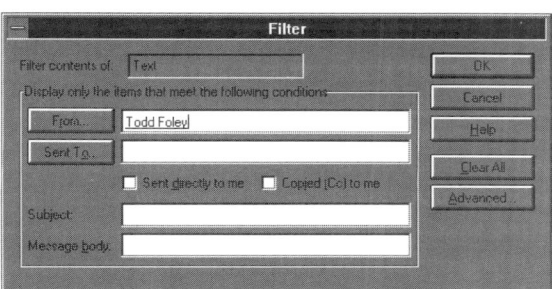

Figure 5.2: The Filter Window

directly to you (as opposed to messages you were copied in on) are displayed.

Filters are great to use when a particular person (like your boss) sends you a lot of unimportant mail (Do this, do that, blah, blah, blah…). Just create a Filter that has your boss's name in the "From:" text box, and then check the "Only items that do not match these conditions" box in the Advanced window. Once created, a Filter will apply to the folder it was created in until cleared. You need never look at a message from your boss again! Of course, this inspired use of Filters might be unappreciated by your boss, and forgetting that a Filter was on might lead to some small disagreements (such as, "Were you fired or did you quit?"). Fortunately, Exchange displays a special Filter icon (shaped like a funnel) in the status bar at the bottom of the Viewer window when you open a folder with an active Filter. If you think that you might be missing something, just clear the Filter by clicking on the **Clear All** button in the Filter window.

Sorting Messages

Once you've found all of the messages you want to read (or filtered out all those you don't) you still may be left with a sizable list of messages. That's where Exchange's sophisticated sorting features come into play. To sort messages simply, you can click on the column header in the folder contents listing. One mouse click on the default "From" or "Subject" header will sort all messages instantly by (you guessed it!) who the message was from or the text in the

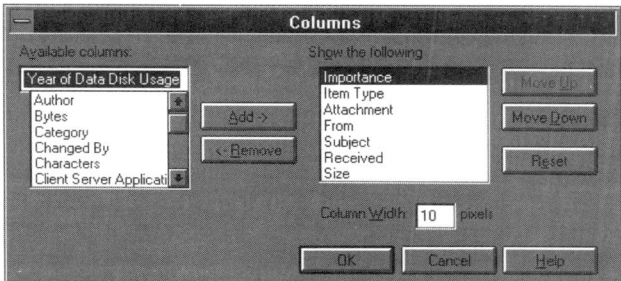

Figure 5.3: Adding and Removing Columns

Subject: field of the message. If you wish to sort the messages differently, you can use the **VIEW...SORT** menu option to open the Sort window, which will let you sort messages by any of the available *columns* (fields of information about a message or document displayed in the folder contents listing) in ascending or descending order.

Changing Displayed Columns

You may change the information available in the display window by modifying the columns displayed. To do so, use the **VIEW...COLUMNS** menu option to open up the Column Selection window (Figure 5.3). All the columns available throughout all Exchange Public Folders are listed in the Available Columns box. You'll notice field names for Microsoft Office Summary Information, as well as every field from every Exchange form created for organization-wide use. Don't be daunted by the huge selection, but don't bother selecting columns for display if you know the column isn't present in the folder—you'll just get a blank listing in the display.

88 Keeping It Under Control

 To prevent listing empty columns in your Viewer window, stick to fields you know are included in your folder contents. At a minimum, you'll always have information from the normal message fields: Importance, Subject, the To: and From: fields, etc.

Selecting an item in the Available Columns box and clicking on the **Add** button will add the column information to the folder contents listing. You may also change the order (left to right) in which the columns are displayed in the Viewer window by selecting the column in question in the "Show the Following" box and using the **Move Up** and **Move Down** buttons to alter its display order.

Grouping Messages

If you have too many messages to simply sort, or if you just want greater control over how your messages are organized within a folder, you might want to try *grouping* your messages (clumping like messages together in outline format).

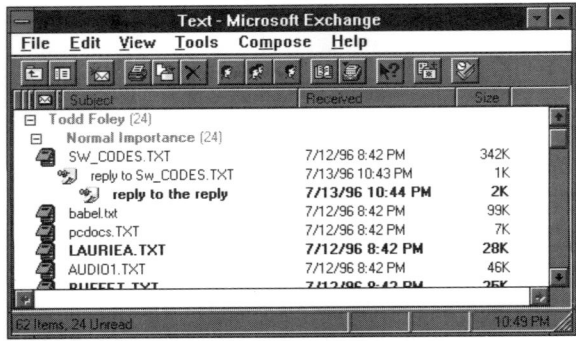

Figure 5.4: Messages Grouped by Sender and Importance

To group messages together, use the **VIEW...GROUP BY** menu option to open the Group By window.

The Group By window allows you to select up to four "outline" levels of grouping for your messages and documents, using any of the available columns as grouping criteria. To create a single level of grouping, just select a column in the top "Group items by:" selection box, and click on the **OK** button. Once you do so, the folder contents listing will no longer display all available column information. Instead, only the column information for the field you are grouping the messages by will be displayed. As an example, say you decided to group all of your messages by subject (Figure 5.4). Only the subjects of messages will be visible in your folder contents listing. The subject will be displayed slightly differently if it is a grouping criterion, however. It will be displayed in a different color text and have a plus sign just to the left of it. Clicking on the plus sign will "expand" the outline format, displaying the message in normal fashion within. If multiple messages have the same subject, then more than one message will be displayed once the plus sign is clicked. This ability to group several messages beneath one heading allows you to organize like messages quickly and simply.

The Group By window allows you to create deeper, nested groupings as well. Once you've selected a column in the "Group items by:" box, you may select a second (and third and fourth) grouping criterion as well. This allows you to create secondary groupings for replies to messages, for example—the bases for threaded discussion groups online. There is even a "conversation thread" sorting option in the "Sort by:" box at the bottom of the Group By window that will *thread* (keep replies to a particular message grouped underneath the original) messages for you!

Once you've grouped messages by as many criteria as desired, you can still sort and filter messages as well. When used together, these features can allow you to have instant access to the messages you need to see—while keeping the unimportant ones on hold.

The Importance of Importance

When sending messages, you may specify how important the message is by using the FILE...PROPERTIES menu option in the New Message window. Make sure that you use this property appropriately! Remember that other users will be sorting, filtering, and grouping messages as well—often on the basis of how important the message is. When urgent, setting the importance to HIGH will ensure it is read promptly. When not so crucial, leaving the importance set to normal or even changing it to low will allow other users to prioritize their messages properly.

Using Views

Once you've isolated the messages you wish to read and identified what columns you wish displayed and how the messages should be sorted, you may find yourself wishing for different ways to look at different messages. While looking at your Inbox, you'll want to know who a message is from, when it arrived, and how important it was. While looking at a collection of Microsoft Word documents in a Public Folder, you'll want to know the author, the title, the revision number, etc. Although you could change the columns displayed in each folder in question, it might be easier to create a custom way of looking at messages or documents that you could instantly apply to any folder when desired. Exchange allows you to build custom display methods for any single folder or for all folders. These custom display methods are called *Views*.

Views come in two flavors—Personal Views that you (and only you—that's what makes them *Personal*) can apply to any folder or mailbox, and Folder Views that apply only to a specific folder but may be used by others if located in a Public Folder. Views are applied by using the **VIEW...PERSONAL VIEWS** or **VIEW...FOLDER VIEWS** menu option. All available Views will be displayed underneath these options, and selecting a View immediately applies it to the currently opened Folder. Without doing a lick of work, you'll already have access to Exchange's four default Personal Views, as follows:

The Default Personal Views

View	Function
Normal	Sorts messages by time received
Group By From	Groups messages by sender, then sorts by time received
Group By Subject	Groups messages by subject, then sorts by time received
Group By Conversation Topic	Groups messages by conversation topic, then sorts by conversation thread

All the default Views use the following columns: Subject, Importance, Item Type, Attachment, From, Received, and Size. In addition, the Group By Conversation Topic adds the Conversation Topic column. These Views are very useful and should help you to quickly sort through messages and documents. You also have access to any special Folder Views that the creator of a Public Folder may already have designed—but what if you want to create your own Views?

To create a new View, use the **VIEW...DEFINE VIEWS** menu option to open the Define Views window. This window will allow you to specify whether or not you wish to create a Folder View or a Personal View. After doing so, click on the **New** button to create your first View. You'll open up the View Options window that will allow you to change Available Columns, alter the sorting and grouping message criteria, and apply Filters. You'll notice that a View allows you to pull together all of the different message management tools into one tidy package. Once you've specified your custom display View, type in a description for it in the View Name: box and click on the **OK** button. This View will now be permanently available to you from the **VIEW..PERSONAL VIEW** or **VIEW...FOLDER VIEW** menu options, just like the defaults.

Using Your Assistants

How would you like an assistant who would read all of your messages for you, figure out which ones were most important, and place them in a "READ ME NOW!" folder for you to examine? Or perhaps you'd like to take Mondays off and play a little golf—but you don't want your boss to know. If your boss called, your assistant could tell your boss that you

Using Your Assistants   93

were in a meeting and forward his message to a friend of yours who knew how to reach you on the golf course! Sound ideal? Exchange gives you all of this functionality and more through the use of your Inbox Assistant, accessible from the **TOOLS...INBOX ASSISTANT** menu option.

The Inbox Assistant allows sophisticated rules-based processing of all incoming messages. You can specify all kinds of conditions that might trigger a Rule to be used and (unlike Filters, where the action is always to filter out messages) wide latitude as to the types of actions that can occur as a result of those conditions being met. When the Inbox Assistant window first opens, you are presented with a list of existing Rules (if there are any) and a **New** button you can use to add additional Rules. Clicking on the **New** button brings up the Edit Rule window (Figure 5.5) with

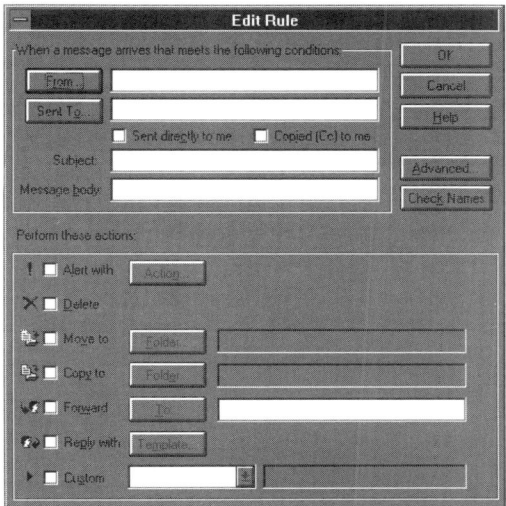

Figure 5.5: Editing a Rule for the Inbox Assistant

options for setting conditions and actions for the Rule. The condition options are the same as for the other rules-based features, searching and filtering. There is a basic conditions section that allows you to base rules on the sender of a message, the recipient, the subject, and the main message text. There is also an **Advanced** button that brings up the same advanced condition options that searching or filtering offer: the size (or range of sizes) of messages, whether or not a message has been read, how important a message was, when the message was received, etc.

The key difference in Rules created for the Inbox Assistant and rules-based searching and filtering of messages is that the Inbox Assistant allows creation of Rules with many different actions resulting from conditions being met. With filtering or searching, the action taken as a result of the Rule is always the same—filtering or searching. With the Inbox Assistant, Rules can cause selected types of incoming messages to cause all kinds of things to occur, as indicated below:

Inbox Assistant Actions

Action	Function
Alert with:	Triggers a pop-up message to be displayed on your screen, plays a sound, or does both. Good for letting you know when high-priority messages have arrived.
Delete	Will automatically delete the message. You should probably move or copy the message first, unless you really don't ever want to see it.
Move to:	Will move the message automatically to another folder. You could create a "READ ME NOW!" folder and write a rule moving all high-importance messages into it.

Copy to: Will copy a message to another folder.
Forward   Will forward a message to another user or group of users. Use this to have all messages from your boss sent to a coworker who knows how to reach you on the golf course!
Reply with: An extremely powerful action, this action allows you to send an automatic custom reply back to the sender.
Custom   Won't do anything. Microsoft included this option for other, third-party software companies to write options for. If you have only Exchange, this action won't do a thing.

There are unlimited possibilities as to what you can ask Rules to do. Actions can be performed in any combination, in any sequence (although you can't delete a message and then move it!). Some useful combinations include:

1. **The "I've been trying to get a hold of you" action**—perhaps you're waiting for a remote laptop user to log on and send you some important information. You could create a Rule that says "Whenever this user sends me a message, alert me with a pop-up message and beep at me. Also, send a copy immediately to Joe Smith, who is also waiting to hear from the remote user. Finally, send the remote user a custom reply that let's him know our meeting time has changed to one hour earlier."
2. **The "I don't deal with that stuff any more" action**—perhaps you used to be Grand Marshall of the Cheese Committee, but Joe Smith now has that position. You are still receiving e-mail about Cheese Committee activities, and you've been forwarding the messages to Joe, but it's starting to get annoying.

Create a Rule that takes any message with the word "cheese" in the subject line, forwards it to Joe Smith, and deletes it from your Mailbox. You'll never see cheesy messages again!
3. The **"This guy bugs me"** action—perhaps there's a particular person who barrages you with unimportant e-mail. Create a Rule to automatically move all messages from this person to a special "Annoying Messages" Folder, where you can look at them whenever you really want to waste time.
4. The **"Ultimate yes-man"** action—want to make a special impression on your boss? Create a special custom reply that is sent automatically in response to every message from your boss. Make sure it has an audio clip saying "Yes Sir!" and text saying "Thank you, sir, for your electronic communication. I will give the matter in question my immediate and undivided attention!" As soon as you create this Rule and reply template, go ahead and take a long lunch break—you've got Brownie points to burn!

The "Reply with:" option permits automatic custom replies to messages meeting your Rule's conditions. To actually create one of these custom replies, all you have to do is select the Reply with: option and click on the **Template** button. A normal-looking New Message window will appear. Go ahead and create your custom message in this window (you can even add additional recipients to the **CC:** field if you like) as if you were creating a normal e-mail message. Once complete, use the **FILE...SAVE & CLOSE** menu option to complete your custom response and return to the Edit Rule window. Next time the conditions of the Rule are met, the custom message will be automatically sent to the sender of the initial message.

The Exchange Inbox Assistant allows you complete control over processing incoming messages. Exchange also provides you with a special Out of Office Assistant with an even simpler way of automatically responding to incoming messages when you would be most likely to want to do so—when you're not there.

The Out of Office Assistant

What if you're at lunch, in a meeting, or otherwise temporarily unable to read your incoming messages? Microsoft Exchange's Out of Office Assistant is a simple solution to these issues (Figure 5.6). With the Out of Office Assistant, you can let people know that you are temporarily unavailable and even forward important messages to a secretary or coworker, all without creating a custom Rule every time you leave your desk.

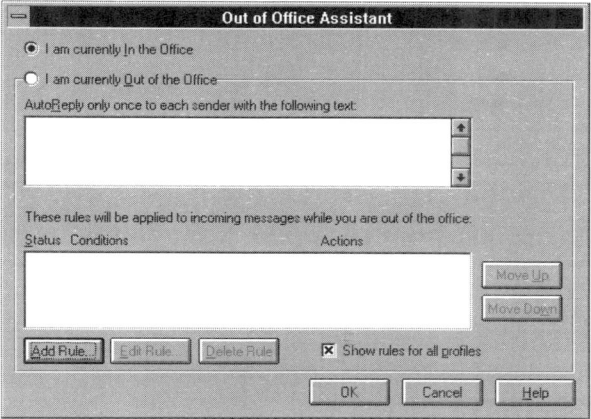

Figure 5.6: The Out of Office Assistant

To open the Out of Office Assistant window, use the **TOOLS...OUT OF OFFICE ASSISTANT** menu option. You'll notice that the bottom half of the window contains the same Rules options that the Inbox Assistant offers. Actually, the Out of Office Assistant is exactly the same as the Inbox Assistant with two exceptions—both immediately visible in the top half of the Out of Office Assistant window. The first difference between the two assistants is pretty obvious—the Out of Office Assistant is active only when you tell Exchange that you are out of the office by selecting the "I am currently Out of the Office" option in the Out of Office Assistant window. The second difference is that you don't need to create a Rule at all to use the Out of Office Assistant.

To use the Out of Office Assistant without creating a Rule, just enter in an appropriate message in the "AutoReply only once to each sender with the following text:" box. You might type in "Out to lunch—back at 1:00 pm" or just "Gone fishing." Once you select the "I am currently Out of the Office" option, anyone who sends you a message will receive an instant e-mail reply containing the text in the "AutoReply only once to each sender with the following text:" box. To disable this AutoReply once you return to your desk, open the Out of Office Assistant window and select the "I am currently In the Office" option. Of course, if you wish to create special message-processing Rules to handle or forward messages to another user when you are away, you may do so in the same manner you would in the Inbox Assistant. This type of Rules processing is especially useful if you are on vacation.

To set up your Out of Office Assistant while you are on vacation to forward important messages to someone else and let people know that you are away, follow these simple steps:

1. Open the Out of Office Assistant window and select the "I am currently Out of the Office" option.
2. Type in an appropriate message in the "AutoReply only once to each sender with the following text:" box. A good message might be: "I will be on vacation from Aug. 17–24. If your message was marked as High Importance then it was just forwarded to Joe Smith, who is handling matters while I am away."
3. Click on the **Add Rule** button and then the **Advanced** button in the Edit Rule window. Check the Importance condition and choose High as the criterion for applying this Rule to incoming messages. Click on the **OK** button to return to the Edit Rule window.
4. Click on the Forward action and then click the **To:** button to select Joe Smith or whoever will be handling your responsibilities while you are away. Click on the **OK** button to complete the Rule and return to the Out of Office Assistant window, then click on the **OK** button to complete the process and return to the Exchange Viewer.

If used consistently by all members of an organization, the Out of Office Assistant allows Exchange to be as instantly reliable as telephone communications—you know that someone has received your message and is available to read it unless you receive an AutoReply stating they are away from their desk. As we'll see in the next chapter, the use of delivery and read receipts, which allow you to know exactly when a message was read, further adds to the rock-solid reliability of Exchange messaging.

Let Someone Else Do It: Secretarial Access

You've seen all of the ways that Exchange allows you to manage your messages—but what about letting other people manage your messages? If you have a secretary or someone who helps you to review your messages, then Exchange gives you a simple method of allowing them to do so, without having to give them all of your passwords and let them use your machine to "log on" as you. Exchange also gives you the ability to let a secretary send messages on your behalf, replies to which, if desired, can show up in your Mailbox for you to review. How does all of this happen? There are three steps involved: allowing your secretary access to your Mailbox, allowing your secretary to send mail for you, and setting your secretary up to do both things.

Delegate Access

To allow your secretary (or someone else) access to your Mailbox, select your Inbox from the folder listing in the Exchange Viewer and use the **FILE...PROPERTIES** menu option to open up the Inbox Properties window. Select the Permissions tab—you'll see a listing of people who have access to your mailbox and what their *Role*, or level of permissions, is (Figure 5.7). Initially there will be only a name of "Default" and a Role of "None" listed in the User List box. To add your secretary to the User List for your mailbox, click on the **Add** button and select his or her name from the Global Address List. Once selected, hit

Let Someone Else Do It: Secretarial Access 101

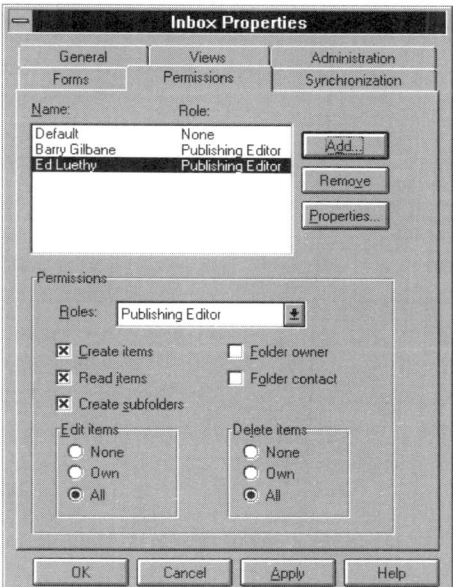

Figure 5.7: Inbox Properties—Permissions

the **OK** button to return to the Permissions tab. You're not done yet, however—you still need to define the Role for your secretary. You'll notice that the User List now displays your secretary's name with a Role of None. Select your secretary's name in the User List, and choose the Publishing Editor option from the Role: selection box in the middle of the window. You'll notice that the boxes checked in the lower half of the window change, indicating that your secretary now has the following permissions:

1. The ability to create new items in your mailbox
2. The ability to read items in your mailbox

3. The ability to create subfolders in your mailbox
4. The ability to edit all items in your mailbox
5. The ability to delete all items in your mailbox

If you wish to limit your secretary's access to your mailbox, perhaps to prevent them from deleting items, you may do so by directly altering the option. For example, you might change the Delete Items option to None (denying the ability to delete) or to Own (allowing them to delete only items they create). You'll notice when you do so that the listed Role changes to something other than Publishing Editor, perhaps to "Custom." The names of the Roles available—Editor, Custom, Author, etc.—are just descriptions of predefined collections of permissions for an object. You may select what permissions you wish to assign à la carte without worrying about the name Microsoft assigned to that particular collection of permissions.

Once you have granted your secretary the appropriate permissions (at a minimum the Read Items option must be checked), click on the **OK** button to complete the first step.

Allowing Others to Send Mail on Your Behalf

To grant your secretary the ability to send mail on your behalf, use the **TOOLS...OPTIONS** menu option to open the Options window. Select the Exchange Server tab (Figure 5.8). You'll see a User List labeled "Give Send on Behalf Permission to:", which should be empty. Click on the **Add** button and select your secretary's name from the Global Address List. Click on the **OK** button to complete the action and return to the Viewer window. Your secretary will now have the ability to click on the From box in a New Message window and select your name. When people

Let Someone Else Do It: Secretarial Access 103

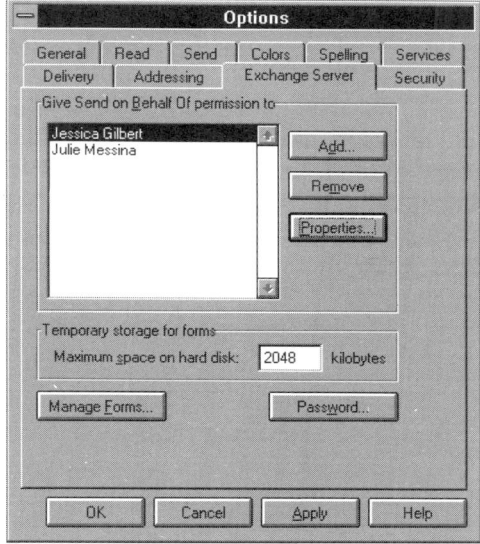

Figure 5.8: Granting Send on Behalf Permission

receive a message sent in this manner, your secretary's name will still appear in the From box, but it will be followed by the statement "on Behalf of *Your Name*."

It is also possible to have your secretary send mail as you without the "on Behalf of" line, but an Exchange administrator must configure your Mailbox properties using the Exchange Administration program to do so.

Setting up Delegate Access

Once the appropriate permissions have been assigned, one more step remains. You must set up your secretary's profile to open your Mailbox as well as his or her own when he or she starts Exchange, or else the secretary will not be able to read your messages. Have your secretary start Exchange and use the **TOOLS...SERVICES** menu option. This will display the Service window listing all Services installed in the secretary's profile. Have him or her select the Microsoft Exchange Server service and hit the **Properties** button. This will open the Microsoft Exchange Server Properties window. Select the Advanced tab. The top half of the window is taken up by Mailbox properties information, and a large Mailbox list box labeled "Open these additional Mailboxes." Click on the **Add** button to the right of this box, and type your name exactly as it appears in the Global Address List into the Add Mailbox window, then hit the **OK** button. You'll see your Mailbox name listed in the "Open these additional Mailboxes" box. Click on the **OK** button to commit the change and return to the Viewer.

When adding an additional mailbox to open, the Global Address List is not used. You must type in the user's alias, or NT Login ID, or their name exactly as it is displayed in the Global Address List. If you do not do so, the mailbox will not be added to the "Open these additional Mailboxes" box in the Advanced tab of the Microsoft Exchange Server Properties window.

Adding Folders to Your Mailbox

In addition to or in place of your Inbox, you can grant your secretary access to your other Mailbox folders as well. Your Mailbox, by default, contains an Inbox, an Outbox, a Sent Items, and a Deleted Items folder. You can create additional folders at any time by selecting your Mailbox in the folder listing and using the **FILE...NEW FOLDER** menu option. Any new folder created in your Mailbox is visible only to you and can't be shared with other users—unless you grant them delegate access to it in the same manner as we reviewed granting delegate access to your Inbox. Additional Mailbox folders are often useful for organizing old messages or messages of a special nature. Remember the Rule we talked about that would automatically move all important files to a "READ ME NOW!" folder? Before it could do so, you would have to create a new folder called READ ME NOW! in your Mailbox. You can also create new folders in places other than the top level of your Mailbox. Selecting your Inbox and creating a new folder will create the folder within your Inbox—one level down. Creating *subfolders* in this way allows you to organize messages in outline-like format—useful for quickly locating old messages.

From Here

You now have seen how to use the powerful organizational and information management tools that Exchange has to offer. You've even learned how to get Exchange to cover for you if you've taken a long lunch break! At this point, we've covered most of the features of the MS Exchange Client as it is installed on your system. Next we'll look at how to make the Exchange Client uniquely yours through customization, how to make certain a message has been delivered or read, even how to make Exchange simpler by removing esoteric or rarely used functions from display.

106 Keeping It Under Control

After that we'll concentrate on how to share information simultaneously with thousands of users using Public Folders—and how to create sophisticated Exchange programs without knowing anything about programming by using the Exchange Forms Designer.

Customizing the Microsoft Exchange Client

Now that you have mastered Microsoft Exchange's Rules and Views, you have complete control over the messages that you receive and store for later use. Next you'll see how to use the tremendous flexibility Exchange offers to gain control over the Exchange Client itself. Practically every button on the toolbar, every field on a message form, even the way in which folders and messages are presented can be customized to your specifications. Do you want Exchange to alert you when you have new mail? Let you know if someone you've sent a message to has actually read the message? Perhaps you just want all of your messages to be the color pink. Exchange will let you make using the Exchange Viewer a uniquely personal (or just very pink) experience.

Setting Defaults

Whenever you open the New Message form to create a new e-mail message, Exchange checks to see how you would like the message to be displayed, spell-checked, colored, and generally created. The default "Send Message" settings for the New Message form are as follows:

Setting	Function	Default Value
Font	Basic font used for text in messages	Arial
Font Style	Basic font style (bold, regular, italics, etc.)	Regular
Font Size	How large the displayed text should be (point size)	10
Font Color	Color of message text	Auto (same as your normal Windows text color)
Delivery Receipt	Sends you a notification when a message is delivered	Off
Read Receipt	Sends you a notification when a message is read	Off
Importance	Priority of message (high, normal, low)	Normal
Save Copy	Keeps a copy of all sent messages in your Sent Items folder	Off

To change any of these settings, use the **Tools...Options** menu option to open the Options window, and then select the Send tab to adjust New Message form defaults (Figure 6.1).

Setting Defaults 109

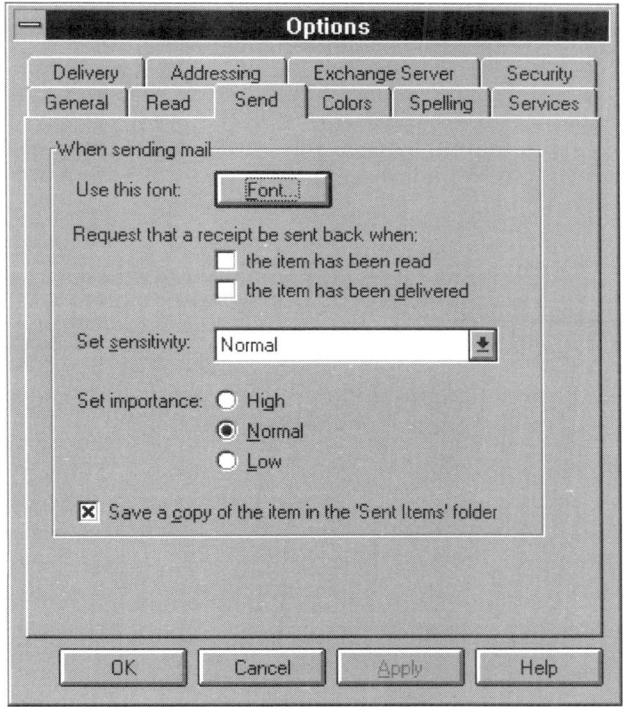

Figure 6.1: Options Window Send Tab

Colors and Fonts

To change the color of text used in new messages, click on the **Font** button in the Send tab of the Options window. Selecting the Auto option will cause the New Message form to automatically use the normal Windows default text color, as defined in your Control Panel setting. Remember that you will still have the option of changing the text manually to some other color while composing an actual message.

The procedure for changing the font and font size is just like that for changing the default text color. Open the Options window using the **Tools...Options** menu item, select the Send tab, and click on the **Font** button. You will also have the opportunity to change the font style (bold, italics, or regular) and add effects such as strikeout and underlining.

The font type you use will become your Exchange "handwriting"—a unique font can be just as expressive as your normal handwriting can be (Figure 6.2). Feeling loud and abrasive? Make certain you use a bright red, large size, bold font, and type everything in capital letters. Feeling anxious and overworked? A jagged, bold-italicized font might let your boss know how overworked you feel. Remember that any font available on your system can be used by Exchange—be creative!

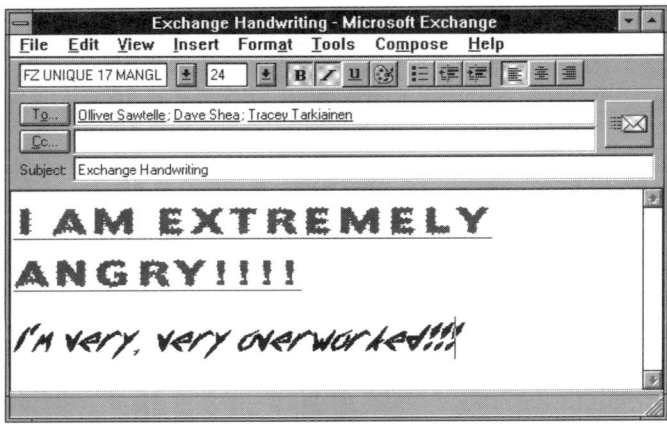

Figure 6.2: Using Different Fonts

Delivery Receipts

Once you've chosen how your message will look when someone receives it, how about checking on when the message was received? Exchange offers you the ability to send messages via "certified mail" and actually receive an electronic notification of when your message was delivered. To ask Exchange to send you a confirmation *delivery receipt* e-mail message stating the exact time your message was delivered, use the **TOOLS...OPTIONS** menu item to open the Options window. Select the Send tab and check the delivery receipt option.

Normally, Exchange delivers messages instantly (or at least within a few seconds), and delivery receipts are unnecessary. Sometimes, however, people to whom you send messages might not be hooked directly to the Exchange Server you are using. A recipient might be using a laptop at home and dialing into the office once a day, or a recipient might be in an office 3000 miles away that receives messages from your office only every 15 minutes or so. Delivery receipts are your opportunity to make certain that important messages are delivered to the person to whom you sent them.

Read Receipts

Exchange actually goes one step further in letting you know how your message was received. Besides delivery receipts, which tell you when a message was delivered, you can request *read receipts*, which tell you when a message was actually opened and read. If you are sending someone an important message, and you don't want them to be able to say, "Oh, I might have gotten it, but I never read it," request a read receipt for the message. To do so,

112   Customizing the Microsoft Exchange Client

use the **TOOLS...OPTIONS** menu item to open the Options window. Select the Send tab and check the read receipt option.

A read receipt will wait until your recipient actually opens the message and views the contents (rather than just the header) to generate an e-mail message to you. Knowing when someone has actually read your message can be very useful if your recipient normally gets too many e-mail messages to read them all right away.

Mail Alerts

Does your mailman ring the doorbell at your house when he drops off your mail? No? Perhaps he flips a flag up on your mailbox to let you know mail has arrived? Exchange can do these things as well as your postman can if you set New Mail alerts. To ask Exchange to alert you when new mail is received, click on the **TOOLS...OPTIONS** menu item to open the Options window. Select the Read tab to display your alert options. You can choose to have Exchange play a sound, pop up a "You Have New Mail" message window on your screen (Figure 6.3), or just leave

Figure 6.3:   A Mail Alert Message

you alone. If you choose to have Exchange keep quiet about new messages, you'll still be able to check on new mail quickly just by using the Exchange Viewer. By default, all new unread message headers in your folder contents listing appear in bold.

Emptying Deleted Items

Don't you hate having to take out the trash? Isn't it easier to leave the pizza boxes in the corner and use them as end tables? You'll be glad to know that Exchange can take the trash out for you—by emptying your Deleted Items folder automatically whenever you exit the Exchange Viewer.

You'll remember that Exchange has a safety feature that allows you to recover deleted messages if you think twice about something you've thrown away. Deleted messages are automatically moved to a Deleted Items folder in your Mailbox, and you may recover them from there if need be. Exchange gives you the option of permanently deleting all items in your deleted items folder either automatically upon exiting the Exchange Viewer or manually whenever you're ready to "take out the trash." Unless you absolutely never want to throw anything away (pack rat!), set Exchange to empty your Deleted Items folder automatically by clicking on the **TOOLS...OPTIONS** menu item to open the Options window. Select the General tab and check the "Empty the Deleted Items folder upon exiting" option.

Setting a Default Address Book

When addressing messages, you have the option of choosing recipients from the Global Address List (the default) or choosing someone from your Personal Address Book. If you would prefer to use your own Personal Address Book by default, just click the **TOOLS...OPTIONS** menu item to open the Options window. Select the Addressing tab and choose the Personal Address Book option in the "Show this address list first:" selection box. You'll still be able to use the Global Address List by manually switching to it when addressing messages, but the custom addresses in your Personal Address Book will be the ones easiest to access.

Adjusting the Spell Checker

For those of us who have to look up the word C-A-T in the dictionary, Exchange's spell checker is just what the doctor ordered. You can adjust the spell checker to suit your taste, or turn it off altogether (show-off!). To alter the spell checker default settings, just click the **TOOLS...OPTIONS** menu item to open the Options window. Select the Spelling tab and make adjustments as desired. Spell checker options and their functional descriptions are as follows:

Option	Function
Always suggest replacements for misspelled words	When a spelling check is performed manually or automatically, if a misspelled word is found, will suggest up to six variant spellings for correction
Always check spelling before sending	Automatically runs the spell checker on new messages or posts just before sending

When checking, always ignore: Words in UPPERCASE	Will not spell-check words containing uppercase letters (like proper names)
When checking, always ignore: Words with numbers	Will not spell-check words containing numbers
When checking, always ignore: The original text in a reply or forward	When you reply to or forward a message, the text of the original message is included. Selecting this option disables spell checking on the original message content

Remember that even if you turn automatic spell checking of messages off completely you may still manually check spelling by using the **TOOLS...SPELLING** menu item or the **F7** HotKey from within the New Message form.

Changing Toolbar Items

Although there are menu options for almost all Exchange functions, and HotKeys for many of them, the simplest way to perform common Exchange functions is by clicking on a toolbar icon. You have complete control over what icons are and are not found on the Exchange Viewer toolbar, simply by using the **TOOLS...CUSTOMIZE TOOLBAR** menu item within the Exchange Viewer. This will bring up the Customize Toolbar window, which lists all of the available toolbar buttons in a box on the left side and all current toolbar buttons on the right (Figure 6.4). Clicking on the **Add** button adds an icon to the toolbar. The

116 Customizing the Microsoft Exchange Client

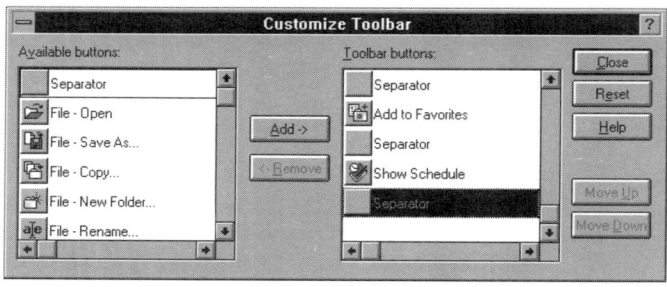

Figure 6.4: Customizing the Toolbar

toolbar icons visible by default when the Viewer is first installed are as follows:

Toolbar Icon	Function
Up a Folder Level	Goes to the folder one level up
View—Folders	Toggles off/on the display of the folder listing
Compose—New Message	Opens the New Message form
File—Print	Prints the currently selected file
File—Move	Moves the currently selected file to another folder
File—Delete	Moves the currently selected file to the Deleted Items folder
Compose—Reply to Sender	Formats a reply to the sender of the currently selected file using the New Message form
Compose—Reply to All	Formats a reply to the sender and all addressees of the currently selected file using the New Message form
Compose—Forward	Opens and formats the New Message form to forward the selected file

Changing Toolbar Items 117

Tools—Address Book	Opens the Address Book
Goes to Inbox	Makes your Inbox the current folder
Add to Favorites	Adds the currently selected folder to your Favorites folder
Show Schedule	Opens Schedule +

Almost all of the default toolbar icons may be removed, if desired, without creating problems—there are menu item or HotKey equivalents for almost all of them. Removing the Show Schedule Toolbar icon, however, would eliminate your ability to run the Schedule + program directly from within Exchange (although even then you would be able to run the program from outside Exchange) and should probably not be done if Schedule + is utilized.

The visible toolbar icons are by no means the only ones that can be displayed. The additional icons that can be added to make the toolbar more useful to you are as follows:

Toolbar Icon	**Function**
File—Open	Opens the currently selected file
File—Save As	Saves the currently selected file to a disk (external to Exchange)
File—Copy	Copies the currently selected file to another folder
File—New Folder	Creates a subfolder within the currently selected folder
File—Rename	Renames the currently selected file
File—Properties	Opens the Properties window for the currently selected item
Edit—Select All	Selects all files within the folder contents listing

Edit — Mark as Read	Marks the currently selected file as "read" and changes the message header from a bold to regular font style
Tools — Find	Opens the Find window
Compose New Post in This Folder	Opens the New Post form
Compose Reply in This Folder	Formats a reply to the folder of the currently selected file using the New Post form
Goes to Outbox	Makes your Outbox the current folder
Tools — Deliver Now	Delivers outbound messages immediately to the Exchange Server. If a remote laptop user, will use remote mail to dial in and log on.
Create Exchange Forms	Will launch the Microsoft Exchange Forms Designer application, if installed
Remove from Favorites	Will remove the currently selected Favorites listing
Folder Design Cue Cards	Will open the Folder Design cue cards, which can walk you through the creation of Public Folders

Some of the optional toolbar icons aren't very useful for most users. There is no need, for example, to use the Goes to Outbox icon if you aren't a remote laptop user, because messages are normally transferred from your Outbox to the Exchange Server within seconds of being sent. Similarly, the Deliver Now icon is unnecessary unless you are a remote user who is working offline. It is even possible that an optional toolbar icon will not work at all. The Create Exchange Forms icon won't do anything unless the Microsoft Exchange Forms Designer, a separate application from Exchange, has been installed on your machine.

Other optional icons are very useful for normal use—the Tools—Find and File—Properties icons are good examples. It's up to you to determine what your most commonly used functions are, but whatever you decide, Exchange will let you alter your environment to make things easier and quicker to do.

Hiding Unwanted Screen Elements

For some people, the tremendous amount of functionality that Exchange offers can make basic operation somewhat distracting. Exchange offers you the ability to hide from display seldom used functions. Some items are already hidden by default when Exchange is installed. These hidden items include the optional toolbar icons mentioned in the previous section, as well as the **BCC:** field on the New Message form.

If you wish to hide or display Exchange items, most items can be selected from the **VIEW** menu option in the Exchange Viewer or the New Message form. While in either the Exchange Viewer or the New Message form, you have the option of selecting the Toolbar and Status Bar options under the **VIEW** menu item. Selecting either option will toggle display of that item off and on. The Exchange Viewer uniquely offers the ability to toggle display of the folder listing using the **VIEW...FOLDERS** menu item or the "Show/Hide Folder List" toolbar icon. The New Message form offers the ability to toggle display of the Formatting Toolbar, **BCC:** field, and **From:** field using options within the **VIEW** menu item. By removing little used functions from display, you will not only avoid "distraction" but you will also gain more room on the New Message form to view and edit your messages. When it comes to displaying functions, sometimes less is more!

From Here

You've seen how to make Exchange do everything you might want it to do for yourself—even including how to make all of your messages your favorite color! Next we'll take a look at how to use Exchange to do things with other Exchange users, simultaneously. Microsoft Exchange Public Folders let you share documents, messages, thoughts, and information with thousands of users at once. Online meetings, document sharing, all of the more advanced Exchange applications are based on Public Folders, and it's high time we took a look at how to use them! After that, we'll take a quick peek at the powerful Microsoft Exchange Forms Designer, which lets you develop sophisticated messaging-enabled programs without having to know anything about programming. Get ready for the good stuff!

Public and Personal Folders: Sharing and Organizing Information

Exchange offers much more functionality than advanced e-mail alone. Using Public Folders you have the ability to share anything with anybody—instantly. What are Public Folders exactly? Think of Public Folders as rooms in a building. Some rooms are used for specific things, a bedroom for sleeping, a living room for watching TV, a kitchen for making a mess in, etc. Other rooms are not quite so well defined or serve primarily as a "catchall" for junk (e.g., the guest room, the attic). It helps to think of Public Folders as a physical location, like a room in a building, because of their "fixed" nature. You put things into Public Folders, just like putting old sneakers into a closet. Public Folders exist in a constant, fixed location (as in, " top of the stairs, on the right"). Most important, more than one person can fit into a Public Folder at once in order to see everything in it. The big difference between Public Folders and your living room is that while you might be able to fit a dozen people into your living room if they stood really close together, you can fit as many people as you like—thousands upon thousands—into a Public Folder.

Although *Public Folder Applications* (a Public Folder dedicated to some specific function, as well as its contents and any Exchange forms used in the folder) can grow to be very sophisticated in implementation, Public Folders themselves are simple and straightforward. They are just rooms that anybody can enter, use what's in them, even leave something in them if they wish. An "online discussion forum" (sounds fancy, huh?) is nothing more than a basic Public Folder. Since anyone can read and post messages to a Public Folder, and Exchange instantly updates your display when someone else posts a message, you can actually hold a conversation by *posting* (sending a message to a folder rather than a person) messages back and forth within a Public Folder. In contrast to just sending messages back and forth to one person (or group), anyone who is looking at that Public Folder can see what you are talking about and join in the conversation by posting a message of their own. A sample use of Public Folders for important online discussions follows:

1. You post a message saying "I like fish!" to the "Important Business" folder
2. Joe Smith, who happens to be looking at the folder at the same time, posts a reply saying "I like fish too!"
3. You post a reply saying "What kinds of fish do you like?"

4. Steve Miller, who happens to be looking at the folder, posts "Fish-shmish! I like breads and cereals!"
5. Joe Smith replies to your post with "I especially like haddock!"
6. Your boss, who has been looking at the folder as well, posts "Enough with the fish! Go back to work!"
7. The next day, your boss's boss looks at the folder, sees the old postings, and posts a new message, "Something fishy is going on here…."

It is also possible to use Public Folders for things other than fish. Just as with your Exchange Inbox, you can put documents, graphics, audio clips—almost anything—into a Public Folder. You can then apply Views, sorting, Filters, Find, and all of the other tools you use to manage messages to the contents of the Public Folder. This means that you could filter out all of the "fishy" stuff and just jump to (for example) the monthly sales report for the Puerto Rico Division for August 1978. No need to hunt through file cabinets or call someone in the records department to print something out from microfiche—just go to the "Sales Reports" Public Folder. Sound like it might be useful? Online meetings, document storage—these Public Folders can do some pretty powerful stuff!

Navigating Public Folders

Before you start creating and posting to Public Folders, it makes sense to figure out how to get around in them. Public Folders use a "top-down" directory structure, just like

124 Public and Personal Folders

normal file directories in MS-DOS (Figure 7.1). In fact, the basic navigation of Public Folders is very similar to navigation using the Windows File Manager or Windows 95 Windows Explorer applications. A limited number of "top-level" Public Folders exists at the "top" or "root" of the Public Folder structure, and then any folder can contain other folders inside it (called *subfolders*), which can in turn contain subfolders of their own. You open Public Folders the same way you open other folders in your Mailbox, by double-clicking on the folder. If a folder has subfolders, then clicking on the plus sign to the left of the folder will display all subfolders in the folder listing, while clicking on the minus sign will collapse the folder listing display. By double-clicking a folder, then a subfolder, then another subfolder, etc., you can travel deep into the Exchange Public Folder structure, stopping anywhere along the way to take advantage of a particular resource or discussion.

Once you have selected the folder in which you wish to post a message or just open up to see what's inside, click on it once with the mouse, or use the **FILE...OPEN** menu option. Doing so will open up the folder and display its

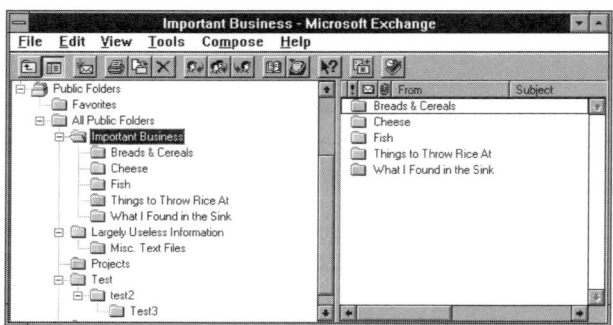

Figure 7.1: Navigating Public Folders

contents in the folder contents listing (otherwise known as the right side of the window). Done reading what's inside the folder? At any time you can click on any other visible Public Folder to examine its contents and subfolders as well. Want to jump from "Great Shortbread Recipes" to "Things to Do with Used Kayaks"? Just click away....

Posting and Replying to Items

So what are you going to do once you've opened up a Public Folder? How about reading what's in it? You can double-click on any item in the folder to open it up and read it (or listen to it, or watch it—depending on whether it's a document or a sound). An item in a Public Folder need not be a normal mail message—it might be a Microsoft Word document, a simple text file, a movie clip, a spreadsheet, almost anything. When you click on an Exchange message (an e-mail or a message posted directly to the folder), then you read the message using the Exchange Viewer. When you click on something else—a Microsoft Word document, for example—then Exchange launches the application used to view that document. It will start up Microsoft Word for you and open the file inside Word. Exchange uses Windows "associations" to determine which application to start for each type of file—adjustable in File Manager if you should care to do so. *Associations* are simple relationships between programs and file extensions, such as "All files ending in the letters T-X-T are text files to be viewed by the NOTEPAD.EXE program." The fact that Exchange utilizes these associations to trigger other programs makes life simple—you don't have to do anything for Exchange to work with all of your existing software! Programs automatically create these associations upon installation, so no additional modification is required.

You can open a document in a Public Folder, edit it in your normal word processing application, and save it right back to the Public Folder. If you have the rights to do so, you can overwrite the existing file, or you may have rights only to create a new version of the file. Here's an example of creating "document versions" that shows how useful this sort of thing can be:

Perhaps you are working on an important presentation with two other people in your office. You write a draft of the document and save it to a Public Folder. Another member of your team opens your document, edits it, and saves it as a new version. The third member of your team reads both versions and does a final edit, saving it as yet another version. If you wish to include something from your original draft, you can open it up and copy it. All the versions can exist in the same folder (even have the same document name!), but you will easily be able to organize them and tell them apart by author, time of creation, size—any of the many different column options.

Sound complicated? It's not—posting to a Public Folder is just as easy as reading items. In fact, you can post items to an Exchange Public Folder without even using Exchange! In the "document versions" example, you might have posted your document to the folder just by using the **FILE...POST TO EXCHANGE FOLDER** menu option from Microsoft Word v7.0 (Figure 7.2). When Exchange is installed, it looks for an existing Microsoft Office installation and actually creates new menu items for these applications that do basic Exchange tasks, such as sending mail or posting items to a folder.

Posting and Replying to Items 127

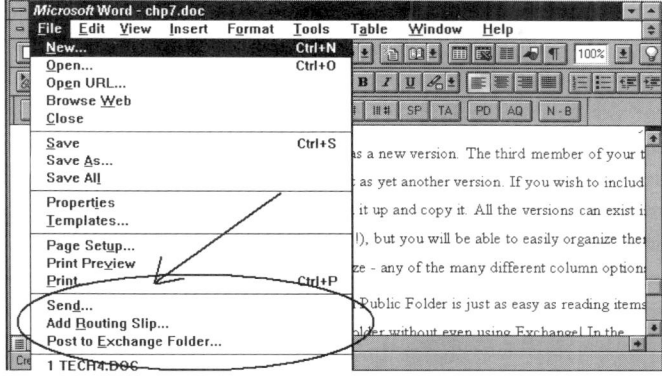

Figure 7.2: Exchange Options in Microsoft Word v7.0

If you happen to find yourself in the "Five Alarm Chili" Public Folder, and you double-click on a document containing the best recipe for Guatemalan Fever Chili you've ever laid eyes on, you may well feel compelled to respond. Exchange offers you two ways to reply to a posting in a Public Folder—**Reply to Sender** or **Post Reply in This Folder**.

If you use the **Reply to Sender** option, using the **CTRL-R** HotKey or the **COMPOSE...REPLY TO SENDER** menu option, then you may compose a normal e-mail response to the person who originally posted the document to the Public Folder, just as if they had sent the document directly to you rather than posting it. They will receive your e-mail in their own Inbox, and your reply will not appear in the Public Folder. This is a useful way to reply to a posting when you wish your remarks to be kept private, or if you simply feel your response would be inappropriate in the Public Folder.

If you wish to leave a public record of your reply, such as you would do if it were an online discussion group, then choose the **Post Reply in This Folder** option, using the **COMPOSE...POST REPLY IN THIS FOLDER** menu option. Your response will go directly to the Public Folder, and no separate message will be sent to the person who posted the original document. If you view the folder by conversation thread, then you will see your reply threaded beneath the original document. You should use this method if you wish to add some comment or content to the original document that all viewers would appreciate, such as "This chili would taste even better if you put more Tabasco sauce in it!"

If you wish to post a brand-new message into a Public Folder, use the **COMPOSE...NEW POST IN THIS FOLDER** menu option to open the New Post window. This window is very similar to the New Message window, with the following two exceptions:

1. Instead of an envelope icon to trigger sending the message, the New Post window has a "pushpin and note" icon that posts the message into the folder.
2. There is a **Keywords:** text box into which you can enter information (such as keywords and phrases describing your posting) that will allow others to perform searching, sorting, and viewing by the **Keywords:** column later on.

Do you want to place an existing file into a Public Folder—perhaps a movie or audio clip? Maybe you have hundreds of files you want to put into a folder—years of reports or documents? The quickest way to put these types of items into a Public Folder is to drag them there, using Exchange's drag and drop support to move files from Windows' File Manager or Windows 95's Windows Explorer directly into Exchange. Just select the file or files you wish

Using Favorites 129

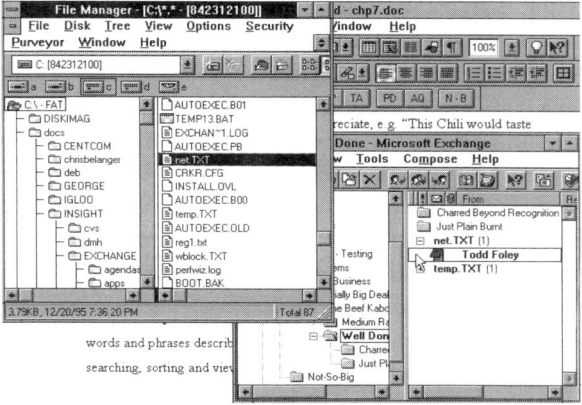

Figure 7.3: Dragging Files into Exchange

to copy or move, click on them once with your mouse, and without releasing the mouse button, drag them into an Exchange folder. Let the mouse button go and voila!— they've "dropped" into place. Of course, to drag and drop files, both applications must be visible at the same time (Figure 7.3). It can be tricky to resize the application windows properly so that both the files you want to copy and the Exchange folder are visible simultaneously. If you find it too great a chore, then you can always use the normal posting method and simply attach or embed the file.

Using Favorites

Sometimes the Public Folders that you use most frequently are buried deeply in the folder directory structure. If the

130 Public and Personal Folders

idea of opening thirty-three folders just to get to the "Things That Make Me Laugh on Tuesdays" folder is a little daunting, then you'll be relieved to know that Exchange offers *Favorites*, a quick way to access even the most deeply nested folders.

Favorites are links, or "shortcuts," to Folders that you use frequently—collected in an easy-access top-level folder (Figure 7.4). Opening a subfolder in the Favorites folder actually opens the folder in its real location—even if it's dozens of folders deep in the folder structure. You can add any folder you like to this useful collection of folder shortcuts simply by opening a folder and using the **FILE...ADD TO FAVORITES** menu option. Once you add the Things That Make Me Laugh on Tuesdays folder to your collection of Favorites, you can access it by double-clicking on it in the Favorites folder rather then having to first open the thirty-three folders of which it is a subfolder.

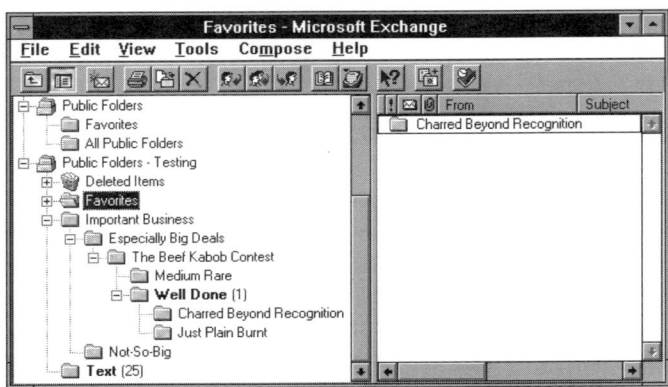

Figure 7.4: Using Favorites

Creating and Using Shortcuts

Your Favorites are personal—no one else has access to them. If you want to tell someone else about a folder of interest that lies deep within the Public Folder structure, you could tell them to go to the "Cheese" folder, which is in the "Dairy Products" folder, which is in the "Food Groups" folder, etc.—or you could create an Exchange *shortcut*. Exchange shortcuts are actually programs that launch Exchange (if it isn't open) and change the focus of the Exchange Viewer to a particular folder. These programs exist outside Exchange and can be run directly from any physical disk drive. They can also be embedded into Exchange messages and used to create World Wide Web–like links to any Public Folder.

To create an Exchange shortcut, highlight the folder to which you would like to create a shortcut, and then use the **FILE...CREATE SHORTCUT** menu option. Exchange will allow you to create a shortcut to any folder, not just Public Folders. If you create a shortcut to a Personal or Mailbox folder (such as your Inbox), then the shortcut will work properly only for you—even if you send the shortcut to another user, they still won't be able to access your Inbox. If you create a shortcut for a Public Folder, then any user who has access to that folder normally will be able to use your shortcut to travel there instantly. The **FILE...CREATE SHORTCUT** menu option will open a **SAVE AS** window prompting you to pick a location on a local or network drive to which to save the shortcut.

Exchange will not allow you to save a shortcut directly to an Exchange folder—you have to drag and drop it there

132 Public and Personal Folders

or attach it to a posting if that's what you desire. Once saved, you may "run" the shortcut the same way you would run any other Windows program—by using the **FILE...RUN** dialog from Windows Program Manager, or double-clicking on the file in the Windows Explorer or File Manager applications. You can even create an icon on your desktop for the shortcut (just like any other Windows program), allowing you to launch Exchange immediately and open the shortcut's target folder—without Exchange having to be running first!

You can also embed Exchange shortcuts into messages, simply by using the **INSERT...FILE** menu option to select and embed the shortcut. When someone reads your message, they will be able to click on the shortcut and immediately open the target folder (Figure 7.5). This makes it a lot easier for someone to locate a particular folder than simply telling them to "go to the *Public Folders\Things Important\Things Not So Important\Stuff* folder"!

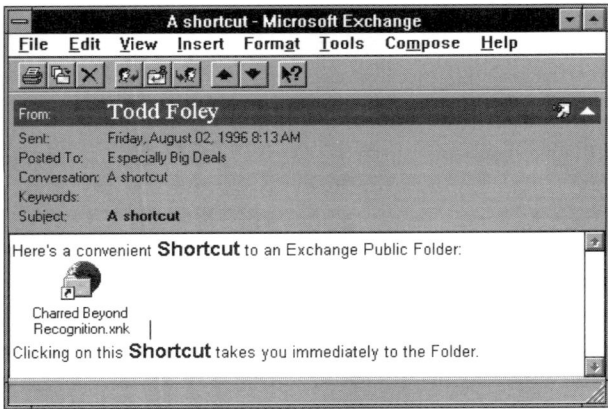

Figure 7.5: A Shortcut Embedded in a Post

Creating Internet Shortcuts

You can create shortcuts not only to Exchange folders but to any Internet Web page as well! In fact, Internet shortcuts are much simpler to use—they're "built in" to Exchange and are automatically created and activated. When you read an Exchange message, any Internet Web page *URL* (the address of the Web page) in the message (in the format "HTTP://WWW.XLCONNECT.COM") will appear in a different color and can be clicked on, launching your Internet browser (such as Microsoft Internet Explorer) and taking you directly to the page. Of course, your computer must be connected to the Internet for this to work—but if it is, you can surf the Web launched from an Exchange Internet shortcut!

To create Internet shortcuts in your own messages, just type the Internet Web page URL in your message. Be sure to use the proper format (use the "HTTP://" part of the URL). That's all there is to it—any Internet URL you type in your message will be automatically recognized by Exchange and linked to the Internet!

Folder Properties

Perhaps you try to open a Public Folder and it doesn't let you—what's going on? You may not have been granted permission to view the contents of the folder. When a Public Folder is created, the *owner* of the folder (the person who created it) has the ability to determine who can see items in a folder, write items to a folder, delete items, etc. They may not have liked you (well, why else wouldn't they let you open it up?). To find out who was responsible for this terrible injustice, you can check the Folder Properties, by highlighting the Folder in question and using the **FILE...PROPERTIES** menu option. The Properties window will have two tabs of information for you to review:

- A General tab containing the name of the folder and any comments or instructions the folder owner has entered.
- A Summary tab telling you the name of the folder contact (the guilty party!) as well as letting you know specifically what permissions you do have within that folder.

If you require additional permissions beyond what the Summary tab tells you are assigned, you may e-mail the folder contact to request them. If they won't give you permission to store all of your essays on "Things You Can Do with Twine and Duct Tape" in their folder, perhaps you can create a Public Folder of your own.

Folder Design

To create a Public Folder, you must first have permission to "Create Subfolders" in a particular folder (check the Folder Properties). If you do, then highlight the folder and use the **FILE...NEW FOLDER** menu option. It will prompt you for a new name for the folder, and then create it. That's it—you're done. Of course, your new folder doesn't do anything fancy or special—it's just a plain vanilla place to put your stuff. If you want to design a more advanced folder, with special Views, Rules, forms—a real Public Folder Application—then you need to use the Folder Design Cue Cards.

The Folder Design Cue Cards are a special "Wizard" program that walks you through every step of creating an advanced Public Folder Application. The Cue Cards also provide instant online help and advice on the different features of Public Folders. Even as an Exchange guru, you will find the Folder Design Cue Cards to be the quickest and easiest way to create new folders. To activate the Cue Cards, use the **TOOLS...APPLICATION DESIGN...FOLDER...DESIGN CUE CARDS** menu option. The Cue Cards will walk you through all of the possible options and features of designing a Public Folder, in the following steps:

Design Step	**Function**
Creating the Folder	Creates an empty, plain folder in a desired location in a set of Personal Folders.
Copy or Install Forms	Associate special forms (that you or others create) not available globally within Exchange, with your new folder.
Create Folder Views	Create special Views that anyone reading items in your folder may use—even create a custom default View that will automatically display your folder contents exactly as you would like.

136 Public and Personal Folders

Test the Forms and Views	Comprehensive testing of your folder's options to make sure it works the way you want it to.
Copy the Folder to the Public Folders	Install your new folder application.
Designate the Forms Allowable in the Folder	Specify all of the Exchange forms that may be used in your new folder.
Grant Permissions	Keep people you don't like from using your folder (or just protect the contents so they can't be deleted or overwritten).
Set Administration Options	Miscellaneous stuff—this step will let you temporarily restrict your folder from use for testing purposes, or change what the default View for your folder is, or change how drag and drop actions work with your folder.
Create Rules for Your Folder	Just as with your Inbox Assistant, you can create special rules that will do almost anything when a message or document is posted to your folder.
Test and Release the Folder	In this step you are told to have other people test your folder before you let everybody use it—even though you know it's already perfect!

The Folder Design Cue Cards actually teach you how to set options in the Folder Designer window, accessible from the **TOOLS...APPLICATION DESIGN...FOLDER DESIGNER** menu option. Once you've created your folder using the Cue Cards, you can return at any time to the Folder Designer window to alter your settings. The Folder Designer window is actually a fancy version of the Folder Properties window, with additional tabs that allow you to manage Rules, Views, forms, and permissions for the folder.

Personal Folders

The Folder Design Cue Cards have you take the step of creating your new Folder Application first in a Personal Folder and then moving it into a Public Folder. Personal Folders are similar to Public Folders in almost every way except:

- They really are personal—they exist as separate files that you can password protect.
- They are saved to a local drive as a *.PST file—they don't stay on the Exchange Server the way Public Folders do.

The reason the Folder Design Cue Cards prompt you to create your new Folder Application in a Personal Folder first, rather than directly into a Public Folder, is twofold. First, keeping your application in a Personal Folder keeps it private—other users won't be able to use it until it has been tested and is ready for installation. Second, you may not have permission to create any Public Folders at all (the Exchange administrators must really dislike you, if that's the case!). Using a Personal Folder allows you to develop and test the application fully, then give it to someone authorized to install it.

138   Public and Personal Folders

You may not have any Personal Folders at all when you first install Exchange. To add Personal Folders to your Exchange Viewer so that you can use them to create new applications, use the **TOOLS...SERVICES** menu option to open the Services window. Click on the **ADD** button to see a listing of available services. Select "Personal Folders" from the list and click on the **OK** button. You will be prompted for a file name for the new *.PST file that will contain your Personal Folders (Figure 7.6). Once you've named and located your file, you will be given the opportunity to password protect it for privacy, and then you'll be able to see and use the Personal Folders in your Exchange Viewer.

Because Personal Folders are saved to a local file, they offer interesting functionality that Public Folders do not provide. You can give another Exchange user a copy of your Personal Folder *.PST file, and they can (provided they know your password or it is not password protected) use the **TOOLS...SERVICES** steps for adding

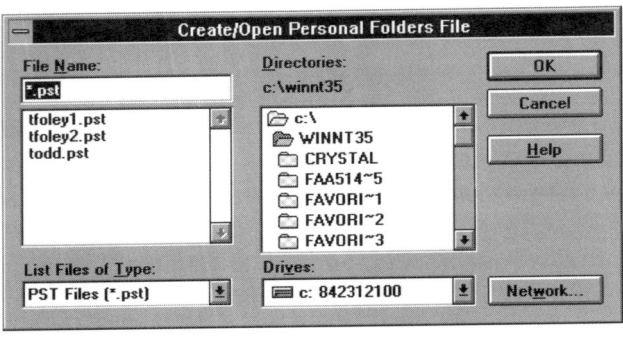

Figure 7.6: Creating a Personal Folder File

Personal Folders to add your Personal Folders to their Exchange Client. To do so, they just select your existing *.PST file rather than creating a new one. This is how you would give a completed Folder Application to an administrator for installation in a Public Folder—or how you might share a private Folder Application with a friend without using Public Folders at all.

Remote Access to Folders

For remote and laptop users, Personal Folders solve an important issue with Exchange—when you are not connected to the Exchange Server, Public Folders are not accessible unless they are in your Favorites folder and you have specifically set them up to be available offline using the Synchronization tab in the Folder Properties window. You may copy the contents of any (or all) of the Public Folders to a Personal Folder and use it for reference whether offline or connected to the network. For information kept in Public Folders that isn't frequently updated, this is the easiest way to make Public Folder resources available to remote users offline.

For information that is frequently updated, remote users will want to add the Public Folder holding the information to their Favorites folder (while they are connected to the server) and then highlight the Favorites Folder and use the **FILE...PROPERTIES** menu option to open the Folder Properties window. Selecting the Synchronization tab will allow them to select the folder as available "When offline or online." Once this is done, the folder contents will be available offline and can be automatically updated when they connect to the server.

From Here

You've seen all there is to see of the Exchange Client, learned how to link your Exchange messages to Internet Web pages, even learned how to develop advanced Public Folder Applications. In the next chapter we'll take a look at the Microsoft Exchange Forms Designer, a separate program that lets you develop Exchange forms for use in Public Folders or throughout all of Exchange ("global" forms). Best of all, the Exchange Forms Designer does not require any programming knowledge to create sophisticated messaging applications! After that we'll get into the really geeky stuff—administration of Microsoft Exchange Server.

THE MICROSOFT EXCHANGE FORMS DESIGNER

You've already mastered the Microsoft Exchange Client and seen how to develop Public Folder Applications using the same Rules and Views that help you manage your personal messages so effectively. Microsoft Exchange also offers you the ability to develop sophisticated programs that can automatically post information to Public Folders, route workflow processes from one person to another— even whistle Dixie (provided you have an audio clip of someone whistling Dixie). Believe it or not, to accomplish all these advanced programming functions you don't need to know a thing about programming. The Microsoft Exchange Forms Designer is a codeless application design environment—you can build applications by running the

Form Template Wizard and dragging a few controls onto a new form with your mouse.

Drag and Drop Programming: The Application Design Environment

The Microsoft Exchange Forms Designer (or EFD for short) is a separate application from the Exchange Viewer and must be installed on your machine after installation of the Exchange Client in order to use its advanced development environment (Figure 8.1). The installation can be performed directly from the Exchange Server Client Software CD, or from a network drive that an administrator has set up for this purpose. Simply run the SETUP.EXE program, and the EFD will be installed to your local hard drive. Installation will add the Microsoft Exchange Forms

Figure 8.1: The Exchange Forms Designer

Drag and Drop Programming   143

Designer icon to your Microsoft Exchange Program Group. Double-clicking this icon or running the EFD.EXE file in the new EFDFORMS directory will start up the EFD and open the Form Template Wizard.

The Form Template Wizard is a special program-within-a-program that prompts you for answers to simple design questions, then generates a "blank" Exchange form based on your responses. This blank form will have all of the messaging functionality (what the form does, how many windows it has) already defined for you and will allow you to add whatever fields and functions you desire.

When first launched, the EFD gives you the option of using the Form Template Wizard, manually choosing a form template, or opening an existing Exchange form project. If you decide to manually choose a form template, then you can pick from one of the eight predefined Exchange form templates. If you use the Form Template Wizard, it will pick one of these eight templates for you. If you decide to open an existing form project, you may open a project you have already started, or you might open one of the sample applications shipped with Exchange to use as a starting point for a new application of your own. The simplest way to begin developing an Exchange form application, however, is to use the Form Template Wizard (Figure 8.2).

The Form Template Wizard initially asks you where the information contained in your form will be sent. An Exchange form is not unlike an Exchange message—it can be sent directly to a specific user or posted directly to a Public Folder. Which method you choose will undoubtedly vary depending on the function of the form you are developing. If you are creating a form to store employee names, addresses, birth dates, and shoe sizes, then you will want to have the information posted to a Public Folder

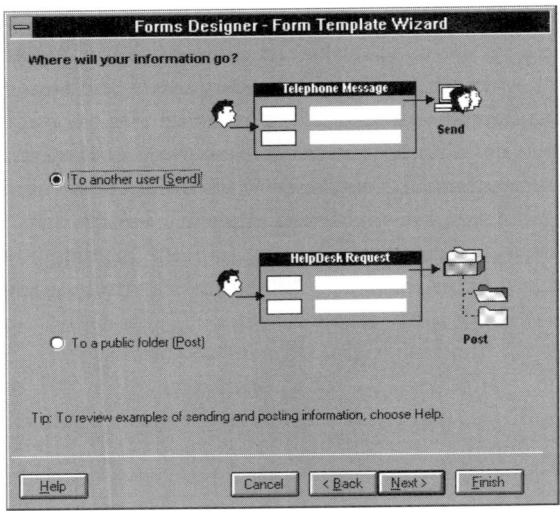

Figure 8.2: The Form Template Wizard

where it can be sorted, grouped, and searched on later. If you are creating a "New Hire" form that will collect all of the information for setting up a payroll account for a new employee, then you may wish the form's contents to be sent directly to the person responsible for setting up payroll accounts. Remember that it is possible to daisy-chain forms or have one form respond to another, so that if you did send a form's contents to a person responsible for setting up payroll accounts, that person could have their own response form that posted the information to a Public Folder when they were done with it.

Once you have decided where the information from the form will be sent, click on the **Next** button at the bottom of the Form Template Wizard to answer how your form will be used—to send original information or to respond to another form. If you were creating a form that was to be a later stage in a workflow process (e.g., new employee information is entered and sent to the person who creates payroll accounts, a payroll account is created, the information is stored in a Public Folder), then you would select "Respond to Another Form." If you were creating the first stage of a workflow process, or a single stand-alone form, then you would choose "To Send Information."

Once you've decided whether or not your form will be used to respond to another form, click on the **Next** button again, and you will be prompted for the number of windows your form will use—one or two. You may wish to select two windows for your single form if for some reason you would like to display information in a manner different from the way it is entered. For example, if you create a form that will be used to enter personal information about a new employee, then send that information to someone who will set up a payroll account for them, you may not want the person creating the payroll account to be able to alter the personal information or be able to see certain unnecessary information, such as the person's shoe size. In this situation, you could create a form with two windows. The first window would allow data entry of all required information. The second window would be a "display" window, with some fields marked as "read only" so that they could not be changed and some fields not displayed at all. You could then create a new form that was a response to the original form that did allow viewing and editing information, but set permissions so that only certain people could do so—but that's getting a little fancy for a first look at the Exchange Forms development environment.

Once you've chosen where the information will be sent, how the form will be used, and how many windows it will

146 The Microsoft Exchange Forms Designer

have, the only thing left to do with the Form Template Wizard is click on the **Next** button, enter a name and brief description of the form, and click on the **Finish** button. The Form Template Wizard will create a new "blank" form project using a template that matches your responses to the Wizard's questions. You could also have started a form project by directly choosing one of the eight template files, located in the TEMPLATE subdirectory of the main EFD directory, EFDFORMS. The eight template files and their functionality are described below:

Template File	Functionality
PSTN1WND.EFP	1. The form posts information to an Exchange folder. 2. The form creates new information. 3. The form uses a single window.
PSTN2WND.EFP	1. The form posts information to an Exchange folder. 2. The form creates new information. 3. The form uses a single window.
PSTR1WND.EFP	1. The form posts information to an Exchange folder. 2. The form is used to respond to another form. 3. The form uses a single window.
PSTR2WND.EFP	1. The form posts information to an Exchange folder. 2. The form is used to respond to another form. 3. The form uses a single window.
SNDN1WND.EFP	1. The form e-mails information to a user's mailbox. 2. The form creates new information. 3. The form uses a single window.

Drag and Drop Programming 147

SNDN2WND.EFP
1. The form e-mails information to a user's mailbox.
2. The form creates new information.
3. The form uses two windows.

SNDR1WND.EFP
1. The form e-mails information to a user's mailbox.
2. The form is used to respond to another form.
3. The form uses a single window.

SNDR2WND.EFP
1. The form e-mails information to a user's mailbox.
2. The form is used to respond to another form.
3. The form uses two windows.

What do you do once you've completed the Wizard and created your "blank" form? The next step is to add fields to your form—boxes where people can enter information and labels to describe the boxes (Figure 8.3). To do so within the EFD, you drag and drop *controls*, objects that perform particular functions, such as a "text box" to enter information into or a "label" to label the text box. All of the controls available to you for dragging and dropping onto the blank form are within the *Toolbox*, a separate window that appears initially at the far left side of your screen and contains several small squares, each representing a different control. The Toolbox also contains the normal e-mail fields that you may add to your form—a **From:** field, a **Date:** field, a **To:** field, etc. Clicking on any of the normal e-mail fields in the Toolbox toggles their appearance on the form.

Before you get further involved in creating a new application, however, it makes sense to take a look at what Exchange forms can do.

148 The Microsoft Exchange Forms Designer

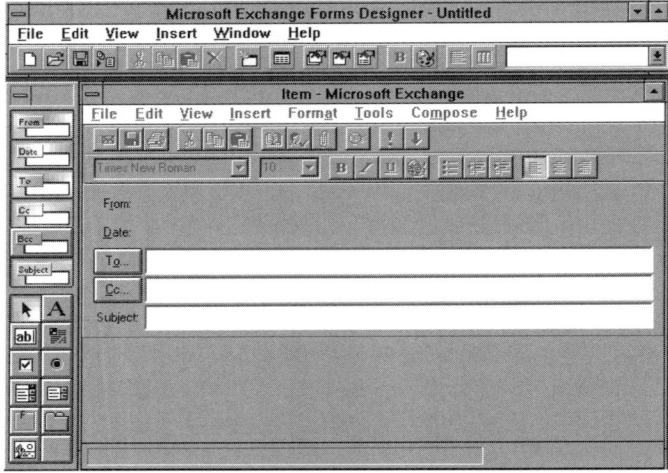

Figure 8.3: A Blank Form

Installing the Microsoft Exchange Sample Applications

Microsoft Exchange ships with several sample applications that display all of the basic EFD development options. These sample applications may already be installed in an Exchange Public Folder for you to review. If they are not available in a Public Folder, then you may install them as a Personal Folder directly from the Exchange Client Software CD or from their default installation location in the Exchange Server's EXCH-SRVR\SAMPAPPS\CLIENT directory. The Personal

Installing the Microsoft Exchange Sample Applications

Folder *.PST file containing all of the sample applications is called, appropriately enough, SAMPAPPS.PST.

 If installing the SAMPAPPS.PST file locally as a Personal Folder, be sure that you have enough disk space—the SAMPAPPS.PST file is 17.5 megabytes in size. If you have enough disk space, copy the file to your local hard drive and use the Exchange Client's **TOOLS...SERVICES** *option to add a new Personal Folder service, then select the SAMPAPPS.PST file as the *.PST file.*

To use the sample applications (or any form, for that matter), open the application folder and use the **COMPOSE...NEW FORM** option to see a list of forms available both globally and within the folder. With folder-specific applications you will also see an extra option under the COMPOSE menu for a specific form (e.g., "Compose New Classified Ad"). Some sample applications, their functionality, and what they demonstrate from a design perspective are listed below:

Sample Application	Function	Example of:
Classified Ads	Allows you to place or respond to an "Item for Sale" classified ad.	Two-form application: one form is a two-window form (one to enter and one to read it) used to enter an ad and post it to a folder; the other form is a response to the original form which mails an offer directly to the original poster of the ad.

Contact Tracking	Used to create and view: • Company and customer profiles • Action items • Correspondence and activity reports	Custom folder Views, two-window forms, multiple-form applications (the application uses five different forms).
Discussion & Response	Threaded discussion group	Uses special folder Views to group by conversation thread, also uses two forms, one to post and one to respond to posts.
Document Filer	Document management and archiving	One-form application that uses custom Views in the folder. Good example of working with other application files: word processors, spreadsheets, etc.
HelpDesk	Online Help desk call logging, tracking, and history	Excellent example of a simple, single form/folder application with strong functionality.
HotTopics	Online newsletter submissions and publishing	Two-form application that uses two different folders so that a news moderator can screen submissions before publishing them in a public area. Good example of folder security.

In addition to serving as operational examples, many of the Exchange sample applications are available as Exchange Forms Designer source code so that you can use the applications as starting points for your own projects—or just modify them slightly to fit your needs. Source code for sample applications is installed along with the Exchange Forms Designer in the EFDFORMS\SAMPLES directory. You can open any of these applications for review or modification by choosing to "Open an Existing Application" when starting the EFD, rather than running the Form Template Wizard.

Creating a Microsoft Exchange Application

With the Exchange Forms Designer, it's a simple matter to create a basic form that will allow quick routing of information from one user to another. As an example, let's walk through creation of a form for the recording of telephone messages. To begin, launch the EFD and start by using the Form Template Wizard. Specify the Wizard options as follows:

Wizard Step	Answer
Where will your information go?	To another user (Send).
How will your Send form be used?	To send information.
One window or two?	One window.
Title/Description	Call the form "Telephone Messages" and type a brief description.

After completing the Form Template Wizard, you will have a new blank form ready for new fields (Figure 8.4). You will need to add a label to the top of the form that says "Telephone Messages." To do so, click on the Label control in the Toolbox (the square with the large capital "A"). If you are uncertain about which control is which, just hold your mouse over any of the squares in the Toolbox. After a second, a "ToolTip" will pop up with a description of the square your mouse is over. Once you've clicked on the Label control, click again on the blank form to place the label. Once placed, the label will say "Label1." To change it to "Telephone Message," click on the label and type over the Label1 caption.

To add fields for who called, what the caller's phone number is, and a description of the message, first click on the Entry field control (the icon shows the letters "a" and "b" in a text box). After selecting the control, click on the

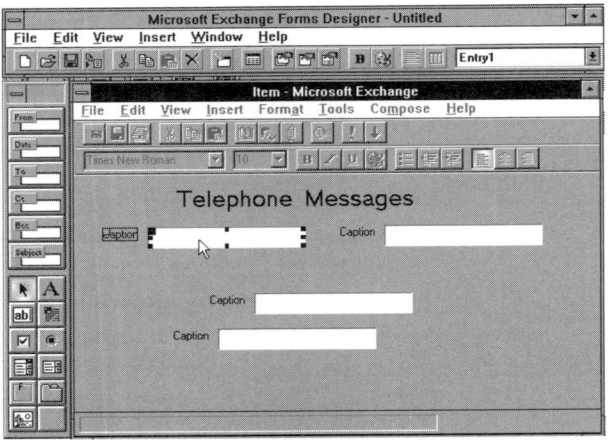

Figure 8.4: Building an Exchange Form

form to place the empty fields. To change the caption of each field from "caption" to "Who Called:" just click on the caption and overtype.

You should now have a form with a Telephone Message label that is probably too small to read and three entry fields that don't quite look right. You also have some unnecessary e-mail fields on the form (**CC:**, **Date:**, **Subject:**). To eliminate the e-mail fields, just click on them once in the Toolbox. Get rid of all of them except for the **To:** field. To complete the other fields, you need to select each field and then set its properties by using the **VIEW...FIELD PROPERTIES** menu option or the **F4** HotKey. This will open up the Field Properties window for the selected field. Use the Format tab to change the font or alignment of the field and the Initial Value field to set up default contents for one of the Entry fields (e.g., if you want the "Description of Message:" field to read "Please Return Their Call" unless you manually change it, enter that as your initial value for the field).

The form should be starting to shape up, with maybe a few small adjustments required. To resize any of the fields, use the mouse to drag the corners of the field—just like resizing a window. If done properly, your form should be ready for installation, as shown in Figure 8.5.

Installing a Form in the Global Forms Registry

At this point your phone message form is ready for installation. You may install it into a Personal Folder or get your

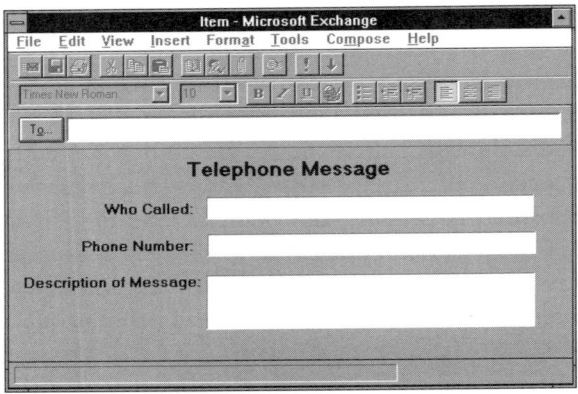

Figure 8.5: A Telephone Message Form

Exchange administrator's permission to install the form into the *Global Forms Registry*, a collection of forms that all Exchange users can use from anywhere in Exchange. This would be the best place for a telephone message application, since it would allow all users to create and view phone messages. In case you cannot install the form there and you use your Telephone Message form to send a message to another user who does not have access to the form, the other user will still receive the information, but it will look like a normal e-mail message. If they have access to your form, they will see the form, just like you do when you enter information. For purposes of this example, let's install the form to the Global Forms Registry.

To install an Exchange form once you've completed it, use the **FILE...INSTALL** menu option within the EFD. If you have not yet saved the application, it will do so for you, prompting you for a name for the *.EFD file that contains your project information. Give the file a name such as "Phone1.EFD" and hit the **OK** button. The Exchange

Forms Designer will save your file and then do something amazing—it will actually write out Visual Basic source code for your form based on what you did using the EFD. You've just written a sophisticated Visual Basic messaging application! And not one line of programming! The EFD will then call its version of Visual Basic to compile your application and prompt you to select a location for the installation of the form. Select "Global Forms Registry" and click on the **OK** button. Feel good? You should—you've just installed an Exchange form that other users can use to create and view phone messages. Not bad for a little bit of mouse clicking!

From Here

You've now had an exhaustive look at the Microsoft Exchange Client and should be able to consider yourself an Exchange wizard. You've also had a first look at the Exchange Forms Designer and a taste of how easy it is to develop applications within Exchange. If you have some experience with Microsoft's Visual Basic Development Environment, you also have the ability to open Exchange projects directly with Visual Basic and modify the application to do some sophisticated things: database access, Internet connectivity, links to other applications—anything you could program outside Exchange, you can program within Exchange as well.

Next we'll take a look at the installation of an Exchange Server—how to get up and running quickly with Microsoft Exchange. The target audience for the Administration section of this book is different from that for the User section. It is assumed that the administrator of an Exchange environment will be familiar with Windows NT and network issues related to Exchange. If that sounds like you, and you're ready for more—read on!

MICROSOFT EXCHANGE SERVER ADMINISTRATION

This section of *The Microsoft Exchange Guide* is for system administrators and network managers who need a ready reference for Microsoft Exchange installation, configuration, administration, and maintenance. A basic knowledge of Windows NT Server is assumed, as is a working knowledge of the Microsoft Exchange Client. The previous section of this guide deals extensively with basic Exchange Client functionality and concepts and should provide ample background for those already skilled in Windows NT Server and basic messaging and network concepts.

Installation and Configuration

Microsoft Exchange is a client/server messaging system, not a client/polling, file-based messaging system such as Microsoft Mail and other older mail systems. The distinction is fairly important. Older mail systems would keep mail messages stored in flat files on either a file server or local hard drive. Queued messages would wait on the mail server in a queue directory until the client would "poll," or actively look for messages in the queue area. Once found, messages would be transferred to the mailbox file in the user's personal directory on the file server, or to their local hard drive. This meant that the mail client software would be frequently polling the mail server for new messages (typically at 10-minute intervals), creating network traffic and using desktop resources, even if no new messages were present. Also, mail messages would consume fair amounts of space on local drives or on file servers. Perhaps most annoying, the polling delay (between when a message was created, then polled to the mail server, then polled to the receiving client) could be as much as 20 minutes—not exactly the lightning-quick response you would expect from an electronic messaging system.

Exchange is a client/server messaging system. The Exchange Server (Figure 9.1) is active and automatically routes messages and alerts clients when new mail arrives. This eliminates the need for regular polling and can greatly reduce network traffic. The Exchange Server, rather than the client, does the work of checking for new messages and moving them to the appropriate mailbox. The mailbox structure itself is very different as well. It is

Installation and Configuration 159

Figure 9.1: Microsoft Exchange Server

based on a relational database rather than a flat-file system. All mail (except for Personal and offline folders) is kept in the Exchange Server's database. The database structure provides indexing for quick retrieval and enables the Exchange Server to save tremendous amounts of file space through the elimination of duplicate messages. When you send the same message to thirty people, the message actually exists in only one spot in the database—all recipients receive only a reference to that message, greatly reducing the disk space required.

Of course, the advantages of a client/server messaging system don't come without a price tag. Because the server does so much more of the work in a client/server system, it needs significantly more resources than your average file server. With the constant database access required by a production Exchange Server system, it is better to configure the hardware for an Exchange Server as you would for a large database server, rather than a normal file server or post office server for an older mail system.

160 Microsoft Exchange Server Administration

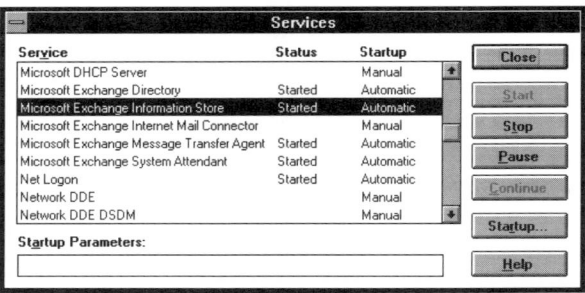

Figure 9.2: The Exchange Services

The Exchange Server is also, like a database and unlike older messaging systems, a real application. It is not simply a "post office" upon which message files reside. It continually runs the sophisticated Exchange Server Services (Figure 9.2), each of which consumes memory and other server resources to perform its functions. The Exchange Server NT Services and their functionality are described below:

Exchange Service	Function
Microsoft Exchange System Attendant	The "master" maintenance service—handles monitors, alerts, routing tables, directory replication consistency, and message logging. Must be running for Exchange to work at all.
Microsoft Exchange Directory	Another essential service, Directory maintains information on all mailboxes, folders, and servers for other services to use to resolve addresses and route messages.

Installation and Configuration   161

Microsoft Exchange Information Store	Another essential service, the Information Store maintains both the Public and Private Information Store databases, controlling storage and access to all Exchange data.
Microsoft Exchange Message Transfer Agent	The MTA manages connections to other servers and systems. You must run the MTA if you are using more than one Exchange Server or if you are using a connector or gateway, such as the Internet Mail Connector.
Microsoft Exchange Internet Mail Connector	An SMTP gateway that connects Exchange to the Internet. An optional component.
Microsoft Mail Connector	The Microsoft Mail Connector allows Exchange to act as a Microsoft Mail post office, permitting messaging and address list interaction with existing MS Mail systems. An optional component.
Schedule + Free/Busy Connector	The Schedule + Free/Busy Connector allows Exchange's version of Schedule + to interact with older Microsoft Mail and Schedule + systems. An optional component, used with the Microsoft Mail Connector.
Microsoft Exchange X.400 Connector	An X.400 gateway that connects Exchange to compliant systems. An optional component.

Microsoft Exchange Directory Synchronization	The Directory Synchronization Service allows Exchange to transfer directory information with Microsoft Mail post offices using the MS Mail 3.x directory synchronization protocol. An optional component, used with the Microsoft Mail Connector.
Microsoft Exchange Key Management Server	Maintains the security database for digital encryption of Exchange messages. An optional component.

It is important to remember when configuring hardware resources for an Exchange Server that these services will be running all of the time—and will always require resources to do so. Also, these services interact dynamically with all network clients. They require Domain Administrator level rights to function, and (because their performance will be visible from the Exchange Client) their performance will affect every desktop within your organization. It is impossible to overemphasize the importance of high-performance hardware, optimized for Exchange Server production use, in the success of any Exchange messaging installation.

Setting Up the First Server in a Site

Exchange is implemented as a three-level system (Figure 9.3). At the topmost level is the Exchange organization, the entire collection of all connected entities within your mes-

Setting Up the First Server in a Site 163

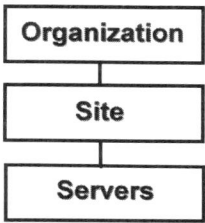

Figure 9.3: The Exchange Hierarchy

saging system. Beneath the organization is the collection of Exchange sites. Sites are collections of Exchange servers, usually within the same geographic area. These servers are connected by high-speed LAN connections (minimally as little as 56kbs in bandwidth, but normally T1 or Ethernet speeds), allowing for constant folder replication and messaging traffic. Different Exchange sites can replicate folder information to each other at scheduled intervals, based on traffic and bandwidth considerations, while servers within the same Exchange site automatically propagate such information within five minutes of its creation (hence the high-speed LAN connection requirement). The basic unit of an Exchange Server organization is the server, the box that runs the Exchange Server Services.

It is tempting (and beneficial for training purposes) to take the Exchange Server CD, put it in the CD-ROM drive of an unused file server, and run the SETUP.EXE program found within the appropriate platform (Intel, Alpha, MIPS) directory. It is as simple an installation as Microsoft Office or any other Windows-based program. After completion of the normal setup program, the Microsoft Exchange Performance Optimizer, an Exchange configuration Wizard, is automatically run, doing the tough work of tweaking Exchange file locations and memory utilization ceilings for you. Sounds pretty simple—and it is. Unfortunately, the setup program will not optimize the Windows NT Server configuration for you, nor will it assist you in planning your organization's structure.

Prior to installation of Microsoft Exchange on a target server, the NT system configuration must be optimized for Exchange Server in order to prevent such evils as *thrashing* (severe disk access overloading), severe *page faults* (heavy virtual memory disk access, symptomatic of insufficient RAM), and other system evils that can occur when a heavily memory- and disk-intensive system such as Microsoft Exchange is running. It is important to ensure that the near-mission-critical functionality of messaging runs smoothly and performance bottlenecks are addressed before they occur.

Hardware Configuration

Microsoft lists the minimum and recommended hardware configuration to run Microsoft Exchange at all as follows:

Hardware	Minimum	Recommended
Processor	Intel 486 or supported RISC-based processor	Intel Pentium 90 MHz or supported RISC-based processor
RAM	At least 32 MB	at least 64 MB
Disk	500 MB	1 GB—preferably multiple physical drives

Remember, these are Microsoft's recommendations for hardware configuration. A prudent administrator will arrange for hardware superior to these recommendations. It is worthy to note that currently very few other applica-

Setting Up the First Server in a Site 165

tions must have 64 MB of RAM to run effectively in production. Microsoft Exchange requires significantly higher server resources than older messaging systems, reflecting its "active server" role in the client/server model. Skimp on server resources at your own peril—an effective Exchange implementation centers around properly configured servers and well-thought-out site deployment. Be sure to use components of true "production server" quality—little things like bus architecture, disk controller specifications, and onboard cache can become serious bottlenecks to performance if inferior products are used.

The most important areas to concentrate on in configuring a system for Microsoft Exchange are physical disk performance and RAM. Windows NT's naturally heavy use of virtual memory makes physical disk performance an important part of any server configuration, but when you add the constant database access and heavy peak virtual memory utilization that Exchange can demand, it becomes absolutely crucial to optimize the disk configuration. Likewise, extra RAM will reduce virtual memory usage, speeding performance and reducing disk access. These needs are reflected in the following system recommendations:

Exchange System Configuration Recommendations

Component	Recommended
RAM	128 MB or greater.
Processor	At least a single "latest and greatest chip" processor (currently an Intel Pentium Pro, but give it a week or two…). Multiple processors are an excellent upgrade, as Exchange will use them to their fullest capacity.

Disk controllers	Fast SCSI-2 controllers, preferably multiple controllers for redundancy and performance.
Hard drives	Fast SCSI-2 drives. Performance counts—get the fastest access-time drives you can. Get at least three separate physical disks to allow for separation of paging files and optimal distribution of Exchange databases and logs.
Redundancy	Consider a hardware-based approach to disk mirroring or RAID solutions. Using NT's functionality to do so will usually provide inferior performance.

As long as you pick your equipment wisely and get as far above the minimum requirements as you can, you will be rewarded with top-notch system execution. However, if budgetary limits restrict your initial configuration to something less than optimum, don't worry. Exchange, just like Windows NT itself, is completely scalable. If you add more RAM, or an extra disk controller, or more drives to an Exchange Server, you can simply rerun the Microsoft Exchange Performance Optimizer to have Exchange instantly reconfigure itself to take advantage of the new resources.

Disk Drive Configuration

Once you've got your "best possible box" assembled and you're ready to install Windows NT on it, there are a number of configuration steps you should take to ensure proper Exchange performance. First of all, think about how you will configure your drives before you install Windows NT. Disk drive access needs should determine your configuration. The main components of disk access in an Exchange system are:

1. Exchange Information Store access
2. Paging file access
3. System access

Optimally, you will dedicate separate disks for Information Store access and system access. However, not everyone will have multiple high-speed disks available, and priority decisions must be made. Exchange Information Store database and log distribution are important to performance but will be handled automatically by Exchange, which tests your hardware and chooses the best location for its files. However, Exchange makes these decisions after the rest of your system has already been configured. If improperly done, Exchange will be presented with unfortunate choices for file locations. If you can leave Exchange two physically separate, empty (no system or other applications on the disks) high-speed disks to work with, optimal performance will be reached. If not, don't worry—as long as the system was configured optimally, Exchange will optimize placement of its files for performance.

Paging file access is crucial to performance in two ways. First, virtual memory is frequently used in Windows NT, and optimizing disks for paging file access is an essential part of Windows NT performance tuning. Second, since virtual memory is frequently used, paging file access can compete with application and system access—a paging file exclusively located on the same drive as a database will actually slow the database access down (and vice versa). Of course, when writing to a single paging file, Windows NT must wait for its read/write operations to complete on that drive before executing others. If paging files exist on separate physical drives, then read/write operations can be occurring on each of them simultaneously, greatly increasing performance. This means that the optimal paging file performance is obtained by having all physical drives contain paging files.

Are the drive requirements starting to sound a little excessive yet? If you follow this logic you will also dedicate a separate drive for system files, two dedicated high-capacity drives for Exchange to distribute files on, and of course you'll use multiple disk controllers for load balancing...and we haven't even talked about mirroring. We've just identified a basic Exchange Server installation, with disk mirroring for redundancy, as requiring half a dozen high-performance fast SCSI-2 drives. Don't worry, though—there is a happy minimum. You can run Exchange Server successfully for limited numbers of users on a single hard drive, using tape backups for disaster recovery. A good production implementation will use three physical drives (four with mirroring), configured as follows:

Example of Production Drive Configuration

Drive 0: Logical drive C 1–2 GB	Boot disk—System files Paging file (Approx. min. = RAM; Max., all available space)
Drive 1: Logical drive D 2 GB	Paging file (Approx. min. = RAM; Max., all available space) Exchange logs
Drive 2: Logical drive E 4 GB	Paging file (Approx. min. = RAM; Max., all available space) Exchange installation Exchange Information Store

Setting Up the First Server in a Site 169

In the example configuration above, optimal performance for virtual memory access is obtained by creating multiple paging files spanning drives. Conflict with Exchange database access is avoided by not placing a paging file on the same drive as the Exchange installation or data. Likewise, the system need not compete with Exchange for disk access.

The Exchange logs are frequently placed on active drives since they require limited disk access normally. This means that we have effectively dedicated Drive 1 to paging file use. The only conflict not addressed by this configuration is that between system and paging file access on Drive 0, which has the least affect upon performance. In fact, despite the theoretical performance increase, failure to create a paging file on the same drive as the system files actually would cause a problem with memory dumps upon system errors. We can therefore avoid dedicating a separate drive to system files, combining it instead with paging file access.

This configuration also has the advantage of requiring full fault tolerance measures only on Drive 2. The system files and Exchange logs on Drive 0 and Drive 1 can be quickly restored from tape in the event of failure, while all of the up-to-the-minute data is isolated on Drive 2. In conjunction with tape backups, mirroring Drive 2 will provide sufficient fault tolerance for most production implementations.

So we've narrowed down the required drives to a count of four (if you mirror Drive 2 in the example above). If you had a smaller production implementation (say a few dozen users), you might eliminate Drive 1 entirely, placing Exchange logs on Drive 0 and creating a paging file on Drive 2. Such an implementation, using mirroring for fault tolerance, would take the following appearance:

Drive 0: Logical drive C Boot disk—System files
2 GB Paging file (Approx. min., RAM + 22 MB; Max., all available space)
  Exchange logs
Drive 1: Logical drive D Exchange installation
4 GB Exchange Information Store
  Paging file (Approx. min., RAM + 22 MB; Max., all available space)

Again, using an additional drive and mirroring the Exchange Information Store drive would provide fault tolerance, but you might also (rather than mirroring) use the additional drive to create a stripe set with parity.

In a stripe set with parity configuration, using just three physical drives, the drives would be configured as follows:

Drive 0: Logical drive C Boot disk—System files
2 GB Paging file (Min., RAM + 150 MB; Max., all available space)
  Exchange logs
Drive 1 and Drive 2: Exchange installation
Logical drive D Exchange Information Store
(stripe set with parity)
4–8 GB total (Drive 1 and Drive 2)

Fault Tolerance and Redundancy

The disk striping with parity configuration has two disadvantages when compared to a mirroring solution, and one large advantage. The first disadvantage is that disk striping with parity is slower than mirroring in writing to the disk. Mirroring actually speeds up disk reads, since NT can read from both halves of a mirror set at once. Disk striping with parity also offers an improvement in data reading, but slows down disk writes. Disk writes are not significantly affected by disk mirroring, since both disks can be written to at the same time. The second disadvantage to disk striping with parity over mirroring is that in the event of disk failure, a mirror set may be broken, and production operation restored, with a click or two of your mouse. With disk striping with parity, a replacement drive must be installed and the data automatically recovered from parity information before production is restored. Slower and not as simple to recover from—doesn't sound too good for disk striping with parity, huh? Wait a minute before judging it too harshly—disk striping with parity is not that much slower than mirroring, and if you keep a spare drive available, not much harder to recover from (you'd be replacing a mirrored drive too, as soon as you could). Striping with parity also offers the major advantage of allowing you to use all available disk space. A mirrored drive requires twice as much space—the production data is "mirrored" to an extra, invisible disk. Mirroring a 4-GB drive requires two 4-GB drives—one for data, one for the mirrored data. Disk striping with parity allows you to use both drives, all 8 GB, and still be fault tolerant.

Server Service Configuration

Microsoft Exchange requires a dedicated machine on which to run. It should not be configured as a PDC, or even a BDC, unless absolutely necessary. Any operation not essential to Exchange Server operation and network connectivity should be removed from the NT configuration and all services that remain should be optimized for Exchange performance. Most important among these running services is the Server service, accessible from the Network icon in Windows NT's Control Panel. To properly configure the Server service, select Server from the list of installed software, and click on the **Configure** button. The Server Configuration window will appear (Figure 9.4). To optimize for Exchange, set the Optimization option to "Maximize Throughput for Network Applications." Also, unless you are running LAN Manager servers on your network, make sure that the checkbox labeled "Make Browser Broadcasts to LAN Manager 2.x Clients" is deselected. Making these changes will ensure that memory allocation will be optimized for Exchange Server.

Server Installation

Time for that installation CD yet? Almost. Once you have your server configured and the Windows NT Server service

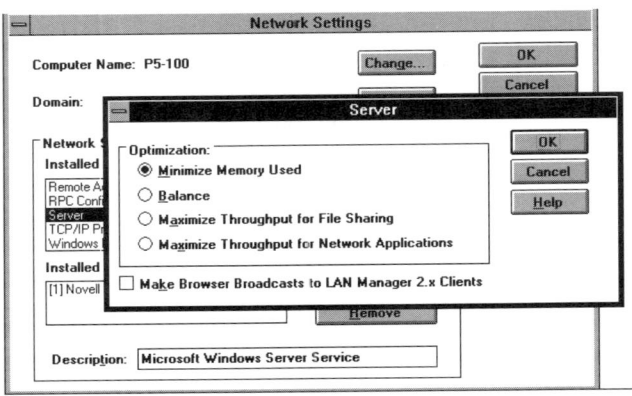

Figure 9.4: Server Service Configuration

Setting Up the First Server in a Site 173

set up properly, you'll want to configure the Windows NT domain account for Exchange and set up a group account for Exchange administrators. These steps complete the "prep" work for an Exchange installation and allow you to get on with the serious business of watching that blue progress bar crawl across the Setup window.

Creating the Service Account

Exchange needs to interact with the entire NT domain, so Exchange Services must be configured to run as a user with domain administration rights (Figure 9.5). Exchange requests the account information to use during setup, so you want to configure it prior to running SETUP.EXE on the installation CD. You are probably already logged on as a user with domain administrator rights (you'd better be — Exchange won't install unless you are!), but don't just use your account for the Exchange Services. If you use a normal administrator's account or your own account and you ever change your password, then the Exchange Services

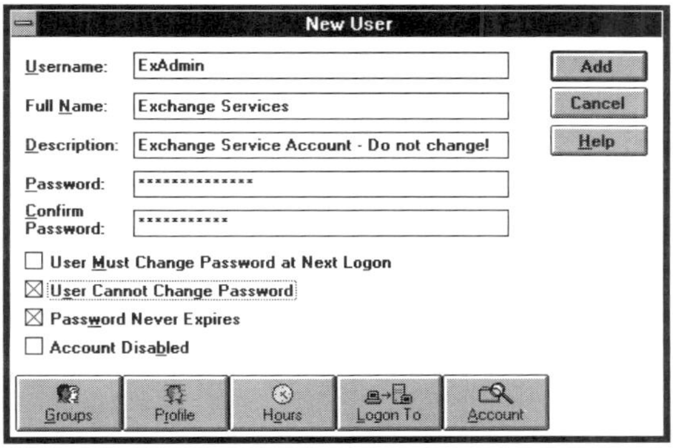

Figure 9.5: Creating the Service Account

will be unable to start from that point on. Don't bring down your mail system just because your 45-day-old password has expired—create a special account, with a password that does not expire, just for Exchange. Be sure to call it "ExAdmin," or something recognizable, so that you can identify it in the user list if you ever need to edit it. For security, you will want to explicitly deny this account access to sensitive areas of your LAN (remember, you just created a domain administrator's account with a password that does not expire). NT will allow this account access to every place you do not specifically deny it. For this reason, you should still regularly change the password (but don't force the change automatically—you don't want to bring down Exchange) by manually editing the Startup As... dialog for each of the Exchange services, accessible by using the Services icon from the Control Panel.

Setting Up the Server Administrator's Group

Once the Exchange Server account has been created, you will also want to create an Exchange Administrators group. You will grant this group full administrative rights to Exchange once installed. By using a group, rather than specific users, you will easily be able to control access to Exchange functions without redoing Exchange permissions—you can just add or delete members from the NT group. In general, use NT domain groups rather than specific accounts when granting Exchange permissions—it makes it easier to administer.

Installation from CD-ROM

Last (but not least): Before installing Exchange, make sure that the version of Windows NT that you are running is the

Setting Up the First Server in a Site 175

latest and greatest one supported by Exchange. This means that all service packs and upgrades must be applied, if they have not been already. The initial commercial release of Exchange included Service Pack 4 for Windows NT v3.51 in the \PATCHES subdirectory of the server installation CD. Run the service pack prior to installing Exchange. If you are not certain if the NT Service pack is appropriate for the version of Exchange you are installing, go ahead and start to install Exchange—no harm will occur if you have not applied a service pack, you will simply receive an error message saying "Microsoft Exchange Requires at Least Service Pack 4 Be Installed," or words to that effect, and you may then cancel setup, upgrade NT, and rerun setup.

If your Windows NT version is current, then you should now be ready to install Microsoft Exchange from CD. You have a Windows NT Server configured for optimal Exchange performance, and all that remains is inserting the disk into the drive and running the SETUP.EXE file, located in the appropriate platform subdirectory (e.g., \SETUP\I386 for Intel-based servers).

What's that? No CD-ROM drive? Stop immediately and get one! Although Exchange can be installed from a shared network CD-ROM, or even a parallel port portable CD-ROM drive, the lack of an internal CD-ROM drive recognized by Windows NT will be a constant irritant during the life of the machine and will undoubtedly slow upgrades, prevent disaster recovery, and affect almost everything. The Exchange Server Install CD would occupy roughly three hundred and thirty 1.44 MB floppy disks (and we didn't even count the client software CD). The days when a CD-ROM was a luxury are long past. If there isn't a CD-ROM drive in the machine, then get one.

The first option the Exchange Setup Program presents is whether to choose a Typical, Custom, or Minimum installation (Figure 9.6). Choose Typical. The functionality installed is the same on the different options, although the Custom option does permit you the opportunity to not install the sample Exchange applications. Install them—they're very useful as examples and some might serve as actual production applications.

Next, you will be prompted to enter the licensing information for Exchange Server. Be very careful when entering licenses not to enter too few licenses—when concurrent connections to an NT server exceed your stated licensing limits, the License Logging Service (accessible from the Services icon in Control Panel) can lock out further users. This can be a major annoyance to Exchange users trying to log on.

Figure 9.6: Installing from CD

Setting Up the First Server in a Site 177

Now comes the real nitty-gritty of the Setup Program—the site and organization definition. Your options are to "Join an Existing Site" or to "Create a New Site." If this were an addition to an existing site, you would select Join an Existing Site and simply enter the machine name of an existing Exchange Server within the site. If this is the first server in a site (and that's what we're talking about here, in case you've forgotten), then select Create a New Site, and fill in your chosen organization name and site name. Be very, very, very, VERY careful about your choice of organization and site names. They cannot be changed once entered without completely reinstalling Exchange—on all the Exchange Servers in the grouping! If you start out with an organization name of "Joe's Company," get Exchange up and running on twelve servers in nine different locations around the world, and then decide to change the organization name to "Joe's Company, Inc.," you will have to reinstall Exchange on every server! Save yourself a lot of heartache later on and run all naming choices by the powers-that-be prior to installation.

After naming your organization and site, you will be prompted for the account information for the Exchange Services Account. Enter the ExAdmin account created earlier.

The installation from CD-ROM is now complete, and the Microsoft Exchange Services will start. At this point, the Microsoft Exchange Performance Optimizer will automatically be launched (Figure 9.7). The Microsoft Exchange Server Performance Optimizer asks you to answer multiple questions about how the Microsoft Exchange Server will be used. Using this information, the Performance Optimizer moves files to optimize disk access. Take the time to click the **Next** button and run the

178 Microsoft Exchange Server Administration

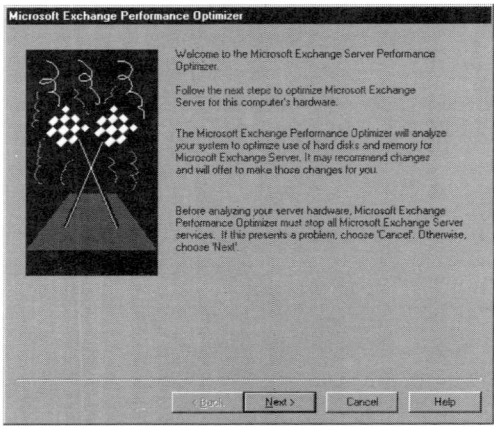

Figure 9.7: The Microsoft Exchange Performance Optimizer

Performance Optimizer right away, rather than hitting the **Cancel** button to postpone it.

The Performance Optimizer will ask you a few questions to help it optimize your Exchange Server configuration. It will ask you to enter in the estimated number of user mailboxes for the particular server you are installing, the estimated total users in your organization, the type of server you are installing, and a memory usage limit, if desired. The estimated server and organization user counts are straightforward enough, but the other parameters are a little more slippery.

The Memory Usage field is actually asking you to enter in the maximum amount of memory that Exchange will be allowed to use. Do *not* enter any value in this field at all, unless you are running other production systems, such as a database server, on the same machine (a very bad idea—Exchange should be run on dedicated hardware). If no value is entered into this field, then Exchange will have

Setting Up the First Server in a Site   179

access to all available resources. If you enter a value (in megabytes), then Exchange will use only up to that amount of available RAM. Be sure to leave it blank.

The type of Exchange server you are running is broken down into four options, any or all of which may be selected. The options are as follows:

Option	Description
Private Store	Some (any at all) user mailboxes will be located on this server, i.e., a Private Information Store.
Public Store	Some (any at all) Public Folders will be located on or replicated to this server, i.e., a Public Information Store.
Connector/Directory Import	This server will be used as a dedicated backbone connection server.
Multi-server	One of two or more total servers within the Exchange site.

In a standard configuration, check the Public Store and Private Store options. If you anticipate installing more than one server in the site, also check the Multi-server box. You would check the Connector/Directory Import box only if you were using this server as a dedicated connector machine between sites with high inter-site traffic. In such a case, you would not use the machine for Public or Private Information Store, and would not check either option.

Once you've answered the questions as best you can, click on the **Next** button. The Performance Optimizer will analyze your drives and calculate the best locations for Exchange files.

Once the file locations have been calculated, a report of suggested locations will be displayed. Make a note of where Exchange is moving your data and files for later reference, and then click the **Next** button to implement the changes. Congratulations! You have successfully configured Exchange for optimal performance.

Granting Initial Permissions

Even though Exchange has now been installed and tweaked for optimal performance, it is still unusable. All that work for nothing! Well, not really nothing—all that remains to be done is to set up the initial permissions on the Exchange Server for Exchange administrators and then install client software to access the Exchange Server.

To grant access to administrative functions on the Exchange Server to the Exchange Administrators group, you will need to launch the Microsoft Exchange Administrator program, newly installed within the Microsoft Exchange Program Group. Go ahead and start the program by double-clicking on the icon or the entry in the Start menu (if using NT v4.0). You will be prompted to enter the name of the server to which you wish to connect. You may click on the **Browse** button to select the server name from a list of all servers in the site, or simply type in the machine's name. Once you've done so, click on the Set as Default checkbox so that you won't need to choose a server name again the next time you run the program. Now click on the **OK** button to connect to the Microsoft Exchange Server.

If unable to connect to the Exchange Server using the Microsoft Exchange Administrator program, check to make sure you entered a valid server name

Setting Up the First Server in a Site 181

by using the Browse button to select a server rather than typing in the name directly. If your server's name does not appear in the Browse list, check the services (accessible from the Control Panel) to make sure they are running—you can't connect to the Exchange Server if the Microsoft Exchange Directory Service is not running.

For the first server in a site, you will need to set access permissions for the organization and for the entire site as well as for the particular server you are installing. To do so, highlight the appropriate object (organization, then site, then server), and use the **FILE...PROPERTIES** menu option to open the appropriate Properties window. The Microsoft Exchange Administrator program mirrors the top-down directory structure of Exchange, with the organization at the top level. Objects in the Exchange hierarchy are also marked by icons to make distinguishing them easier. The icons representing the organization, site, and server objects that need to have their permissions configured are as follows:

 The Exchange organization

 An Exchange site

 An Exchange server

Once you've opened the Properties window for any of the Exchange objects, click on the Permissions tab to begin adding the Exchange Administrators group to the list of permitted users for the object. The ExAdmin account will already be listed with a *role* of "Service Account Admin." A *role* in Exchange is a predefined set of rights that represents a particular imagined function. For instance, a user assigned the "View Only Admin." role will be able to access all administrative detail for an object but will not be able to change any settings. A user assigned the "Permissions Admin." role will be able to perform administrative functions, as well as change the rights of others. You will want to assign the Exchange administrators the "Permissions Admin." role so that they will later be able to adjust permissions themselves without having to log on as the Service Account. To do so, click on the **Add** button to bring up a list of all groups in the domain, select the Exchange Administrator group, and click on the **Add** and then the **OK** button. The Exchange Administrator group will appear in the "Windows NT Accounts with Permissions" listing on the Permissions tab. Select the group in the listing, and change the selected role to be "Permissions Admin." Click on the **OK** button to complete the process. Once you've done this for the organization object, repeat the process for the site and server objects. The basic permission assignments are then complete.

You still need to perform a few tasks in the Microsoft Exchange Administrator program to complete your server setup. First of all, you will need to import or create some mailboxes for your users. You will need to generate an Offline Address Book so that remote users will be able to download the Address Book for offline use. You will also need to create an Organizational Forms Library to allow global-usage forms to be installed, and grant permissions to that registry based on mailbox rather than NT account. Fortunately, all of these things can be quickly configured, with any desired fine-tuning being done when convenient.

Setting Up the First Server in a Site 183

Creating Mailboxes and Importing Windows NT Users

To generate mailboxes for every user of your NT domain, simply use the **TOOLS...EXTRACT WINDOWS NT ACCOUNT LIST** menu option. This option will ask you for the name of your domain controller (you must be logged on to the domain as an administrator) and the name of a target file for the export. Generate an NTACCT.CSV file by clicking on the **OK** button. Once this export file has been created, you can use the **TOOLS...DIRECTORY IMPORT** to import the file and create new mailboxes for all NT users. Be sure to set the Directory Import parameters as follows:

Parameter	Proper Settings
Windows NT Domain	Current domain name
Microsoft Exchange Server	Current server name
Container	Recipients
Recipient Template	Blank
Import File	The full path to the NTACCT.CSV export file just created
Account Creation	Leave all boxes blank
Logging Level	Low
Multivalued Properties	Append

Once you've set the import parameters properly, click on the **Import** button and a new Exchange mailbox will be created for each NT user.

Generating the Offline Address Book

To generate an Offline Address Book that remote users can download and use for offline addressing, you have two options. You may manually generate the book on a regular basis, doing so only when changes to the address list are made and an update is needed, or you can schedule the Offline Address Book generation on a regular basis. It's best to automate Offline Address Book generation on a daily basis to ensure accuracy, unless your organization is small enough or static enough to not require regular updates. Either method is configurable from the Properties page of the DS Site Configuration object (Figure 9.8; use the **FILE...PROPERTIES** menu option when the object is highlighted, or just double-click it), found in the Microsoft Exchange Administrator program's directory structure underneath the site in the Configuration container.

To generate the Offline Address Book manually, select the Offline Address Book tab from the DS Site Configura-

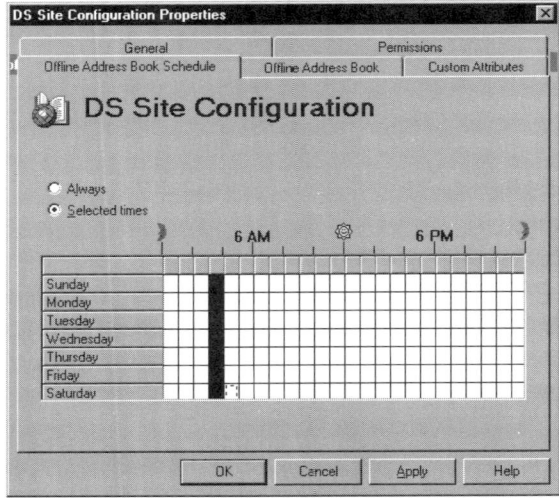

Figure 9.8: Scheduling Offline Address Book Generation

Setting Up the First Server in a Site 185

tion object's Properties page, and click on the **Generate Offline Address Book Now** button. Even if you intend to schedule this operation, it's a good idea to do it right away manually so that you can test it with your first client installation.

To schedule Offline Address Book generation, select the Offline Address Book Schedule tab and click on the Selected Times option. Be careful not to click on the Always option or Offline Address Book generation will occur every 15 minutes—a normally unreasonable amount of work for your Exchange Server to be doing. Highlight the time in the schedule grid that you wish the daily (or weekly—it's fully configurable to half-hour intervals) generation to occur—probably in the middle of the night so that it doesn't conflict with normal usage. Click on the **OK** button to complete the process.

Creating an Organization Forms Library

Once you've installed Exchange Server, in order for any forms applications to ever be used as "global" forms, that is, forms accessible from anywhere in Exchange, you must first create the registry of all global forms, the Organization Forms Library. To do so, use the **TOOLS...FORMS ADMINISTRATOR** menu option to open the Organization Forms Library Administrator window. Click on the **New** button to open a selection window, assign a name to the Organization Forms Library (personally, I think that "Organization Forms Library" is pretty catchy) and choose the language (English or otherwise) that you are using. Click on the **OK** button to finish the Library creation.

Once it is created, you must assign permissions to those Exchange users who will be able to install forms into the

Organization Forms Registry. You do so by clicking on the **Permissions** button and choosing authorized users from the Global Address List—the list of all Exchange recipients. These permissions, unlike other permissions in Exchange, are assigned to Exchange mailboxes rather than to NT accounts, preventing you from simply assigning rights to the Windows NT Exchange Administrators group. Rather than assign permissions to individual mailboxes, however, you can use the Exchange equivalent of a user group—the distribution list.

Creating a Distribution List

A distribution list can be selected from the Global Address List for assigning permissions to the Organization Forms Library just as an individual mailbox can be. To create a distribution list of all Exchange administrators, use the **FILE...NEW DISTRIBUTION LIST** menu option or the **CTRL-D** HotKey within the Microsoft Exchange Administrator program. This will open the New Distribution List window, which will prompt you for:

- A display name, which will appear in the Global Address List with other user names (e.g., "Exchange Administrators")
- An alias for internal reference (e.g., "exadmins")
- An owner of the distribution list (select your mailbox)
- All the members of the list

To add members to the list, click on the **Modify** button located just under the Members List, and select the mailboxes of all Exchange administrators from the Global Address List. Once finished, click on the **OK** button to add the list to the Global Address List. You may now add this list to the permissions list of the Organization Forms Library, as well as use it for quick addressing of e-mail to all Exchange administrators.

Setting Up Additional Servers

Once you have a single Exchange Server installed, you've already done most of the work that any server installation will require. Although there are some slight differences in setup (which we'll review soon) for adding servers to a site rather than creating a new site, the procedures are pretty much the same. Installation of additional servers should no longer be a difficult issue. The tougher issue is whether or not you need additional servers, how many, and how they should be configured (not all servers need be installed with both Public and Private Information Stores, for example).

General Guidelines

Planning an Exchange organization should be done carefully and with input from all areas of your organization. Things like future workflow application requirements, scheduling use, and document sharing can have a sudden and unexpected impact on networks prepared only for messaging traffic. To avoid this, current and projected application and scheduling usage should be factored into Exchange planning and the intended users surveyed as to what that usage might become. The client/server nature of Exchange can also represent a significant alteration of existing network traffic patterns, and must be accounted for. Every installation of Exchange is different, since no two companies will typically have the same network infrastructure, workflow patterns, development and messaging needs, and user involvement. With these factors in mind, there are some general guidelines to Exchange infrastructure planning that can be helpful. Bear in mind that these are rule-of-thumb guidelines only—your actual mileage may vary.

How to Determine How Many Servers You Need

There are two fairly simple formulas for Microsoft Exchange Server load balancing—which means they're not by any means 100% accurate. The formulas are as follows:

1. P200 w/64 MB RAM = 100 users
2. Every building = 1 server

The first formula is straightforward enough. A basic Exchange Server implementation of 100 average users (of course, there's no such thing) should be maintainable on an average server with a basic system configuration with a single Intel P200 processor, 64 MB of RAM, and enough disk space to prevent any serious I/O bottleneck (as we discussed in the earlier Disk Drive Configuration section). Adding additional hardware will allow more users or heavier utilization. Some guidelines for upgrades:

Adding additional (SMP) processors	+100 per (P100) processor
Doubling the installed RAM	+100 users

Setting Up Additional Servers 189

Using these guidelines, to support 500 Exchange mailboxes on a single Exchange Server you would need a minimum of a quad P200 processor (+100 × 3 processors = +300) machine with 128 MB of RAM (doubling RAM = +100). Again, these are all ballpark numbers—but they ought to get you into the ballpark. Of course, disk access becomes a more likely bottleneck as RAM and processor capacity increase—don't fail to use fast, high-capacity drives and even multiple controllers if possible. Alternatives such as optical flash disks may also affect performance dramatically by providing higher-speed access to data. Also, once the number of users grows large (500+) you will quickly start to run into network bandwidth bottlenecks. Use of fast 100 Mb/s Ethernet connections or other high-speed LAN connections can help to minimize such issues, but be ready to place servers in different LAN segments just to eliminate network traffic.

That final caution brings us to our second formula, "Every building = 1." In general, LAN or WAN connectivity between different physical locations is done through more restricted bandwidth network connections than connections within a particular physical location. If you have 200 users in one building and 300 users in another building connected by a single T1 line, then you most likely will be placing an Exchange Server on each end of the T1 *pipe* (network connection). You may also wish to configure the servers as members of separate sites, in order to be able to increase the replication interval to account for network traffic beyond the five-minute period Exchange uses within a given site. Don't make these decisions quickly—all of these decisions will need to be based on careful analysis of existing network traffic and thoughtful projection of future Exchange usage.

How to Determine In What Site to Place a Server

One of the ways to minimize Exchange's impact on network traffic is to place Exchange Servers in different sites. You need to create multiple sites within your organization if different physical locations are not connected by high-speed LAN connections. For example, you may have an office in New York and an office in Boston, connected by a T1 line that analysis reveals has as little as 45 K of available bandwidth after normal, non-messaging traffic is accounted for. You would configure each office as a separate Exchange site, and configure the Exchange Site Connector to *replicate*, or copy, messages or changes made to Public Folders on a measured, scheduled basis that allowed you to exchange as

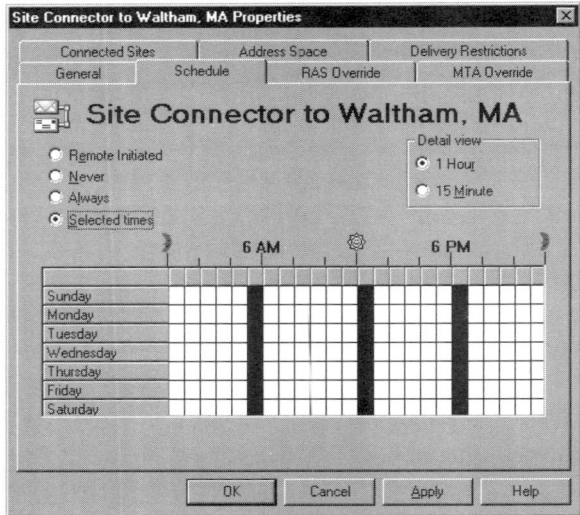

Figure 9.9: Scheduling Site Connectivity

Setting Up Additional Servers 191

much data as possible without saturating the connection. Exchange only allows you to adjust the replication between servers if they are in different sites. Exchange Servers within the same site automatically replicate all information from one to another server within five-minute intervals—too much traffic to be occurring over a small pipe.

The same factors that might mandate the creation of multiple sites for Exchange Servers in different cities might mandate the creation of multiple sites for Exchange Servers in different LAN segments. Make certain that all of your Exchange Servers have ample available bandwidth for connectivity. A good rule of thumb is at least 56 Kb/s for a half-dozen or so users—much more (1.25–16 Mb/s) for higher production use.

Where to Install the Public Information Store

One of the easiest ways to minimize replication traffic within a site is to not replicate at all. Microsoft Exchange's intersite replication traffic is primarily concerned with keeping Public Folders synchronized between all of the Public Information Stores on all of the Exchange Servers within the site. Exchange allows you to dedicate a single machine to Public Folder data, eliminating the need to replicate at all.

To make one Exchange Server a dedicated Public Folder server, simply delete the Private Information Store from the server, found beneath the server object in the Administrator program hierarchy. Of course, you will want to move any existing mailboxes in the Private Information Store to another server before deletion, using the **TOOLS...MOVE MAILBOX** option within the Administrator program (Figure 9.10).

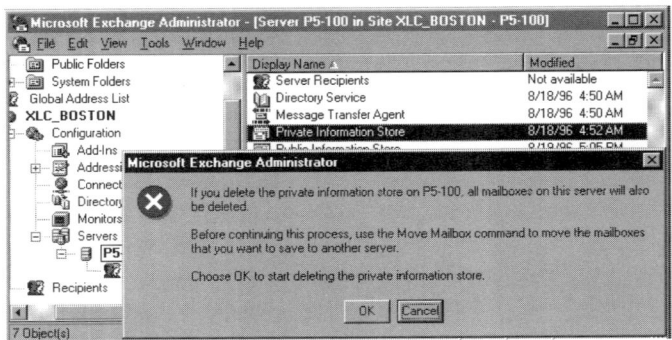

Figure 9.10: Creating a Dedicated Public Folder Server

Once the Private Information Store has been deleted on the dedicated Public Folder server, you will want to similarly delete the Public Information Stores from the other servers in the site. When you do so, you will be prompted to specify the dedicated Public Folder server as the server to which the other servers have *Public Folder affinity*—this will allow users with mailboxes on these machines to access Public Folders on the dedicated Public Folder server as if they were on the same machine as the mailboxes.

In addition to the decrease in network traffic caused by the elimination of internal site Public Folder replication, there is a substantial increase in Exchange Server performance on the servers from which Public Folders were removed. This is because normal Private Information Store disk access is no longer competing with Public Folder access for resources. Overall, creating a dedicated Public Folder server within a site is often the quickest and most rewarding way to scale a production Exchange system.

Additional Server Installation

The actual mechanics of installing an additional server to a site using the Microsoft Exchange Server Installation CD-ROM are fairly straightforward, insofar as they are nearly identical to the procedures used to install the first server to an Exchange site. The main difference is that when asked whether to "Join an Existing Site" or to "Create a New Site," you should select Join an Existing Site and enter in the server name of an existing (and running) Microsoft Exchange Server for that site which is accessible from your installation machine. It is important to remember that if you are offline, or just unable to connect to an existing Exchange Server for the site, then you will be completely unable to add the server to the existing Exchange site. In such a case, choosing the Create a New Site option and naming it the same as the existing site will not allow you to rejoin the site later on, but will rather create a conflicting Exchange site. Avoid doing this and make sure you have LAN connectivity to an existing server before trying to install an additional Exchange Server to an existing site.

Other than choosing Join an Existing Site, the main difference between installing an additional server and installing the first server in an Exchange site is that you do not need to repeat any of the organizational and site configuration tasks you had done earlier. The organization and site permissions have already been assigned, you should have been able to use the same service account, the Organization Forms Library was already created, and so forth. The only task that will be different is the creation or movement of mailboxes. If creating mailboxes, you may do so manually, using a migration tool or reimporting the NT account list after manually editing out unwanted names from the

*.CSV file. In the more likely event that the mailboxes already exist on the first site server, you may simply move them by connecting with the Administrator program to the server on which the mailboxes reside and then using the Administrator program's **TOOLS...MOVE MAILBOX** function to move the mailboxes to the new server.

Setting Up Additional Sites

If you do set up additional sites within your organization, the site and server configuration will be identical to your initial site installation—but you'll need to find a way to connect the two sites. To do so you need to add and configure a site connector between each two sites. It is important to remember that you must configure a separate site connector between each site to which you wish to replicate directly. This requirement obviously involves a certain amount of administrative effort, both for configuration and maintenance. It is for this reason that you should create separate Exchange sites only when performance needs dictate it—unnecessary segmentation of an Exchange organization into separate Exchange sites increases administrative overhead considerably.

Installing Site Connectors

To install a site connector, first choose a server in each site that will be able to handle the replication traffic without performance problems. It may make sense to dedicate a server in each site to be used only for the site connection,

Setting Up Additional Sites 195

if traffic is exceptionally high between the sites. Once the machines have been chosen, connect to the local site server using the Administrator program. Make certain that you have domain administrator rights on both the local and the *target*, or remote, server. Use the **FILE...NEW OTHER...SITE CONNECTOR** menu option to begin adding the site connector. A New Site Connector window will pop up, requesting the name of the target server (Figure 9.11). Enter the target machine's name and click the **OK** button to continue.

The Administrator program will attempt to locate the target server (make sure you have LAN connectivity supporting RPC, or it will fail at this point). Once it is successful, the new site connector will be created and the Site Connector Properties page will be displayed, set on the General tab. The General tab allows you to configure the "cost" of the site connector. Set this field to zero so that it is always used—in Exchange, "cost" is a numerical value used to determine which of two or more connectors is to be

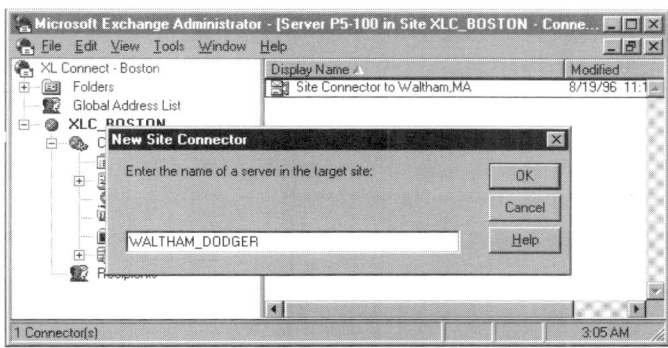

Figure 9.11: Installing a Site Connector

used to make an actual connection. The lowest-cost connector available is always used. For example, if you wanted to configure a normal WAN connection site connector and a backup dynamic RAS connector that dialed out via modem only when the LAN connection went down, you would set the LAN connection's cost to 1, and the RAS connector's cost to 99.

The site connector properties are set automatically when you first connect using the network. An X.400 address space is created for you, and all properties that need to be set to allow for connectivity are set for you—no need to be mucking around with them. The exception to this is when the local and remote Exchange Servers are in different NT domains. In such a case, you will want to click on the Override tab on the Site Connector Properties page. This page will allow you to enter a Windows NT account and password to be used to log on to the target server's domain.

Site Connector Options

An RPC-based site connector is created automatically using the **FILE...NEW OTHER...SITE CONNECTOR** option, and you can create a dynamic RAS Connector to use ISDN or dial-up for site connectivity. Exchange also allows you to create site connections using the same X.400 Connector you can use to connect to foreign systems—and it will run over any of three different MTA transport stacks: X.25, TCP/IP, or TP4/CLNP.

The Dynamic RAS Connector

RAS is an excellent tool for cheap connections and connection backups. You wouldn't want to route messaging and Public Folder replication between two large Exchange sites over a 28.8 modem normally—but in the event of a main connection's failure, a dynamic RAS connector with a higher cost than the main connection that failed will dial out and allow connectivity, albeit at a much slower rate. Multiple RAS connectors can be configured to make connectivity performance increase, and the growing availability of ISDN makes RAS connector performance viable for even normal traffic connections.

To configure a RAS connector, you must first install the RAS MTA transport stack. This needs to be done just once for all of your RAS connections. To do so, use the **FILE...NEW OTHER...RAS TRANSPORT STACK** menu option. This will open the New MTA Transport Stack window. Select RAS MTA Transport Stack from the Type text box, and select the server on which you wish to install the dynamic RAS connector from the Server text box. Click on the **OK** button to continue the installation and set the RAS MTA transport stack properties. The RAS Properties window will be displayed, prompting you for a name for the MTA stack and for an MTA callback number. Leave the MTA stack name set on the default name of "RAS (*Server*)" and enter in the telephone number of the RAS connection of the server on which you are setting up the stack, that is, the phone number of the local box on which you are working. Be sure to enter the phone number's area code and any prefixes that the remote target server will have to dial to get a connection on your local machine. Click on the **OK** button to complete the installation.

Once the RAS MTA transport stack is installed, you can create a dynamic RAS connector using the **FILE...NEW OTHER...DYNAMIC RAS CONNECTOR** option.

You will need to set the following properties on the General tab of the RAS Connector Properties window (Figure 9.12) that will be displayed:

Dynamic RAS Connector Properties

Property	Setting
Display Name	Type in a name for the RAS connector that will be displayed in the Administrator program's Directory ("RAS Connector" works pretty well).
Directory Name	Type in a shorter name (no more than 64 characters), used for Event Log entries.
MTA Transport Stack	The name of the MTA transport stack you just created, selected by default.
Phone Book Entry	The RAS phone book entry for connecting to the other site. Don't have one yet? Click on the **RAS Phone Book** button to add one.
Message Size	Set to No Limit by default, you may enter a number (in kilobytes) to limit the maximum message size (a good idea if over a dial-up line). For example, enter "3000" to set the maximum message size to 3 MB.

You will also want to adjust the frequency at which the RAS connector dials the target server on the Schedule tab, and you can enter in login information on the Override tab if the target server is located within a different NT domain. Once done, click on the **OK** button to complete the dynamic RAS connector creation.

Connecting Sites Together Using X.400

You can use the X.400 Connector to connect different Exchange sites together using TCP/IP. Of course, both the

Setting Up Additional Sites 199

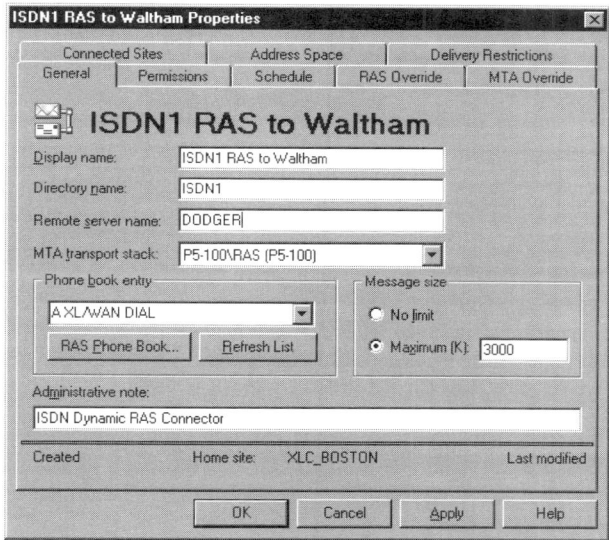

Figure 9.12: Configuring a Dynamic RAS Connector

local and target server must already be running TCP/IP and be routing to each other. It won't mean a thing if it ain't got that ping—so check to make sure that you can ping from one machine to the other before setting up the X.400 Connector. To do so, first you'll need to install the TCP/IP MTA transport stack on both the remote and local machines. Unlike a site connector, you must configure each machine separately in the same manner in order to get a connection. Use the **FILE...NEW OTHER...MTA TRANSPORT STACK** option to do so, selecting TCP/IP MTA Transport Stack from the Type text box and your local server from the Server text box of the New MTA Transport Stack window. Click on the **OK** button to continue and open the TCP Properties window. The TCP/IP

MTA Properties window will already have a default name ("TCP (*Server*)") and the appropriate local server name displayed. Click on the **OK** button to complete the MTA installation.

Now you're ready to create the X.400 Connector. Use the **FILE...NEW OTHER....X.400 CONNECTOR** option to open the X.400 Connector Properties window. Click on the General Tab to begin, and set the following properties:

Internet X.400 Connector Properties

Tab	Property	Setting
General	Name	Type in a name for the X.400 Connector that will be displayed in the Administrator program's Directory (the default is "X.400 Connector X").
	Remote MTA Name	Name of the target server MTA (as displayed on the target server's Message Transfer Agent object's General Properties tab).
	Remote MTA Password	Password of the target server MTA (as displayed on the target server's Message Transfer Agent object's General Properties tab). The Remote MTA Password can be a blank password.
	MTA Transport Stack	The name of the TCP/IP MTA transport stack you just created, selected by default.

Setting Up Additional Sites 201

	Message Text Word-Wrap	Set this to Never—you would enter a column number only if you were using the X.400 Connector to connect to a non-Exchange system with odd text handling.
	Remote Client MAPI Support	Check this box—it would be unchecked only if you were using the X.400 Connector to connect to a non-Exchange system.
Stack	Address	Enter either a resolvable (via DNS or LMHOSTS) host name for the target server, or an IP address.
Address Space	Address Space	Click the **New X.400** button to bring up the General tab and enter the X.400 address of the target server. Assign the connection a Routing Cost ("1" unless it's a backup connection).
Advanced Properties	All fields...	Entries on this tab must be the same for both systems—leave them at the defaults and all will be fine. Change them and I'll be calling to say, "I told you so...."

Once the X.400 properties have been set, click on the **OK** button to complete the installation. Remember that this process must be repeated on the target server before a connection is made.

Installing Microsoft Exchange Clients from the Network

We've covered setting up multiple Exchange Servers within a site, setting up multiple sites within an organization, even routing between sites using the Internet—but does any of it work? You need to run a client against a server after installation to verify operation, and it's a good idea in general to install the Windows NT client on each Exchange Server in order to be able to troubleshoot directly from the server. So how do you install the client, anyhow?

You could just install the client software directly from the Exchange Client Software CD. Just put the disk in a CD-ROM drive and run the SETUP.EXE file found within the appropriate platform directory (WINNT, WIN16, etc.). This could quickly become a problem, however, when you roll the software out to hundreds of users. Fortunately, the Client Software Installation CD has a setup program (Found in the \ENG\SETUP\I386 directory for an English Language Intel installation, or the \ENG\SETUP\ALPHA directory for an Alpha install) that will install a shared network installation point on an NT Server. Running this setup program will allow you to specify to what directory the client software setup programs should be copied and sets that directory up as a network share called "Exchange." Afterwards, you can connect to that share and install the Exchange Client for any available platform—no CD required.

 The setup program that creates the Client Installation Point fails to copy the Exchange Forms Designer software along with the client software.

Installing Microsoft Exchange Clients 203
from the Network

Save yourself some time later on and manually copy the \EFDSETUP directory tree to the Client Installation Share as well.

Once the Client Installation Point has been set up, you can use the Microsoft Exchange Setup Editor (installed with the server) to modify the default settings of the client software (Figure 9.13). To do so, run the Setup Editor and use the **FILE...SELECT CLIENT INSTALLATION POINT** to select one of the available platforms' Client Software Setup Directories. The Setup Editor will only modify one setup program at a time. This is an advantage if you wish different parameters for Windows 3.11 and Windows 95 Client users and a disadvantage (you must configure each one separately) if you do not.

Once you've selected a setup directory to modify, use the **FILE...SET USER OPTIONS** menu option to open the

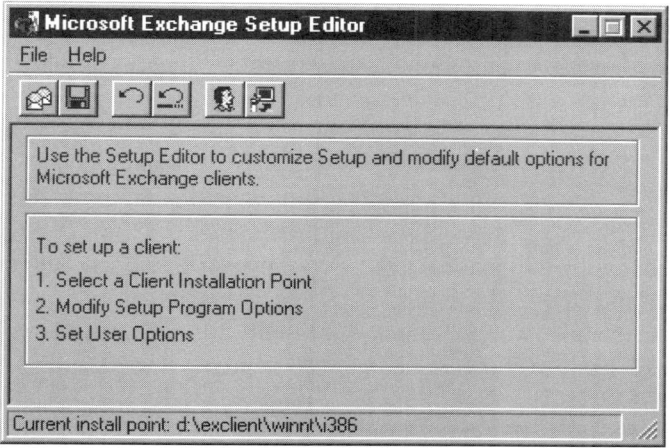

Figure 9.13: The Microsoft Exchange Setup Editor

User Options window. The General tab gives you the opportunity to choose the default user options for the client software. These are options that users may change themselves later on, such as whether or not they get a pop-up message when new mail arrives and how the spell checker behaves. As an administrator, it makes sense to select the "Empty the 'Deleted Items' Folder Upon Exiting" option on the General tab to help limit database storage of deleted messages. Likewise, you might deselect the "Save a Copy of the Item in the 'Sent Items' Folder" option on the Send tab in order to reduce database storage. In any case, be sure to enter a default Exchange Server name on the Home Server tab in order to speed profile creation.

When you've tweaked the user options to your specifications, be sure to save the changes you've made by using the **FILE...SAVE** menu option. You will see a pop-up message saying "Information Saved Successfully" if all goes well. Remember that you've only saved changes for one platform's client setup. Additional client setup directories—every client used in your organization—will need to have the same changes made to them in order for the changes to be universal.

Once the user options are saved, use the **FILE...MODIFY SETUP PROGRAM OPTIONS** to make changes to the setup program itself. This menu option will open the Setup Program Options window, which will allow you to specify the default client software installation directory, program group for icons, even whether or not the Custom and Laptop installation options are displayed during setup. You may also prevent components (such as the Schedule+ "Seven Habits Tools") from being set up at all.

The Services tab in the Setup Program Options window allows you to choose which Exchange Services—

Installing Microsoft Exchange Clients from the Network

Personal Folders, Microsoft Mail, Exchange Server, and the Personal Address Book—are installed during setup. The Binding Order tab allows you to substantially improve client performance by removing unnecessary network protocol support and moving up the primary connectivity protocol in the binding order. At the very least, be certain to remove the "RPC for Banyan Vines" protocol support if you are not on a Banyan network. Remember this tab—if client performance becomes an issue, be sure to revisit the client software bindings for quick performance enhancement through removal of unnecessary protocols.

To dramatically speed up Exchange Client performance, remove all unnecessary protocol support through use of the Microsoft Exchange Setup Editor, and then reinstall the client.

Installing Shared Network Versions of Client Software

If you are using a shared network installation of your desktop operating system, Microsoft Exchange allows you to install a partially shared version of the client software in order to minimize hard drive usage. To set up the Client Installation Point for a shared version of an Exchange Client, simply run the Client Setup program using the "/A" switch (e.g., SETUP.EXE /A).

Be certain to upgrade Microsoft Exchange whenever updates are available, using any Service Packs released by Microsoft. Having the latest version of both Exchange and Windows NT ensures that Exchange will function as it is supposed to.

Installing Microsoft Exchange with NetWare

Not everyone has the luxury of installing Microsoft Exchange into an exclusively Windows NT network. Exchange will support Novell NetWare clients—but some adjustments need to be made to the NT Server configuration of the Exchange Server in order to optimize the interaction.

If Novell clients are being used, and connecting to the Exchange Server using IPX/SPX instead of TCP/IP, you will need to do the following:

1. Install Windows NT's Gateway Services for NetWare on the Exchange Server.
2. Make certain NetBios is running on the Exchange Server.
3. Install the SAP agent on the Exchange Server.
4. Manually change the NT Server's IPX/SPX frame type to match that of the Novell clients.

Once the NT Server is configured to operate properly in a Novell environment, you will need to configure the Novell environment to interact with Exchange. First, make certain that a drive is mapped directly to the user's home directory, rather than to the directory immediately above it. Users must have read/write access to the root directory of the drive their home directory is in, or Exchange will generate errors. Next, make certain that the following statement is added to the NET.CFG file for ODI clients, or to the SHELL.CFG file if IPX.COM is being used:

```
ipx sockets = 50
```

Finally, in order to properly write schedule files, you will need to make certain File Scan is enabled on the NetWare servers.

If these extra configuration steps seem overly complicated or just plain annoying, you could always use TCP/IP—or just migrate to NT!

Migrating from Other Systems

Speaking of migration, Exchange offers substantial migration capabilities, including a Migration Wizard utility (Figure 9.14) that quickly and easily migrates data from cc:Mail or Microsoft Mail post offices or imports data files exported from almost any type of mail system, including IBM PROFS, Digital All-in-1, and Verimation MEMO. In

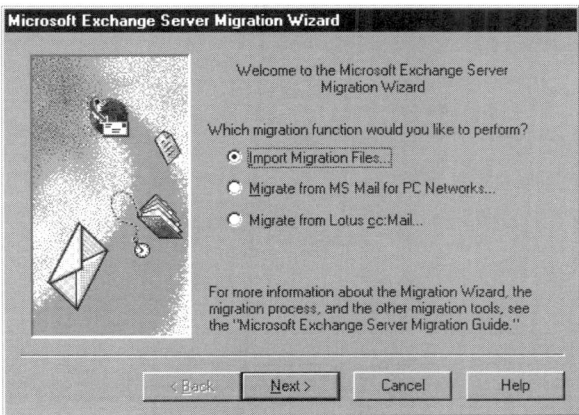

Figure 9.14: The Migration Wizard

addition, the directory import format for Microsoft Exchange is a simple flat-file format that can easily be modified by any extractor program, allowing any mail system to be migrated into Exchange. The Migration Wizard is installed along with Exchange Server's Administrator program.

The Migration Wizard will allow you to extract and import mailboxes, stored messages, bulletin boards, forms, and schedule information. It will also allow you to create Windows NT accounts automatically for users along with their new mailboxes. For some systems (MS Mail, cc:Mail) for which the Migration Wizard has a "source extractor," the Wizard has a two-step mode that allows you to extract all the data desired for migration, edit it in flat-file format, and then import it into Exchange. This is an excellent opportunity to add information into Exchange, such as user phone extensions or other company directory information.

The Microsoft Administrator program is also itself a useful migration tool, its **TOOLS...DIRECTORY IMPORT** option providing much of the flat-file import functionality of the Migration Wizard. It will also allow you to extract a user list from either an NT PDC or the Novell Bindery, to be used for mailbox creation or other import functions.

It is important before any migration utility is used to have a clear plan for rollout of Exchange. Temporary coexistence and interaction of mail systems can become very complicated, and if possible, a clean transition from one system to another should be sought. The tools Exchange provides should allow you to import all of your data from any existing messaging system (though some will require more elbow grease than others).

From Here

You've installed your first server, your first Exchange site, your first X.400 site connector, set up your network Client Installation Point, configured a dynamic RAS connector, and migrated your existing messaging system. That's plenty for now—go take a well-deserved break.

In the next chapter, we'll look at the administration of Microsoft Exchange, from basic configuration to advanced parameter modification—everything you need to know to make Exchange hop the way you want it to. Later, we'll look at how to configure Exchange to run as a Microsoft Mail post office as well as an Internet mail server and examine connections to other systems as well.

Go ahead and relax. Now that you know how to get a server or two up and running, it's all just fun and games from here on in....

Basic Administration

If you've installed and configured Microsoft Exchange Server, then you've started to use the Microsoft Exchange Administrator program, and you've probably realized that the initial administrative tasks you performed to set up Exchange are but the tip of the iceberg when it comes to the functionality available for administering and maintaining Microsoft Exchange Server.

Do not be daunted by the seemingly endless collection of objects and configurable properties visible in the Administrator program—most of these properties are set correctly by default during installation or need be set just once to enable the desired functionality. In this chapter, we'll review the initial administrative tasks that a new Exchange Server might need performed, as well as how to leverage Exchange's sophisticated administrative capabilities to ensure smooth operation of your production system.

Running the Administrator Program

The Administrator program is installed automatically along with Microsoft Exchange Server and can be started by double-clicking on the Microsoft Exchange Administrator program icon in the Microsoft Exchange Program Group or in the Start menu (if using NT v4.0). Once launched, the Administrator program will either prompt you to select the Exchange Server to which you wish to connect, or (if you have already done so and specified your choice as the default) automatically connect to your default Exchange Server. In order to connect, you must at least have Microsoft Exchange user permissions for the Microsoft Exchange Server to which you are trying to connect.

Once connected, you may choose to connect to other Exchange Servers as well, using the **FILE...CONNECT TO SERVER** menu option. The Administrator program allows you to connect to and administrate multiple Exchange Servers simultaneously.

Graphically, the Administrator program is not unlike the Exchange Viewer. Like the Viewer, the Administrator program has a left and right side display window (Figure 10.1). Objects on the left side of the window are "container" objects called *directory objects* (not unlike Exchange folders in the Viewer's folder listing window). Objects on the right side of the window are object "contents"—similar to the folder contents listing in the Viewer. Also as in the Viewer, every object has *properties*, or configurable parameters and settings, accessible by highlighting the object with the mouse and using either the **FILE...PROPERTIES** menu option or the **ALT-ENTER** HotKey.

Running the Administrator Program 213

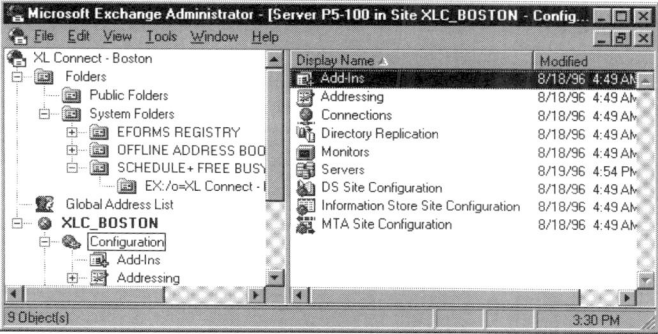

Figure 10.1: Administering Microsoft Exchange

The directory objects in the left window are arranged in a top-down directory structure that matches the Exchange organizational hierarchy, with organization-level objects such as the Global Address List and the Public and System Folders on top, site-level objects such as the Directory Service Site Configuration and Site Addressing directly underneath, and server-level objects such as the Private and Public Information Stores at the bottom of the directory structure.

Running the Administrator Program Remotely

Besides the default Administrator program installation on the Exchange Server itself, you may also install and use the Administrator program separately on any other Windows NT server or workstation (but not on a Windows 95 or 16-bit Windows platform). To do so, you will need to run the Exchange Server installation program on the target workstation, and be sure to use the Custom installation

214 Basic Administration

mode to install only the Administrator program. Be certain to deselect all of the other Exchange Server components for installation, or you will inadvertently install Exchange Server on a machine not able to support it. It can take days for an NT server with 24MB of RAM to stop thrashing and allow you to stop the services, so if you are asked to choose whether to "Join an Existing Site" or "Create a New Site," be sure to choose "Exit Setup" instead!

Once the Administrator program is installed on a remote workstation, running the program and connecting to an Exchange Server is just like running the Administrator program on the server itself—except that you must have network RPC connectivity in order to attach. If for some reason you are unable to connect, you may wish to use the RPC Ping utility (Figure 10.2) provided with Exchange Server to check your connectivity. This utility is not installed automatically during Exchange setup, but is located in the \SUPPORT\RPCPING directory of the Exchange Server Installation CD. This utility has two components—a

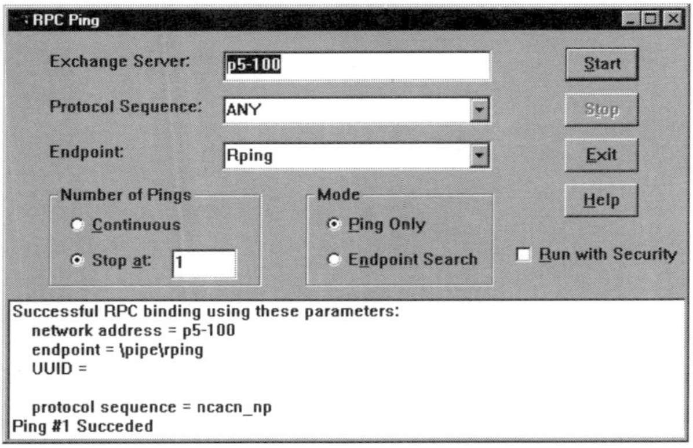

Figure 10.2: The RPC Ping Utility

server-side console application, RPINGS.EXE, that must be run on the target Exchange Server and the RPC Ping client application, RPINGC32.EXE for an NT server or workstation.

To use the RPC Ping utility, run the RPINGS.EXE application from a command line on the target server, and run the RPINGC32.EXE application on the remote server. On the remote server, in the RPC Ping Client window, enter the machine name of the target server in the Exchange Server: text box, then click on the **Start** button. If RPC connectivity exists, a "Successful RPC binding" message will be displayed in the text box at the bottom of the window. If the RPC Ping fails, check your physical connectivity as well as the status of the RPC service on the Exchange Server (accessible from the Services icon in the Control Panel).

Once you've launched the Administrator program and established your connection to the Exchange Server (locally or remotely), you are ready to perform your Exchange administrative tasks.

DS Site Configuration

The Directory Service Site Configuration object in the Exchange Administrator program is contained within the Site Configuration container. The DS Site Configuration object allows you to set parameters affecting all directory objects—including mailboxes, Public Folders, distribution lists, and custom recipients. The three main configuration settings on the Properties page of the DS Site

Configuration object are for the *Offline Address Book*, *tombstones*, *garbage collection*, and *custom attributes*.

We've already seen how to manually generate and schedule the generation of the Offline Address Book in the previous chapter, but it's important to remember that all remote users rely upon the Offline Address Book for sending messages to other users and distribution lists while disconnected from the network. Without a current Offline Address Book, those users will not have access to the Global Address List at all while offline.

Tombstones are "death notices" created every time a directory object, such as a Public Folder, is deleted. Once an item is deleted from its home server, the "news" of that deletion, just like any new posting, must be replicated to all servers within the Exchange organization. If this information is not properly replicated, some servers will think the item still exists, even when it doesn't. By default, a tombstone exists for 30 days after an object is deleted, after which time the tombstone is considered to be "expired." Once it is expired, it will be permanently deleted at the next *garbage collection*, or automatic directory maintenance and compacting. Your Exchange database performance can be improved and disk consumption lessened if you shorten the "Tombstone Lifetime" from 30 days to a period of time just above that required for full organizational replication and system backup—think of it as "defragmentation" of your Exchange database. You want to make sure that the tombstone has time to replicate and that all systems have completed their normal backup after the replication has occurred. If you back up each server nightly, and you have only one Exchange site (so that it takes only five minutes to replicate all information), you could set tombstones to expire in two days. Make it four or five days just in case a server is offline for a day or two, and you will still have gained 25 days and considerable database efficiency and performance. The tombstone lifetime and garbage collection interval are configurable on the General tab of the DS Site Configuration Properties page. By default, garbage collection occurs every 12 hours. Leave this setting at the default unless you find that garbage collection and directory compacting are interfering with Exchange production (possible on a very busy system), in which case you might increase the interval to as much as 24 hours.

Custom attributes are administrator-defined "extra" properties that appear as text box entry options on user mailbox Properties pages. If you would like to list every user's favorite color or shoe size as a property of their mailbox, accessible from the Global Address List, then you will have to manually enter or import that information into the user's mailbox Properties page on the Custom Attributes tab. To set everyone's Custom Attribute field label to a caption of "Shoe Size" or "Favorite Color" rather than the defaults of "Custom Attribute 1" and "Custom Attribute 2," use the Custom Attributes tab on the DS Site Configuration Properties page to alter the default label.

Information Store Configuration

The Information Store Configuration object in the Exchange Administrator program is contained within the Site Configuration container. The Information Store Configuration object allows you to set parameters affecting

218 Basic Administration

Public Folder storage and permissions, as well as allowing diagnostic message tracking.

The Information Store Configuration Properties page (Figure 10.3) allows you to specify which users can create "top-level" Public Folders, schedule the frequency of storage limit warnings for mailboxes and folders, and enable message tracking.

To specify which users can create new Public Folders at the topmost level of the Exchange Folder Listing, click on the Top Level Folder Creation tab. There are two text boxes on this page. The left text box is a list of all those users allowed to create top-level Public Folders. The right text box is a list of all of those users specifically denied the ability to create top-level Public Folders. Each text box has a **Modify** button underneath it that allows you to add

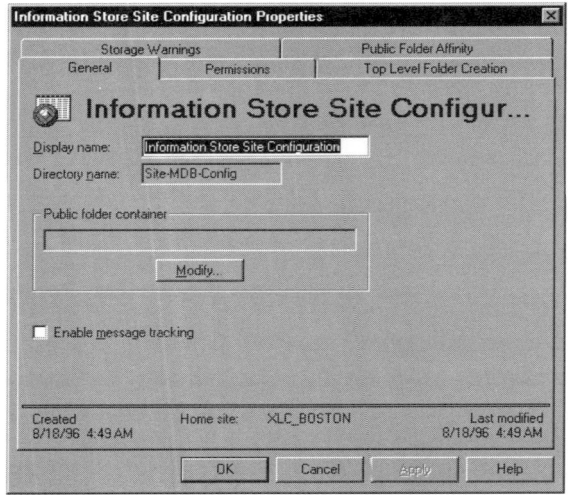

Figure 10.3: Configuring the Information Store

Information Store Configuration   219

users from the Global Address List. By default, both lists are bypassed—the All option is selected for those allowed to create folders and the none option is selected for those denied the ability.

This is very dangerous—unrestricted folder creation at the top level of the Public Folder structure can quickly lead to a hopeless tangle of files and applications that can take an administrator months to sort out and restructure. Make certain that you enable the "list" option for allowing and denying users folder creation rights, and select users from the Global Address List that you wish to have the ability to create folders. Initially, you should select only the "Exchange Administrators" distribution list for the "allowed" list, or alternately create a new distribution list (using the **NEW...DISTRIBUTION LIST** menu option) for "Public Folder Administrators."

Be sure to restrict access on top-level Public Folder creation. Unrestricted Public Folder creation can result in a tangled directory structure that greatly reduces effectiveness and navigational functionality.

Storage limit warnings are scheduled on the Storage Warnings tab. Storage limit warnings are e-mail messages sent out to mailbox or Public Folder owners when their mailboxes or folders exceed size and storage limits set by administrators. These limits can be set on the Properties pages of individual mailboxes or folders, or at the server level on the Properties page of the Public or Private Information Store. You are given the ability to schedule the creation and transmission of these warning messages so that their generation can be done off-hours, not conflicting with production use or backup procedures. Be sure to specify a

220 Basic Administration

low-traffic time for these messages, and generate them on a daily basis.

Message tracking is used only when troubleshooting an Exchange Server, as it generates huge log files in a very short period of time, leading to virtual memory errors and other lack of disk space issues if not carefully monitored. To enable message tracking, simply select the Enable Message Tracking checkbox on the General tab of the Properties page. This will start creating log files of every message that passes through the local Exchange Server's Information Store (MTA logging is separate and enabled from the MTA properties page). You can access these log files using the Message Tracking Center (Figure 10.4), launched using the **TOOLS...TRACK MESSAGE** menu option.

The Message Tracking Center is an excellent diagnostic tool that displays routing and delivery information about every message and offers advanced search capabilities to allow you to quickly locate "missing" messages in the log

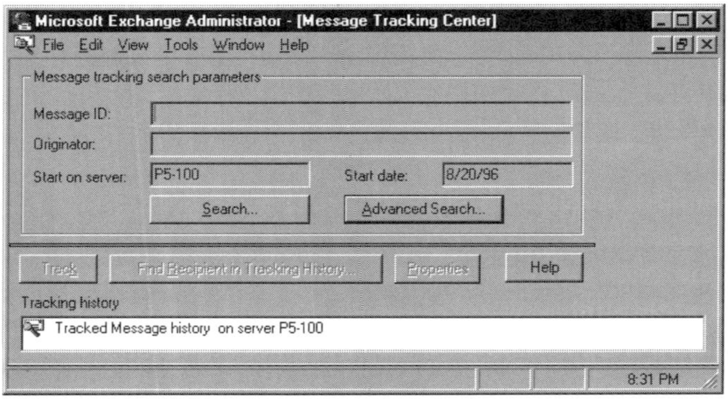

Figure 10.4: The Message Tracking Center

files. For the Message Tracking Center to be able to locate a message, message tracking must have been enabled from the Information Store Properties page during the time the message was sent.

The Information Store properties affect all messaging within the current site, but to track messages going to external sites or foreign systems you will need to enable message tracking on the Message Transfer Agent.

Message Transfer Agent Configuration

The MTA Site Configuration object in the Exchange Administrator program is contained within the Site Configuration container. The MTA Configuration object allows you to modify parameters affecting all traffic between Exchange Servers and other connectors and gateways. By altering settings on the MTA Site Configuration Properties page (Figure 10.5) you can enable message tracking for interserver traffic, or adjust and fine-tune the basic messaging transfer components.

To create log files for messages sent from server to server or to other sites and systems, select the Enable Message Tracking option on the General tab of the Properties page. Remember to do so only while monitoring and troubleshooting the Exchange Server—the log files can quickly grow to consume large amounts of disk space.

To alter the basic parameters governing message transfer in and from your Exchange Site, use the Messaging Defaults tab. This page will allow you to do some serious

222 Basic Administration

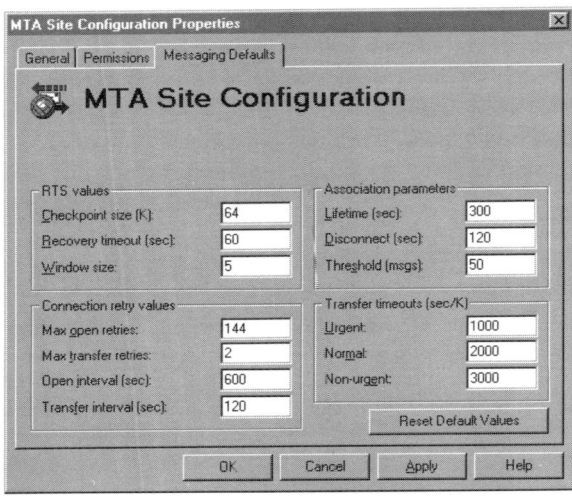

Figure 10.5: Configuring the MTA

damage to message traffic if you play around with the settings—so be sure to hit the **Reset Default Values** button on this tab if you have problems with message transfer between servers. If you feel brave enough to muck around with parameters automatically configured by Exchange, be prepared for trouble. That said, you can gain an increase in message transfer speed by adjusting the Checkpoint Size (K): field in the RTS Values frame from its default setting of 30 K to 64 K, provided you have fairly reliable LAN connectivity to the Exchange Server you are configuring.

Why does adjusting the checkpoint size make a difference? Exchange automatically verifies all message transfers going through the MTA. At set intervals during the transfer (every 30 K by default), Exchange inserts a "checkpoint" into the data that it uses to bookmark its last verified spot in the message transfer. If an error is detected, Exchange only has to retransmit from the last inserted checkpoint. This checkpoint insertion reduces messaging transfer speed slightly. Increasing the checkpoint size from 30 KB to 64 KB improves performance by requiring fewer checkpoint insertions. Of course, if frequent errors are detected, Exchange may have to retransmit more information since the checkpoints are farther apart, slowing down the transfer rate. For this reason, Microsoft recommends decreasing the checkpoint size to below the default 30 K setting if the connection is unreliable. Sound like more of a pain than it is worth? That's why there's a **Reset Default Values** button on this page! Use it in good health.

Setting Up Default Site Addressing

If you are not using a connector or gateway, such as the MS Mail Connector, the X.400 Connector, or the Internet Mail Connector, then you need not worry about site addressing. The Site Addressing object in the Exchange Administrator program is installed into the Site Configuration container only upon installation of one of the aforementioned connectors.

The Site Addressing object allows you to modify the address template that Exchange uses to automatically generate X.400 and Internet e-mail addresses for all users (it generates MS Mail addresses too, but the site address for MS Mail must be modified from the MS Mail Connector directly). The Site Addressing object also allows you to schedule a "catch all" recalculation of the site routing table and view details of all of the site's connectors and gateways.

Microsoft Exchange uses the organization and site names to generate e-mail addresses for other systems. By default, everyone's Internet address is their mailbox alias, the "@" symbol, and then the site name, followed by a period, the organization name, another period, and finally the suffix "com." As an example, if your mailbox alias is "JSMITH" and you work for the XL Connect company and set up an organization named "XL Connect" and a site named "Waltham Offices," your Internet e-mail address will be "jsmith@XL Connect.Waltham Offices.com." Since Internet e-mail addresses can't have spaces in them, and Mr. Smith probably wanted his e-mail address to be "jsmith@xlconnect.com," the default addressing scheme needs to be changed.

To alter the X.400 or Internet e-mail address generated by Exchange for users in the site, click on the Site Addressing tab of the Site Addressing Properties page (Figure 10.6), highlight the address, and click the **Edit** button. Make any changes you like, and then click on the **OK** button to commit them. Exchange will automatically ask if you would like to change all existing mailboxes to use the new addressing scheme—click on the **Yes** button and do so. Make certain that your Internet domain's primary DNS recognizes the address as well. (Did that sound like gobbledygook? We'll get into the Internet Mail Connector in more detail in the next chapter.)

You can use the Site Addressing Properties page to view details of all of the current site connectors and gateways. To do so, click on the Routing tab to display the listing of Connector Routing Items and Costs. Highlight any connector and click the **Details** button to show extended information about the connection. This feature is useful for a "30,000 foot view" overview of all of your site connections

Setting Up Default Site Addressing 225

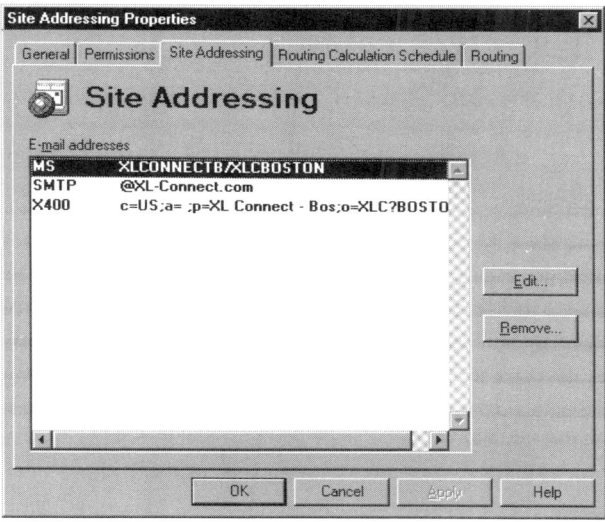

Figure 10.6: Site Addressing

and routing costs. Connector properties cannot be directly edited from this page.

Whenever a connector or gateway is added or reconfigured, the Exchange site automatically recalculates the routing table and applies it to messaging traffic. Occasionally, a server within a site will be offline and not receive this information. It is therefore useful to schedule an automatic recalculation of the site routing table on a routine basis. You will want to schedule the recalculation to occur when production traffic is minimal, as the recalculation does require system resources and can take a few minutes to complete. To schedule an off-hours recalculation of the site routing table, use the Routing Calculation Schedule tab, select the Selected Times option, and specify the time to recalculate.

Configuring the Public Information Store

The Public Information Store object in the Exchange Administrator program is contained within the Server, rather than the Site, container. The Public Information Store object allows you to modify parameters affecting all Public Folders contained on that server, including setting age and size limits and scheduling replication. It will also allow you to view detailed information about each individual folder within the site.

To set global size limits on all Public Folders on the server, enter the size (in Kb) on the General tab of the Public Information Store Properties page, then check the Issue Warning option. Owners of Public Folders whose folders exceed this limit will receive an e-mail to that effect unless you specify a higher limit on the individual folder's property page.

To set an age limit for Public Folder contents, click on the Age Limits tab. Check the "Age Limit for all Folders in this Information Store (days)" option, and enter in a value. This sets a cap on how long messages can remain in a Public Folder before being deleted.

You may also enter in age limits for specific folders or folder replicas, all of which are listed on this tab. To do so, double-click on the folder in question to open an age limit configuration window for that specific folder. Any age limits set on specific folders override the overall age limit.

Not sure what a reasonable limit is on Public Folder size or content age? How about what an unreasonable limit is? Be sure to set limits on

Configuring the Public Information Store 227

everything—even if they must be ridiculously high at first. You might think it unnecessary initially, but if for some reason someone copies their entire hard drive to a single Public Folder, you're going to want them to get a warning! Remember, too, that you can always make exceptions on a folder-by-folder basis later on.

Once you've set age and size limits on Public Folders you can schedule server replication times for all Public Folder replicas on the Replication Schedule tab. You will probably want to configure replication on a folder-by-folder basis, however, instead (from the Properties page of each separate folder). Scheduling replication separately for folders allows you to distinguish between important information that must be updated frequently and fairly static archives of information. Doing so can greatly reduce your overall replication traffic—certainly worth a little extra administrative effort up front when a folder is created.

Once you've configured the Public Folder defaults to suit your liking, click on the Public Folder Resources tab to see a folder-by-folder breakdown of folder size, number of content items, date created, last access time (useful for winnowing out seldom used folders), and number of owners or contacts. This tab is by far your best resource in determining how your Public Folder structure is functioning. You can see at a glance (and sort on demand) which folders are using the highest amount of storage space, which folders are infrequently accessed, and which folders are getting too full to easily navigate.

The Public Information Store also has a Diagnostic Logging tab where you can activate logging of Public Folder usage for troubleshooting purposes. Do not use logging at all unless you are troubleshooting and actively monitoring the Exchange Server. Activity logs can quickly grow to choke available drive space if left unattended.

Setting Mailbox Properties

In the last chapter we touched upon how to use the **TOOLS...EXTRACT WINDOWS NT ACCOUNT LIST** function to create an import file for new mailbox creation. We also looked at the **TOOLS...DIRECTORY IMPORT** function, which is used to import files from other systems in migration or to bulk-add new users and user information. You can greatly reduce the amount of information that needs to be imported or manually entered by specifying the mailbox default options and by using a mailbox template on import.

To specify how Exchange will generate mailbox aliases and NT user IDs upon import or mailbox creation, use the **TOOLS...OPTIONS** menu item to open the Options window (Figure 10.7). From this window's Auto Naming tab you may create a default aliasing scheme based on any combination of letters from a user's first, middle, and last names. Be sure to set this option to match your existing network aliasing standard to simplify integration between Exchange, NT, and any coexisting network operating system.

While still in the Options window, you will also want to click on the Permissions tab to specify the way Permissions pages are displayed throughout the Administrator program. For some reason, the default installation actually hides from display permissions pages for some objects, as well as not displaying the actual breakdown of rights for

Setting Mailbox Properties 229

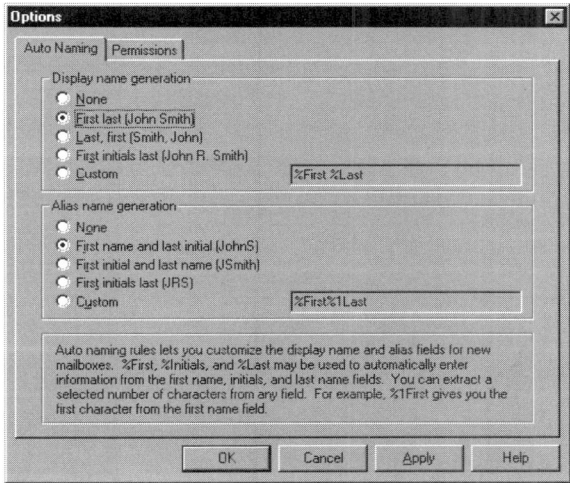

Figure 10.7: Configuring New Mailbox Creation Options

specific roles. Remedy this situation by checking both the "Show Permissions Page for All Objects" and "Display Rights for Roles on Permissions Page" options.

Using a mailbox template upon import is fairly simple. The Directory Import window has a **Recipient Template** button which, when clicked, allows you to select an individual existing mailbox from the Global Address List. Upon import, all of the properties in the existing mailbox which are not included in the import file will be added to every mailbox created. This is a very simple way to add company name, address, and telephone information—anything constant between users can be manually entered in one mailbox and then automatically copied upon import. Doing this can greatly reduce or eliminate development of special source extraction programs or direct import file editing.

230 Basic Administration

Once a mailbox has been created, you can locate it in the Exchange Administrator program in the Global Address List container, found just beneath the organization name at the top of the directory structure. Properties that can be edited directly include the following:

Mailbox Properties

Tab Location	Property	Description
General	Name and Address Information	The user's personal and company information, as well as the NT account alias and association.
Organization	Manager and Reports	Information on the user's position and supervisor.
Phone/Notes	Phone Numbers	Extended contact information for the user.
Distribution Lists	List Membership	This tab allows you to add to or remove the user from any existing distribution list.
E-mail Addresses	Addresses	The e-mail addresses generated by Exchange for foreign systems (such as the Internet).
Delivery Restrictions	Accept From: and Reject From: lists	Allows you to specifically deny all or some users the ability to send mail to the user.
Custom Attributes	Attributes 1–10	Allows you to enter "extra" information about the user, in up to 10 custom fields defined from the DS Site Configuration Properties page.

Advanced	Message Size and Mailbox Storage Limits	Allows you to override the default site values for storage limits and maximum message sizes.
Delivery Options	Assign "Send on" permissions and assign an alternate recipient	Allows you to grant different users the ability to "Send on Behalf of" the mailbox owner and to have a different user receive messages sent to the mailbox (perhaps while the user is on vacation).
Permissions	Send As rights	Allows you to grant another user (such as a secretary) the ability to send and receive messages as if they were the mailbox owner. This function could be used to add several people and create a group mailbox, if desired.

From Here

You've now seen most of the configuration tricks and initial tasks required by an Exchange Server. You should feel qualified to be an Exchange administrator already—though we'll get into the day-to-day business of Exchange administration later. In the next chapter, we'll take a look at connections to foreign systems—which is a fancy way of saying we'll see how to configure the Internet Mail

Connector, as well as taking a look at Microsoft Mail and X.400. Soon you'll be able to engineer seamless coexistence with an existing Microsoft Mail installation, as well as calmly routing enterprise-wide messaging and file attachments to the Internet! (Have you ever seen anyone "excitedly routing"?)

Configuring Connectors to Foreign Systems

Once your Exchange organization is up and running, the issue of how to connect to a client or partner's corporate messaging system, or even the entire Internet, will quickly become an important one. Exchange is unique among messaging systems in its wide support of different messaging standards and protocols. Microsoft licenses a Microsoft Mail Connector for Exchange that allows seamless coexistence between Exchange and any existing Microsoft Mail system—even Microsoft Mail for AppleTalk Networks. It also licenses a fully compliant X.400 Connector, allowing simple connectivity to any system that uses this industry standard for their external messaging. Best of all, Microsoft licenses an excellent Internet Mail Connector for

234 Configuring Connectors to Foreign Systems

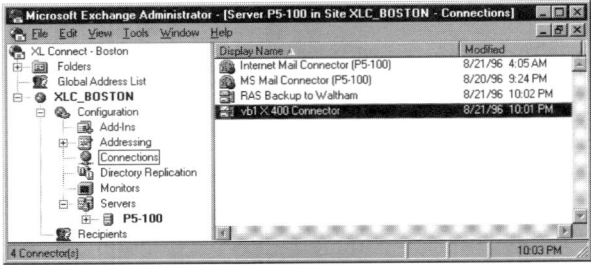

Figure 11.1: The Connections Object

Microsoft Exchange, which delivers immediate Internet connectivity to client desktops.

Installation of any of these connectors creates a new Connector item in the Connections object of the Site Configuration container (Figure 11.1). It will also create a Windows NT service or services for the installed connector. These services must be started for the connector to operate, and the connectors must be configured prior to starting the services successfully. Configuration of each of the available connectors is very similar to the configuration of a site connector, especially a dynamic RAS connector, which we've already reviewed in our look at connecting different Exchange sites.

Configuring the X.400 Connector

Configuring an X.400 connector is something we've already taken a look at—we used the X.400 connector to backbone Exchange site connectivity over the Internet in

Configuring the X.400 Connector 235

an example of how to connect Exchange sites. The process of connecting to an organization using X.400 that is not being routed over the Internet is very similar, the only real difference being the MTA used.

Prior to installing an X.400 connector, an MTA must be installed for the protocol to be used for network connectivity. This is done using the **FILE...NEW OTHER...MTA TRANSPORT STACK** menu option. The available transport stacks are as follows:

MTA Transport Stack	Description
Eicon X.25 MTA Stack	Used for X.25 connectivity to a foreign system. Requires installation of Eicon Port Adapter hardware.
RAS MTA Stack	Used for dynamic RAS connectors only.
TCP/IP MTA Stack	The "workhorse" of stacks—the most commonly used stack, will provide connectivity over any TCP/IP network (including the Internet).
TP4 MTA Stack	Transport Class 4 Connectionless Network Protocol—provides an OSI interface that works with the TP4 interface on Windows NT and the remote server.

To install the appropriate stack, select it from the "type" listing of the New MTA Transport Stack window and click on the **OK** button. When the Properties pages for the stack appear, leave the settings at their defaults and click on the **OK** button to complete the installation.

Once the appropriate MTA stack is installed, the X.400 connector can be created using the **FILE...NEW OTHER...X.400 CONNNECTOR** menu option. Set the Properties pages for the connector as described in the earlier section on "Connecting Sites Together over the Internet," with the exception being that non-Exchange systems will probably not support Message Text Word-Wrap or Remote Client MAPI Support, and these options on the General tab should not be selected.

Configuring the Microsoft Mail Connector

The most important concept to understand about the Microsoft Mail Connector is that once the Microsoft Mail Connector is installed and configured on an Exchange Server, the Exchange Server *is* a Microsoft Mail Server for all practical purposes.

The installation of the connector creates a "shadow" post office that emulates a Microsoft Mail post office exactly—even allowing the Exchange Server to:

- Act as a Dirsync Requestor or Dirsync server
- Replicate Schedule+ Free/Busy information for Microsoft Mail Client Schedule + users

Microsoft Exchange Client users will have access to the MS Mail Post Office Address List, be able to address and send messages and attachments back and forth to any MS Mail client user, even use MS Mail Shared Folders!

The tight integration between Exchange and MS Mail that the Microsoft Mail Connector allows, along with the simple operation of the Migration Wizard in migrating Microsoft Mail and Schedule+ data to Exchange, makes switching from Microsoft Mail to Microsoft Exchange painless and

Configuring the Microsoft Mail Connector 237

easy. You don't even need to migrate in a normal roll-out fashion—Exchange and MS Mail can coexist indefinitely, with MS Mail users never noticing any loss of functionality as members of the organization migrate to Exchange.

To configure the Microsoft Mail Connector, highlight the Connector item and use the **FILE...PROPERTIES** menu option to open the Properties window for the connector (Figure 11.2). After installation, you must use the Properties pages to:

1. Specify the Administrator's Mailbox
2. Connect to a Microsoft Mail post office

These two functions must be completed before the Microsoft Mail Connector Interchange (the main Windows NT Service for the MS Mail Connector) can be started. In addition, there are several other properties of the connector that may be configured to improve performance or adapt to site-specific issues.

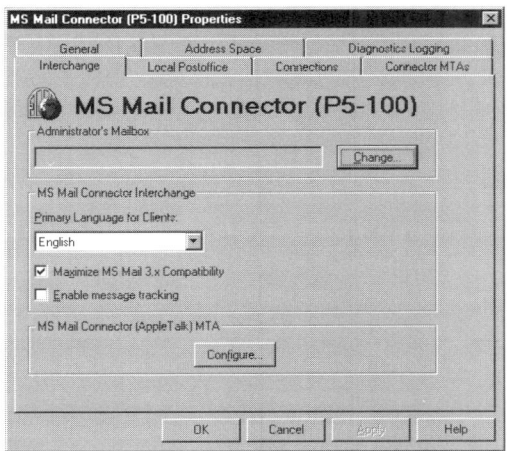

Figure 11.2: The Microsoft Mail Connector

238 Configuring Connectors to Foreign Systems

To specify the Administrator's Mailbox, click on the Interchange tab of the Connector's Properties page and use the **Change...** button to select a mailbox from the Global Address List. The Administrator's Mailbox might be your mailbox, if you wish to receive error messages sent from the Connector, or it might be the Exchange Administrators distribution list, or even a special "Postmaster" mailbox set up for just for this sort of thing. Once you've selected the mailbox or distribution list from the Global Address List, click on the **OK** button to complete the update.

To connect to a Microsoft Mail post office on your LAN, click on the Connections tab and then the **Create...** button. Don't be confused by the fact that a Microsoft Mail post office is listed in the Connections window on that page even before you hit the button—that post office listing represents the shadow post office on the Exchange Server. The **Create...** button will open the Create Connection window, where you can enter information on the Microsoft Mail post office to which you wish to connect. Click on the **Change...** button to enter in the post office path, and a Post Office Path window will appear, allowing you to specify the network path (using the UNC format of "*SERVERNAME\SHARENAME*") as well as the user ID and password of the MS Mail Administrator's account. Enter the information and click on the **OK** button to update the Create Connection window, then click on that window's **OK** button to apply the changes to the Microsoft Mail Connector. That's all that absolutely must be done to configure the Connector—you could now go to Windows NT's Control Panel, click on the Services icon, and start the MS Mail Connector Interchange Service. MS Mail clients can now send messages to Exchange and vice versa (provided

Configuring the Microsoft Mail Connector 239

the Exchange Client has been configured with the Microsoft Mail Service—either manually using the **TOOLS...SERVICES** dialog from within the Exchange Viewer or automatically during installation).

Simply getting the connector up and running is not always the full extent of your configuration requirements. Although the default values set for the rest of the connector properties will never need to be altered, some of the more useful configuration properties for the Microsoft Mail Connector are listed below:

Microsoft Mail Connector Properties

Tab	Property	Setting
General	Message Size Limit	Select the Maximum: (K) option and enter a value in kilobytes for the maximum message size allowed to pass through the connector. If unsure of the limit you wish to set, give 10000 (10MB) a try—better to enter a very high value than to allow someone to mail their hard drive to your MS Mail Server.
Interchange	Administrator's Mailbox	The lucky fellow or distribution list that receives any error messages generated by the connector.
	Enable Message Tracking	Turns on log file generation for the Message Tracking Center. Use only when troubleshooting—logs can quickly choke your disk space.

240 Configuring Connectors to Foreign Systems

Interchange *(cont.)*	Maximize MS Mail 3.x Compatibility	(selected by default) Allows MS Mail users to receive embedded OLE objects in messages sent from Exchange Clients. Turn this off if you do not need to pass embedded objects to MS Mail users (though you probably do). Exchange actually creates a specially formatted copy of OLE objects just for MS Mail clients, doubling the message size, when this option is enabled.
	Configure the MS Mail Connector (AppleTalk) MTA	Allows you to connect Exchange to an MS Mail for AppleTalk Networks Post Office, provided you have installed Macintosh Services for Windows NT and created a Macintosh Accessible Volume to install the post office on.
Connections	Queue	Displays all queued messages sent to the Connector awaiting delivery to MS Mail or Exchange Clients.
	Create	Allows you to add additional connections to different MS Mail post offices.
Address Space	Address Space	Allows you to enter alternate routing and routing cost information for the Connector to use for load balancing or connection redundancy.

Using MS Mail Gateways with Microsoft Exchange

Remember that for all practical purposes an Exchange Server with the Microsoft Mail Connector installed *is* a Microsoft Mail post office. This extends to third-party and gateway products as well. You can install any Microsoft Mail gateway on the Exchange Server, with the exception of the redundant ones—there's no need for the MS Mail SMTP or X.400 gateways with Exchange. The gateways available for MS Mail pretty much all use dedicated (386 or better) PCs to run on, but the Gateway Component installs on the Exchange Server the same way it would on a Microsoft Mail Server. Available gateways include:

- MCI Mail
- AT&T Easylink
- The MS Mail Gateway to Fax
- IBM PROFS and Office Vision
- MHS
- SNADS

The best part of this backward compatibility with MS Mail products is that you don't even need to be running MS Mail to use an available gateway! If you would like to migrate to Exchange from an MHS-based messaging system, you might install the Microsoft Mail Connector and the MS Mail MHS gateway on your Exchange Server—even though you don't use Microsoft Mail. Doing this would allow you to maintain messaging connectivity between all users as you make the transition from the MHS system to Exchange. The large amount of third-party products and utilities designed for MS Mail can therefore be leveraged by Exchange! Pretty nifty thinking on the part of those connector designers, huh? Of course, it would be nice if it could sing, too....

Hooking Up to the Internet: Configuring the Internet Mail Connector

One of the most exciting capabilities of Exchange is its ability to connect nearly transparently to the Internet using the Internet Mail Connector. Internet connectivity allows Exchange to be used to share information and implement workflow processes that literally span the globe. The installation and configuration of the Internet Mail Connector require no additional hardware and can be done simply by running the setup program and configuring the connector properties. Of course, for all of this to work, your Exchange Server must be running TCP/IP and be connected to the Internet.

You need not be an Internet guru or firewall expert to connect Exchange to the Internet. If your company does not yet have an Internet connection, just let your fingers do the walking—almost every Yellow Pages now has several Internet service providers (ISPs) to choose from.

Most ISPs will install and configure your connection for you, as well as installing any firewall hardware and software your business requires.

Besides getting a basic Internet connection, however, you will need to obtain a domain name and a series of routable IP addresses, normally a block of 256 of them called a "Class C License." Your ISP will be able to pro-

Hooking Up to the Internet 243

vide these for you—make sure you request them when ordering your connection. You will also want to make certain that your ISP provides Primary Domain Name Service (DNS) for you. Domain Name Service is a master listing of your IP numbers and the machines they are associated with. Your Exchange Server must be assigned a special DNS entry called an "MX record," short for "Mail Exchange" (pretty appropriate, huh?).

The MX record, along with the normal name-to-IP resolution performed by the standard "A" record, specifies the location of your Internet mail server (your Exchange Server) to the rest of the Internet. It is part of the same Domain Name Service that allows you to get to "www.xl-connect.com" instead of having to type "166.80.22.3." However, it is possible to be able to "ping" the domain name of your Exchange Server without having the proper MX records—so be certain to verify that your ISP has indeed assigned your Exchange Server a proper DNS MX record before configuring the Internet Mail Connector.

To configure the Internet Mail Connector, highlight the Connector item and use the **FILE...PROPERTIES** menu option to open the Properties window for the connector (Figure 11.3). After installation, you must use the Properties pages to:

1. Specify the Administrator's mailbox
2. Specify the Message Delivery Mode
3. Create an Address Space

These three functions must be completed before the Internet Mail Connector Service (the connector's Windows NT Service) can be started. In addition, there are several other properties of the connector that may be configured to improve performance or adapt to your preferences.

244 Configuring Connectors to Foreign Systems

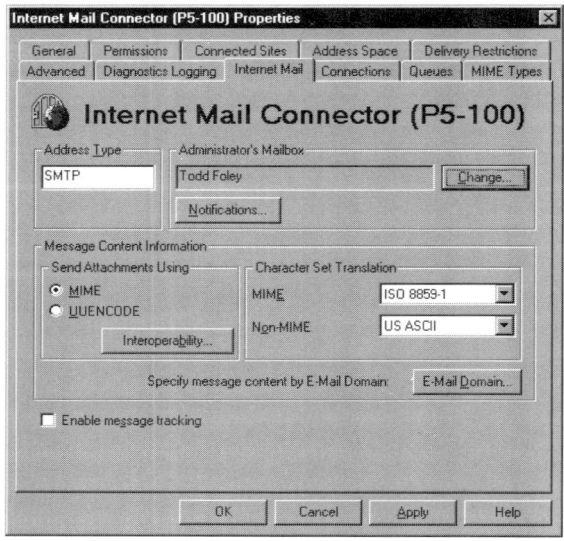

Figure 11.3: The Internet Mail Connector

To specify the Administrator's Mailbox, click on the Internet Mail tab of the Connector's Properties page and use the **Change...** button to select a mailbox from the Global Address List. The Administrator's Mailbox might be your mailbox, if you wish to receive error messages sent from the connector, or it might be the Exchange Administrators distribution list, or even a special "Postmaster" mailbox set up for just for this sort of thing. Once you've selected the mailbox or distribution list from the Global Address List, click on the **OK** button to complete the update. You may now click on the **Notifications** button to bring up a window allowing you to choose what types of nondelivery events will generate an e-mail notification to the Administrator's Mailbox you just specified. When first installing the connector, it is useful to select the "Always send messages when nondelivery reports are generated" option, but once the connector is configured and tested thoroughly you will want to reset this option to the default, which sends messages only if "multiple matches for an e-mail address are found." If you do not reset this option, you (or the Administrator) will receive an e-mail notification every time a user mistypes an Internet mail address and has it returned.

Once the Administrator's Mailbox options are set, click on the Connections tab to set the Message Delivery option. By default, Exchange is set to use DNS to deliver messages. It is fine to keep this option selected, provided your Exchange Server's NT TCP/IP configuration points to a valid DNS server (preferably your ISP's DNS server). Use the Control Panel's Network icon to check the TCP/IP configuration on the server to make certain valid DNS servers are listed. Just to be safe, run the command "PING WWW.MICROSOFT.COM" at the command line. If the PING command hangs or fails to return an IP address for WWW.MICROSOFT.COM, then you have a problem with your DNS (or your TCP/IP configuration, or your Internet connection...be sure to verify connectivity before configuring the Connector).

Alternately, you may arrange with your ISP to use an *SMTP Relay Host* (a fancy name for a pass-through Internet mail server). When you use an SMTP Relay Host, your Exchange Server receives messages normally, but instead of delivering outgoing messages directly, it forwards all outgoing mail to a "smart" mail server run by your ISP which does a DNS lookup for each message and sends it on its merry way. This method has the advantage of not requiring your Exchange Server to use DNS to resolve messages. To use this method of delivery, check the "Forward all messages to host:" option and enter the IP address of your ISP's SMTP Relay Host.

It's worth noting that the SMTP Relay Host need not be provided by your ISP. If you have an existing (non-Exchange) Internet mail server somewhere in your organization, you can continue to use it while using Exchange, and you could even use it as your own SMTP Relay Host by simply entering its IP address in the "Forward all messages to host:" option.

Once your message delivery mode is established, you need to complete the minimum configuration by creating a new Address Space. To do so, select the Address Space tab and click on the **New Internet** button. The SMTP Properties window will appear (Figure 11.4). Click on the General tab—only two parameters will be listed. These two parameters, the E-mail Domain (blank by default) and the Cost (1 by default), should not be touched, altered, folded,

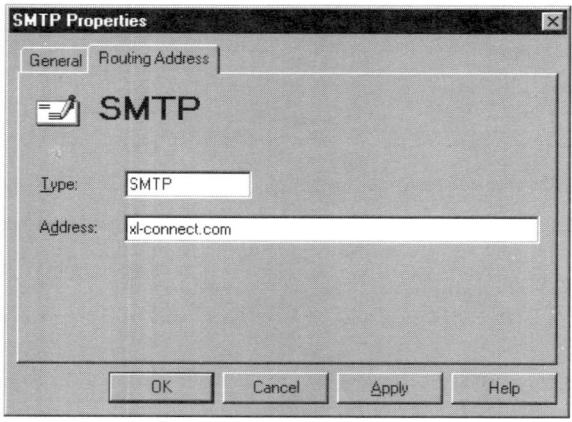

Figure 11.4: The SMTP Properties Window

Hooking Up to the Internet 247

bent, or mutilated in any way. Leave the E-mail Domain field blank and click on the Routing Address tab. This tab again has only two parameters—but these you will need to change. Set the Type field to be "SMTP" (just type the letters S-M-T-P into the field). Set the Address field to be the full DNS name used to resolve the messages—everything after the "@" in a user address. For example, if the Exchange Server will be the Internet mail connector for the XL-CONNECT.COM domain, and all user addresses will be in the form of "jsmith@XL-CONNECT.COM," then type XL-CONNECT.COM into the Address field. Click on the **OK** button in the SMTP Properties window and then the **OK** button on the Address Space tab to complete your configuration.

At this point, start the connector's Windows NT Service. You should now be able to send e-mail back and forth to the Internet. If it doesn't seem to be working, take a look at the nondelivery reports being sent to the Administrator's Mailbox (you did add all the available nondelivery options by using the **Notifications** button, didn't you?) and check with your ISP to make certain your MX records are properly configured. You can also use the Queues tab to look at the status of active undelivered messages.

Finally, if unsuccessful at diagnosing the issue, turn on message tracking from the Internet Mail tab and use the Message Tracking Center to trace the paths of your failed messages. The stage in the routing of Internet mail where a message fails will indicate the cause of the failure. Be sure to turn message logging off after troubleshooting is complete.

Once you have verified operation of the Internet Mail Connector, you can return to the Connector Properties page and alter some of the settings to suit your preferences.

248 Configuring Connectors to Foreign Systems

Some of the most useful parameters of the Internet Mail Connector are listed below:

Internet Mail Connector Properties

Tab	Property	Setting
General	Message Size Limit	Select the Maximum: (K) option and enter a value in kilobytes for the maximum message size allowed to pass through the connector. If unsure of the limit you wish to set, give 10000 (10MB) a try—better to enter a very high value than to allow someone to tie up your Internet connector with huge attachments.
Internet Mail	Administrator's Mailbox	The lucky fellow or distribution list that receives any error messages generated by the connector.
	Notifications	Allows you to specify the types of nondelivery messages, if any, that will generate an e-mail notice to the administrator.
	Enable Message Tracking	Turns on log file generation for the Message Tracking Center. Use only when troubleshooting—logs can quickly choke your disk space.
	Message Content Information	Allows you to choose between the MIME and UUENCODING standards for message attachments (MIME by default).

	Interoperability	Controls how automatic responses are treated by the connector (stopped by default) as well as RTF formatting (user defined by default). Also controls transmission of Display Names.
MIME Types	Edit	Allows you to add to or remove the MIME types Exchange uses to decode Internet attachments and embedded objects.
Queue	Queue	Displays all queued messages sent to the connector awaiting delivery to MS Mail or Exchange Clients.
Address Space	Address Space	Allows you to enter alternate routing and routing cost information for the connector to use for load balancing or connection redundancy.

From Here

You've learned how to connect Exchange up to just about anything—from the Microsoft Mail gateway to fax to the Internet and beyond. At this point, you should be able to get just about any Exchange configuration up and running.

In the next chapter, we'll take a look at just what exactly you do once Exchange is up and running—administrative maintenance. We'll also see how to take advantage of Exchange's advanced Administrative Monitors to make normal administration simpler.

Later, we'll be getting into the powerful simulation package that ships with Exchange and find out how to customize Exchange to make your Exchange installation suit your user base to a T. We'll also delve a little further into Windows NT's tight integration with Exchange.

ADMINISTRATIVE MAINTENANCE TASKS

OK—you've got Exchange working, and it's been perfectly configured to meet the needs of your organization—now what? If you just lock the machine in a closet and visit it on alternate Mondays, you're eventually going to have some real issues to deal with. The Exchange Server database will become fragmented, and automated system maintenance functions may conflict with each other and with backups, affecting even production use. Worst of all, Exchange Servers may go offline or have partial service stoppages—with your only source of notification being the angry end user!

Sound like a nightmare waiting to happen? Well, it's not. It's just a bunch of good reasons to carefully configure your Exchange maintenance schedules, set up offline database compaction, and use Exchange's sophisticated monitoring capabilities to alert you to potential issues before they become serious problems.

Information Store Maintenance

Exchange will do administrative tasks for you—you just have to schedule regular automatic system maintenance functions so they don't conflict with backups or normal production use. Due to the tremendous impact it has on performance, the most important maintenance function Exchange performs is the defragmentation and compaction of the primary Exchange database—the Information Store (IS).

Exchange will automatically check the Information Store and compact it as best it can while the Information Store Service is up and running for production use. This "background" processing can take a considerable amount of your system's resources, however, and should be scheduled for off-peak hours. To schedule the online Information Store maintenance, highlight the particular Exchange Server on which you are working in the Administrator program's directory listing (found in the Servers container), and use the **FILE...PROPERTIES** menu option to open the Properties page for that particular server. Click on the IS Maintenance tab to schedule times when background defragmentation and compaction of the Information Store will be running (Figure 12.1).

By default, IS maintenance processing is scheduled from midnight to 6 AM every day. Increase this period to as

Information Store Maintenance 253

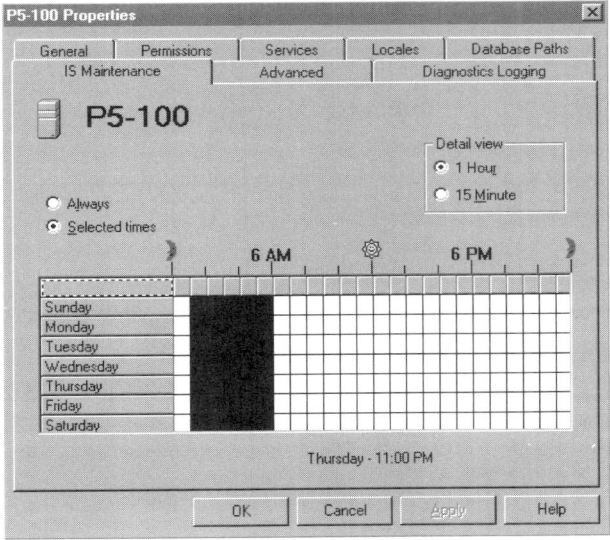

Figure 12.1: Scheduling IS Maintenance

much time as possible outside your normal production use—the Exchange database will perform much better with more frequent maintenance.

Very little can affect Exchange Server performance as much as database defragmentation. Try to allow Exchange to run its background maintenance for as much time as possible every day. If your system receives high usage only between the hours of 9 AM to 5 PM, then schedule IS maintenance from 5:30 PM to 8:30 AM. You will notice a significant decrease in performance when the background processing is running, however, so be sure to take into account any other processes (such as backups or Storage Limit Warning Notice generation) when scheduling IS maintenance. Leave a window open for these other processes during which IS maintenance will not be running. A little bit of coordination between IS maintenance processing, Storage Limit Warnings generation, and regular backups will result in smooth server operation—without competing processes causing the Exchange Server's performance to slow to a deathly crawl.

Offline IS Maintenance

Unfortunately, even if you schedule online IS maintenance to occur every hour of the day, the Exchange Information Store will become fragmented and performance will suffer. At a minimum of once monthly, you should schedule offline IS maintenance.

Offline IS maintenance involves stopping the Microsoft Exchange Information Store Service and running the Microsoft Exchange Server Database Utility Program, EDBUTIL.EXE. This utility is a console application—it only runs from the command line, which allows batch processing. You can write a batch file to stop the Information Store, defragment the database, and restart the Information Store. You can then use Windows NT's AT command (the Schedule Service) to run the batch file at midnight on the 25th of every month (or whenever you like—at least monthly, and possibly as much as weekly, depending on traffic). You do not need to worry about the offline IS maintenance conflicting with the normal online IS maintenance schedule, since the service will be stopped. You do, however, need to take the backup schedule into account so as not to result in overlapping processing.

The EDBUTIL.EXE Utility

The command-line Exchange database utility, EDBUTIL.EXE, can be found in the EXCHSRVR\BIN directory on your Exchange Server (Figure 12.2). This program requires that the full path and name of the Information Store database file (Public or Private) be passed to it as a command-line parameter, along with a name for a backup file of the original Information Store (backup is an "optional" program parameter that you never want to skip—better safe than sorry). If you are uncertain of the path to the Public and Private Information Store database files, look them up on the Database Paths tab of the Server's Properties page.

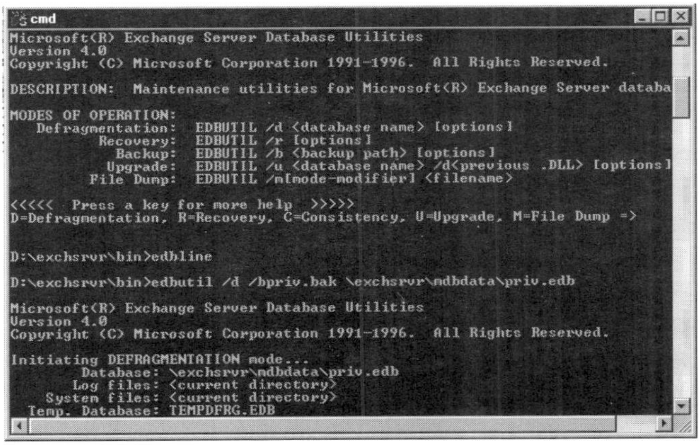

Figure 12.2: Using the EDBUTIL.EXE Utility

256   Administrative Maintenance Tasks

The syntax of the utility is as follows:

```
EDBUTIL /d /b{name of backup file to create}
{ path to public or private database}
```

For example, the command line

```
edbutil /d /bpriv.bak
exchsrvrmdbdatapriv.edb
```

would create a backup of the existing Private Information Store database file called "PRIV.BAK" and then defragment the Private Information Store.

A sample batch file that backed up and defragmented the Public and Private Information Stores on a server would perform the following sequential functions:

1. Stop the Information Store Service
2. Back up and defragment the Private Information Store
3. Back up and defragment the Public Information Store
4. Restart the Information Store Service

The exact syntax of such a batch file would be as follows:

```
net stop "Microsoft Exchange Information
Store"

edbutil /d /bpriv.bak
exchsrvrmdbdatapriv.edb

edbutil /d /bpub.bak exchsrvrmdbdatapub.edb

net start "Microsoft Exchange Information
Store"
```

Running the above batch file on at least a monthly basis will ensure that the Exchange Information Store database is optimally compacted for performance. It is important to note, however, that running the offline IS maintenance requires a fair amount of disk space—at least twice the size of the database files being compacted must be available as free drive space. This is because the process backs up the original database, then uses a temporary file as large as the database file itself to copy information to as it writes out the new file. Make sure there is enough disk space to accommodate offline maintenance before running the utility.

Verifying DS/IS Consistency

Occasionally an item becomes "orphaned" in either the Exchange Directory Service (DS) or the Information Store. A message or other item might exist in the Information Store without a valid directory reference, or a directory reference might refer to an item that no longer exists. This might be the result of a too-short Tombstone Expiration setting, or it might be due to the restoration of an Information Store file from backup tape. In any case, Exchange automatically resynchronizes the Information Store and the Directory Service during replication—but there may be times when this fails, or you may simply wish to reconcile the Directory and Information Store immediately after a tape restoration. If you have done a tape restoration of the Information Store, and there are directory entries for Public Folders created after the backup was made, you will want to adjust the inconsistencies with a latency period equal to the period of time between when the tape

258 Administrative Maintenance Tasks

was made and the last directory entry created. This interval should be long enough to permit Exchange to recreate the objects automatically by replication. If it was a total of three days between backup and restoration, then try setting the DS/IS consistency adjustment interval to adjust inconsistencies automatically over 3 days, and then click on the **Adjust** button on the Advanced tab of the Server Properties page (Figure 12.3). If you wish to reconcile all differences immediately, then set the adjustment option to All Inconsistencies and hit the **Adjust** button.

Even if no tape restoration occurs, a manual DS/IS consistency adjustment should be made at least on a monthly basis. Just go to the Advanced tab of the Server Properties page, and click on the **Adjust** button. This will ensure that

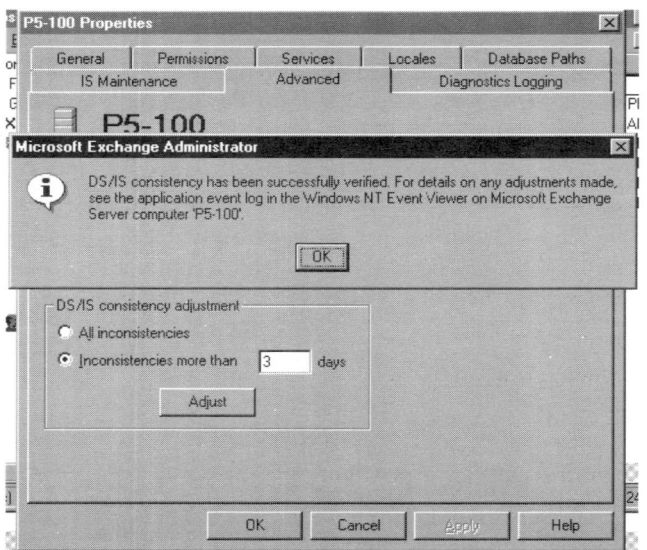

Figure 12.3: Verifying DS/IS Consistency

orphaned objects neither consume disk storage space nor represent phantom items in the Exchange Viewer folder contents listing.

Configuring Administrative Monitors

Exchange has sophisticated monitoring capabilities called *Link Monitors* that allow you to receive notification whenever another Exchange Server or a connection to another site goes down. These notifications can take the form of pager programs, network alert messages, or simple e-mail messages.

Exchange also has monitoring capabilities, called *Server Monitors,* for the individual Exchange services running on different Exchange Servers within a site. These monitors are capable of automatically restarting services and even servers if an important service, such as the Information Store or Directory Service, goes down.

Creating a Link Monitor

Exchange Link Monitors are automated "pings" of other Exchange Servers or foreign mail systems. When creating a Link Monitor, you specify an Exchange Server name or a mailbox on a foreign mail system. If Exchange fails to receive a message back from the remote server or system within a certain amount of time, then it enters an "Alert" state and triggers a notification of some sort to an Exchange administrator. This feature is very useful for being quickly alerted to potentially severe messaging problems.

260 Administrative Maintenance Tasks

Link Monitors are created in the Monitor object in the Site container of the Administrator program. To create a Link Monitor, use the **NEW OTHER...LINK MONITOR** menu option to open the New Link Monitor Properties page. You will need to enter a display name for the new Link Monitor on the General tab of the monitor's Properties page (Figure 12.4).

Next, click on the Servers tab and use your mouse to highlight any and all Exchange Servers in the site to which you wish to apply the Link Monitor. When complete, hit the **Add** button to apply the Link Monitor to the selected servers.

Finally, click on the Notification tab to specify what action the Link Monitor should take when it reaches an

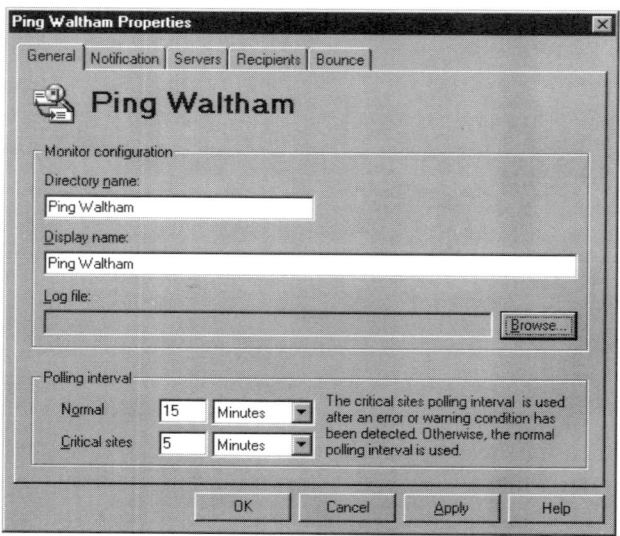

Figure 12.4: Creating a Link Monitor

Alert condition. Click on the **New** button to select a notification option for the monitor. The available notification types are as follows:

1. Launch a Process—triggers any external command-line program; normally used for alphanumeric pager alerts.
2. Mail Message—sends an e-mail message to any Exchange mailbox, distribution list, or custom recipient.
3. Windows NT Alert—sends a Windows NT Network Alert message to a specific NT Server.

Even if you do use a pager program or Network Alert messages as your notification method, you probably still want to have an e-mail message sent, just for historical documentation purposes. Once you've chosen the type of notification, you will be prompted for the needed notification destination information (the e-mail address for a Mail Message notification, the program path for a Launch a Process notification, or the server name for a Network Alert message). Once it has been entered, click on the **OK** button to complete the creation of the Link Monitor—you will now receive notification whenever messages start to fail to make the round trip to another Exchange Server or foreign system recipient.

Creating a Server Monitor

Exchange Server Monitors are RPC-based checks on other Exchange Servers and their component NT Services. When creating a Server Monitor, you specify an Exchange Server name. The Server Monitor will check on that server and all of the services on that machine that have been specified as "Monitored Services" on the Services tab of the Server's Properties page in the Administrator program. If Exchange detects a service stoppage, or detects that the machine is completely down, then it enters an "Alert" state and triggers an Action Response, as well as a notification of some sort to an Exchange administrator. The Action Response feature is very useful for automatically fixing severe messaging problems as soon as they begin, which Exchange does by simply restarting the service or server that has failed.

The Server Monitor also can automatically synchronize the system clocks of monitored servers. This feature allows all servers in the site to maintain consistent time-stamping information, which is crucial to troubleshooting and important for message dating.

Server Monitors are created in the Monitor object in the Site container of the Administrator program. To create a Server Monitor, use the **NEW OTHER...SERVER MONITOR** menu option to open the New Server Monitor Properties page. You will need to enter a display name for the new Server Monitor on the General tab of the monitor's Properties page.

Next, click on the Servers tab and use your mouse to highlight any and all Exchange Servers in the site to which you wish to apply the Server Monitor. When complete, hit the **Add** button to apply the Server Monitor to the selected servers.

After the servers have been selected, click on the Actions tab to specify one of the following actions to be taken if an Alert state is entered:

1. No action
2. Restart the service
3. Restart the remote server

Configuring Administrative Monitors 263

You may specify an action to occur at the first, second, or third instance of failure detected. A logical sequence of action events might be to take no action at the first detection of failure, have the failed service restarted if the failure is detected after the next critical polling interval, and finally, have the server rebooted if a third poll still detects failure. This flexibility allows you to take drastic response measures such as rebooting the server only when necessary.

Finally, click on the Notification tab to specify what action the Server Monitor should take when it reaches an Alert condition. Click on the **New** button to select a notification option for the monitor. The available notification types are as follows:

1. Launch a Process—triggers any external command-line program; normally used for alphanumeric pager alerts.
2. Mail Message—sends an e-mail message to any Exchange mailbox, distribution list, or custom recipient.
3. Windows NT Alert—sends a Windows NT Network Alert message to a specific NT Server.

Even if you do use a pager program or Network Alert messages as your notification method, you probably still want to have an e-mail message sent, just for historical documentation purposes. Once you've chosen the type of notification, you will be prompted for the needed notification destination information (the e-mail address for a Mail Message notification, the program path for a Launch a Process notification, or the server name for a Network Alert message). Once it has been entered, click on the **OK** button to complete the creation of the Server Monitor—you will now receive notification whenever a service failure is detected on another Exchange Server.

From Here

You've now learned the tricks for keeping an Exchange Server healthy and talking to you—even how to have it page you when there's a problem. This knowledge should give you the ability to establish a proper maintenance schedule and prepare emergency response standards for your organization. The tools Exchange offers for administration can make life substantially easier for an Exchange administrator if used properly, and you've had a chance to look at the basics required to implement those tools.

Next, we'll look at the Load Simulator utility. The Load Simulator actually allows you to run exceptionally detailed real-time simulations against Exchange Servers, allowing simple troubleshooting of peak-time issues, as well as giving an administrator an unprecedented ability to predict how a planned Exchange Server will behave in real (production environment) life. Later, we'll see how to customize Exchange to meet almost any company's needs—even if they want to use Exchange only to talk about cheese.

Load Simulator

Microsoft Exchange includes a sophisticated production use simulation tool called Load Simulator (Figure 13.1). This program is run on a Windows NT Exchange Client computer and very accurately simulates the real-time load conditions created by a hundred or more individual clients. This allows you to use very few client computers to do performance analysis or recreate peak load conditions on your Exchange Server. The beauty of Load Simulator is that it actually creates a true production load. When you create a Load Simulator test, the program automatically creates and uses hundreds of temporary mailboxes and Public Folders and accesses them using real message content. It actually sends messages and makes posts to recipients and folders on the Exchange Server.

266 Load Simulator

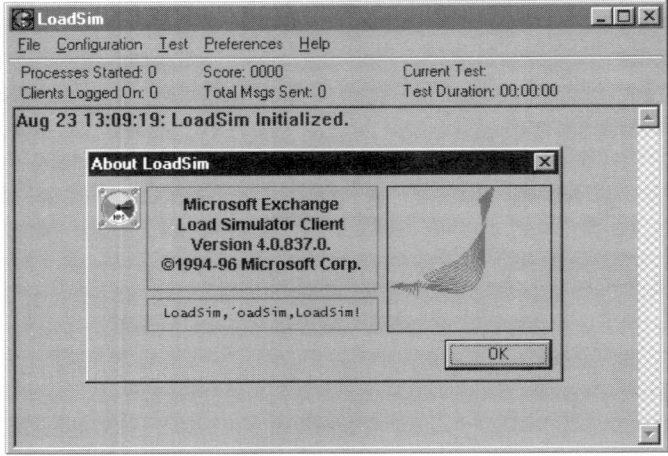

Figure 13.1: Load Simulator

The fact that Load Simulator creates a "real" load on the Exchange Server means that you can do more than just crunch numbers when analyzing the results of a test. It gives you the ability to actually see how performance changes from a client use perspective. If troubleshooting using Load Simulator, you can go to any client workstation that has been experiencing difficulty and run the client as you normally would. Load Simulator will recreate the peak load conditions on the server, and you will be able to resolve issues without having to wait for the "busiest time of day" to recreate those conditions.

There are two things to bear in mind when using Load Simulator for troubleshooting or performance analysis. The first thing to remember is that Load Simulator will not test network bandwidth issues for you—since it is running a hundred or more users off one machine, only the single network connection is being validated. Second, remember the old GIGO (garbage in, garbage out) principle—the simulation is only as accurate as the data you provide it. This last item is particularly important because Load Simulator will accept (and expects) a tremendously granular knowledge of your site's messaging and folder access volume and patterns of use. If using Load Simulator for planning purposes, be certain to develop as exhaustive an analysis of existing and projected messaging, scheduling, and Public Folder use as possible before running Load Simulator. If using Load Simulator for troubleshooting, don't leave anything out or cut any corners in configuring your test profile, or your results will be questionable.

Load Simulator will run from a Windows 95 machine, but several important features and the overall accuracy of the test will be impaired. Use a Windows NT workstation or server with at least 32 MB of RAM to properly run the Load Simulator. On a workstation with 32 MB of RAM you can simulate roughly 100 Exchange users. Use multiple instances of Load Simulator running simultaneously against the same Exchange Server to simulate more, or upgrade the RAM and processors of the testing machine to simulate extra users. Never run more than 250 simulated users from a single processor machine, and use the general hardware guidelines given for number of users on an Exchange Server for a rule of thumb on how many users you can simulate from an NT workstation or server. You will also have to have the Windows NT Exchange Client software installed on the machine running Load Simulator, with a valid profile, and be logged into the domain with domain administrator and Exchange administrator permissions on the test machine.

Setting the Test Topology

The first order of business in creating your first Load Simulator test is to install Load Simulator. You do so by copying the entire SUPPORTLOADSIMI386 directory from the Exchange Server Installation CD to a local hard drive on your test machine. To start Load Simulator, run the LOADSIM.EXE file in that directory.

The next order of business is to configure your test topology. Use the **CONFIGURATION...TEST TOPOLOGY** menu option to open the Test Topology window. Click on the **Add Server** button to begin setting up your test in the Server Properties window.

The Server Properties window requires that you enter the following information about the identity of your Exchange Server, the number of users you wish to simulate in the test from the particular test machine you are on, and some general information about Public Folder replication. The entry fields and their descriptions are as follows:

Frame	Field Label	Description
Basic Topology	Organization	The name of your Exchange organization (spelling counts!).
	Site	The name of the Exchange site in which the server you are testing is located.
	Server	The name of the Exchange Server you are testing.
	No. of Accounts	The number of users you wish to simulate from the test machine you are on.

Public Folders / Replication	Different Public Server	Check this box and enter the name of the dedicated Public Folder server if the server you are testing does not have its own Public Information Store.
	Total Public Folders	Enter the total number of Public Folders on the server you are testing.
	Root Folders	Enter the total number of top-level Public Folders on the server you are testing.
	Replicas in this site of each folder	Enter the minimum, maximum, and average count of folder replicas on other servers within the site.
	Replicas in other sites of each folder	Enter the minimum, maximum, and average count of folder replicas on other servers outside the site. Enter zeros if a single-site organization.

Once the server properties are entered, click on the **OK** button in both the Server Properties and Test Topology windows to complete the Test Topology setup.

Load Simulator will actually create mailboxes and Public Folders for testing in quantities matching the numbers you enter on the Server Properties window (it does not use existing mailboxes or folders) and you will need available disk space on the Exchange Server to permit this. If your server is low on disk space, add more or larger physical drives to the Exchange Server before running Load Simulator.

Distribution Lists

You must next let Load Simulator know how distribution lists are used on the Exchange Server you are testing. Use the **CONFIGURATION...DISTRIBUTION LISTS** menu option (Figure 13.2) to specify the following properties:

Field Label	Description
Size of Lists	Enter the minimum, maximum, and average count of users on any given distribution list.
Cover %	Enter the percentage of the total users on the Exchange Server being tested who are actually on a distribution list at all.
Create Lists	Enter the total number of distribution lists on the server being tested.
% Local	Use this only if you are testing more than one Exchange Server at once from your test client. The field value should represent the percentage of the members of any given distribution list who have mailboxes on the server on which the distribution list is located. If you take the simple way out and just test one server at a time (recommended), you can leave this field blank.

When finished entering the distribution list specifications, hit the **OK** button to commit them to your test configuration.

Completing the Test Configuration

Next, if you are using multiple client machines, each one running its own version of Load Simulator against the

Setting the Test Topology 271

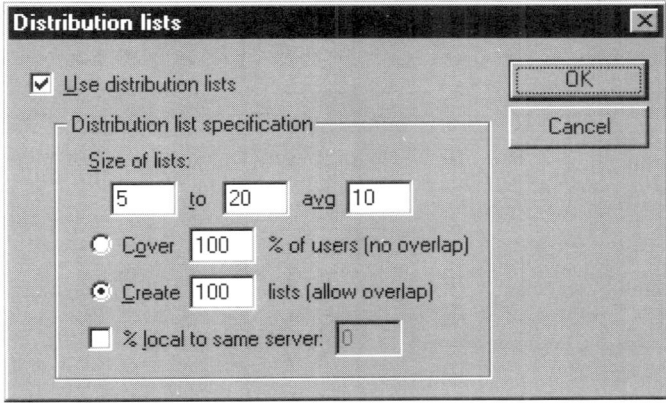

Figure 13.2: Setting Distribution List Properties

Exchange Server you are testing, you will need to use the **CONFIGURATION...CLIENT MACHINES** menu option to list all of the machines being used during the test. Load Simulator expects that any machine you list in this window will be used during testing. If for some reason you remove or don't run a particular machine, remove it from this list. If you decide to use only the client machine you are on, make sure the Use Multiple Client Machines checkbox is cleared. Click on the **OK** button to commit your changes to the test configuration.

All that remains is to create the import files required for all of the test mailboxes, Public Folders, and distribution lists you have specified, and then import them into the Exchange Server you are testing. Use the **CONFIGURATION...GENERATE DIRECTORY IMPORT FILES** menu option to create the import files and then the **CONFIGURATION...IMPORT USERS** menu option to import them into the Exchange Server being tested. Once complete, you will be able to log on to the Exchange Server with the Exchange Client and see all of the test Public Folders which Load Simulator has created, or connect using the Administrator program and see all of the new mailboxes and distribution lists in a new LoadSim object in the site's Configuration container. Your basic test configuration is now complete—now you just have to specify the behavior and content of your test mailboxes and folders in the User Initialization Test and the Public Folder Initialization Test before running the actual load simulation.

Creating the User Initialization Profile

Use the **FILE...USER INITIALIZATION PARAMETERS** menu option to open the User Initialization Profile Properties page. Click on the Parameters tab to begin configuring the User Initialization Profile. This profile is used by the User Initialization Test (not really a test, just a setup program for the actual run of Load Simulator) to generate real content (and consume storage space) in test mailboxes, as well as to specify how messages are sent and received and how big the messages are during the simulation.

The first value you must enter is the Number of Processes Per Server, found on the Parameters tab. This value sets how many users at once will be set up on each server in the Test Topology when the User Initialization Test is run. This affects only the speed at which the setup program runs, since creating multiple users at once greatly speeds up the process. Be careful not to exceed

Creating the User Initialization Profile 273

the processing capacity of the test machine when running the setup, however. Try setting this value at six, and increase or decrease it if the User Initialization Test runs too slowly or fails.

Next, click on the **Low, Medium,** or **High** usage button. These buttons will set the default values for the following properties of each individual mailbox and actually create content when the User Initialization Test is run:

- Number of new folders (within the mailbox—not Public Folders)
- Number of messages per new folder
- Number of messages in Inbox
- Number of messages in Deleted Items

If after clicking one of the usage buttons, the numbers displayed for any of these properties seem inappropriate, you may edit them directly by typing in a new value in the property field.

Next, click on the Senders tab to specify which mailboxes will be used to send test messages. Select the Exchange Server being tested from the Available Servers list and click on the **ADD ALL** button. This will define all of the mailboxes you've created for testing on the test client you are using to be valid senders. Click on the Recipients tab and repeat the server selection process, clicking on **ADD ALL** to select all test mailboxes as valid test message recipients.

Now you need to specify how messages are received during testing. Click on the Recipient Options tab and specify to how many users each message is normally addressed at once. Select the Between option and specify the minimum number of recipients (1), the maximum number of recipients (probably just a half-dozen or so—distribution lists count as one user for purposes of this value), and the average number of recipients (probably one or two—most e-mail messages are generally sent to one person, but your organization's use may differ).

Unless you are testing multiple servers at once, clear (make sure they're not checked) all of the Options settings, including:

- To Local Server
- To Local Site
- To Local Organization

If you have defined any distribution lists in your test topology, check the "Add Distribution List to" option and specify a percentage of all messages that will include distribution lists as message recipients. A high value here will generate substantial traffic, so be sure that your estimation is accurate. Most organizations will have a value well under 10% for this parameter.

Finally, click on the Messages tab to set the average message size used during simulation. Several generic test messages of various sizes are available to choose from, and you may add or remove any or all of them to or from your test, based on your estimation of standard message sizes. Add all message files that represent valid test messages for your Exchange Server by selecting them and clicking on the **Add Files** button, or remove listed files that seem inappropriate by selecting them and clicking on the **Remove** button. For each file selected, you must specify its relative weighting in the simulation with a numerical value. The higher the number entered, the more likely it is to be used. For example, if a message has a weight of 1 and another a weight of 12, then the message weighted at 12 will be used 12 times more often then the message weighted at 1. Be careful not to weight larger messages too highly, as it will greatly affect the load placed on the Exchange Server. Click on the **OK** button to complete the user initialization parameters.

Creating the Public Folder Initialization Profile

The creation of the Public Folder Initialization Profile is very similar to that of the User Initialization Profile, and the method for picking messages on the Pub Fld Msgs tab (Figure 13.3) is identical to that used on the User Profile Initialization Properties page Messages tab.

The method for picking Public Folders to be used for testing is nearly identical to that used in selecting senders on the User Profile Initialization Properties page Senders tab. Just select the server being tested and click on the **ADD ALL** button. The one difference between the User Initialization Profile and Public Folders Initialization Properties configuration is on the Parameters tab.

To set Public Folders Initialization Properties on the Parameters tab, click on the tab and enter in values for the minimum, maximum, and average number of messages to be stored in each test Public Folder as content prior to the simulation. Also specify whether folders should be displayed in the Address Book and what the folder's content age limit might be, if any. When complete, click on the **OK** button to finish the Public Folders Initialization Properties configuration.

276 Load Simulator

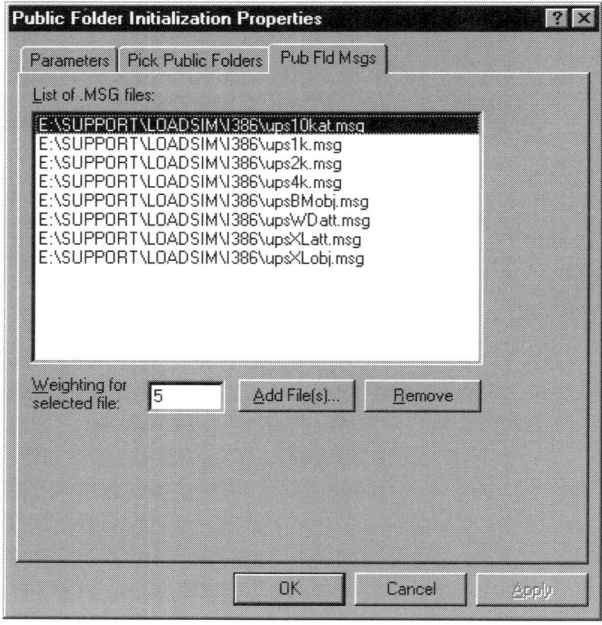

Figure 13.3: Creating the Public Folder Initialization Profile

Setting Load Simulation Parameters

The User Initialization Test and the Public Folder Initialization Test set up mailbox and Public Folder content on the test server before the actual simulation is run. Prior to running the simulation, you will need to use the **TEST...RUN...USERINIT** and **TEST...RUN...PUBLICFOLDERINIT** menu options to prepopulate your test environment. Once this has been done, you may create and run any number of load simulations without repeating these setup tests.

To create a load simulation, use the **TEST…LOAD SIMULATION PARAMETERS** menu option to create a new User Load test. You will be prompted for a name for your first test; go ahead and call it "First Test" (pretty creative name, huh?). You may add additional tests later by clicking on the **New** button on the General tab of the LoadSim User Profile Properties page.

There are twelve separate configuration tabs, allowing you (and requiring you, for the most part) to specify an amazingly detailed variety of parameters for Load Simulation. Remember the garbage in, garbage out principle. Without detailed analysis and planning, the numbers entered in this simulation mean little and will not result in accurate simulation results.

Five of the twelve configuration tabs are identical to those in the user Initialization Profile and Public Folder Initialization Profile Properties pages; you just need to set the same parameters to be specific to the test you are creating. These tabs are as follows:

- Messages
- Pick Senders
- Pick Recipients
- Active Pub Flds
- Pub Fld Msgs

The remaining seven tabs include four very detailed tabs on which you can specify any variation of options for simulation of Public Folder, messaging, and scheduling use. The values on these tabs can be "generally set," however, by specifying the default usage level on the General tab, using the **Low**, **Medium**, or **High** button. The tabs affected by these settings are as follows:

- Read Mail
- Send Mail
- Schedule +
- Public Folders

The three remaining tabs are the General tab, the Logoff tab, and the Test Report tab. As mentioned previously, the General tab contains Low, High, and Medium buttons for setting up the general default values on the Read Mail, Send Mail, Schedule +, and Public Folders tabs. It also has a Task Options listing that will allow you to choose to test (or not test) any combination of sending mail, reading mail, Schedule + use, and Public Folders usage. This latter option is especially useful if you wish to eliminate an item from testing, such as Schedule + or Public Folders use. Just deselect the items in the Task Options listing, and they will not be included in your Load Simulation.

The final option on the General tab is to set the Task Duration—how long the simulation will run. By default this is set for Forever, which will run the load simulation until it is stopped manually. You might choose to specify a fixed amount of hours or a number of cycle iterations as limits to the Task Duration instead. Before specifying a fixed length (or running the simulation at all, for that matter), remember that the load simulation runs real-time against your Exchange Server. It doesn't just run for a few minutes, shut down, and generate a report. It runs forever, constantly simulating normal minute-by-minute load conditions. This means that unless you are troubleshooting a specific time of day, you will want to run your Load Simulation for at least a full day in order to get an accurate picture of load conditions.

Setting Load Simulation Parameters 279

Defining what exactly constitutes a full day is the task of the Logoff tab. By default, the business day is listed as 8 hours. Changing this value dramatically affects the results of the simulation, as all of the message behavior parameters—sending and receiving mail, accessing Public Folders, etc.—are based on occurrences per day. If you make the day shorter, than the server load gets higher as Load Simulator tries to cram all of the messages into the day—even if you reduce the day to 1 hour!

The Logoff tab is also where you configure how the simulated Exchange Clients log on to the network. By default, all clients log on at the beginning of the day and do not log off. This prevents logoff/logon traffic from interfering with the simulation results. Changing this setting is inadvisable, as it will result in logon traffic from the client being displayed in simulation results. This is inappropriate, as the act of logging on 100 or more users is substantially slower on one workstation than on 100 different ones. For this reason, the default setting is configured so that the actual simulation does not begin until all test clients have been logged on. Be prepared for the logon process to take some time, especially on slower test client machines.

Once the parameters have been set, click on the Test Report tab (Figure 13.4) for a final sanity check before running the simulation. The Test Report page will indicate the basic message volume per user for your simulated business day. If these numbers seem abnormally low or high, return to the appropriate properties page and adjust the parameters to more closely reflect your server's traffic.

Once the Test Report looks proper, click on the **OK** button to complete the Load Simulator configuration. You are ready to run the load simulation using the **TEST...RUN...FIRST ONE** menu option (or whatever

280 Load Simulator

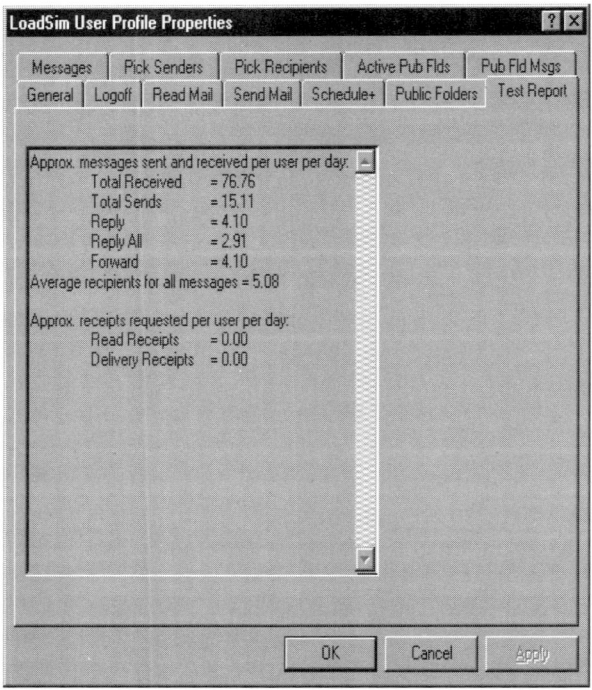

Figure 13.4: The Test Report Tab

you happened to name your first test). The test will begin immediately.

Load Simulator will generate logs and output its console display to a file if you so desire, configurable using the **PREFERENCES** menu option. The best monitor, analysis, and logging service you can use with Load Simulator, however, is the Windows NT Performance Monitor. Run the Performance Monitor on the Exchange Server as the simulation is being run, and save the monitor information to a log for later review. When reviewing the Performance Monitor log data, be sure to set the Time window to begin at the point where all clients were logged in, not just when you started the Load Simulator run. This will ensure that you are measuring only valid simulated messaging activity.

From Here

The load simulation tool we've discussed in this chapter should give you the ability to predict the performance of an Exchange Server accurately prior to its production implementation, as well as serving as a useful tool for troubleshooting and expansion planning. Next we'll take a look at how to customize some of the basic items of Exchange administration to better suit your organization, and later we'll explore the deep integration Exchange has with Windows NT.

Customizing Microsoft Exchange

Now that you have seen how to perform advanced Microsoft Exchange administration and learned how to use the Load Simulator tool for planning and troubleshooting purposes, it might interest you to see how you, as an administrator, can directly alter the way Exchange Server presents information to users logged on with the Exchange Client.

Exchange offers administrators the ability to alter almost all properties pages displayed in the Exchange Address Book, as well as what Custom Attributes are displayed in the Mailbox Properties page.

Modifying Custom Attributes

We've already taken a look at how to modify the labels on every mailbox's Custom Attributes tab for the purposes of configuring imported users and setting up Mailbox import templates. This is the easiest "built-in" way for administrators to add special company-specific information to their Exchange installation.

Microsoft anticipated that administrators would take advantage of the Mailbox Properties pages, accessible to all users just by double-clicking on a name in the Global Address List, to provide detailed information about individual users (Figure 14.1). Doing so allows companies to completely eliminate old paper-bound Company Directo-

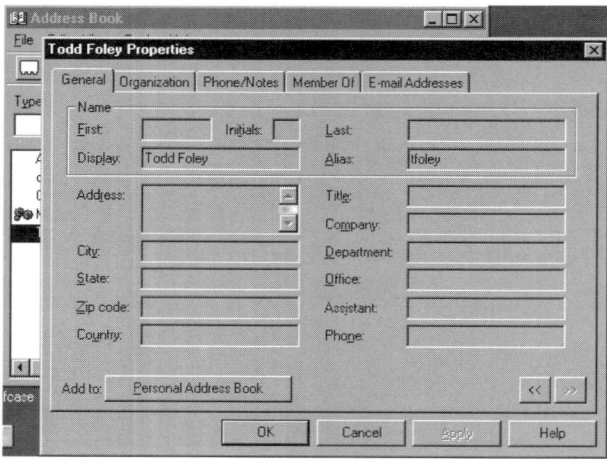

Figure 14.1: Accessing Properties Pages from the Address Book

ries, which quickly become obsolete and require constant updates and redistribution. By maintaining the Company Directory electronically, the information becomes centralized, easy to update, and readily accessible by all. Most important, since everyone already has Exchange running on the desktop, it becomes more convenient as well. Psychologically, accessing a Company Directory to locate a phone extension for an individual may well result in greater messaging use—why call if you've already got an e-mail address ready to be used with the click of a button?

Realizing this functionality would be important to administrators, Microsoft created very detailed Properties pages for each mailbox, structured so that any information that was currently entered into even the most detailed Company Directory could be included. It even created an extra ten Custom Attributes fields to serve as a catch all for unusual entry needs. These ten Custom Attributes can be used for any extra information that does not fit the predefined fields on the properties pages. Their labels are, by default, "Custom Attribute 1," Custom Attribute 2," etc. As we've seen earlier, changing these labels is quite simple. The Properties page of the DS Site Configuration object (found within the Exchange Site's Configuration container in the Administrator program) contains a Custom Attributes tab of its own. On this tab you can just type in whatever label you would like each of the ten fields to have. If, for example, you wished to provide a field for each mailbox user's shoe size, you could change the "Custom Attribute 1" label to "Shoe Size" in the DS Site Configuration properties, and every user would then have a "Shoe Size" field appear on the Custom Attributes tab of their individual mailbox's Properties page. The actual shoe size can then be entered directly, or a custom application could be used to import large blocks of records.

Modifying Details Templates

What if you don't want to use all of the fields Microsoft has predefined on their Properties pages? What if you want to add a field someplace besides the Custom Attributes page? The ability to do so is provided in the Administrator program through use of Details Templates. Exchange builds Properties pages for several Address Book objects from special *Details Templates*, which are special Exchange Form display scripts. These templates are found within the appropriate language subdirectory (e.g., English/USA) of the Details Templates object in the Addressing container of the Site's Configuration container (Figure 14.2). The location in directory path notation would be:

```
ORGANIZATION\SITE\CONFIGURATION\ADDRESSING\
DETAILS TEMPLATES\ENGLISH
```

The templates are pretty deep within the directory structure, but well worth hunting for.

The Mailbox Template

Several Details Templates, each representing a different Address Book object, exist. The Mailbox Template is the template used to generate an individual user's Mailbox Properties pages. To edit the template and add or delete fields, double-click on the Mailbox item in the English/USA (or other language) container. The General tab con-

Modifying Details Templates 287

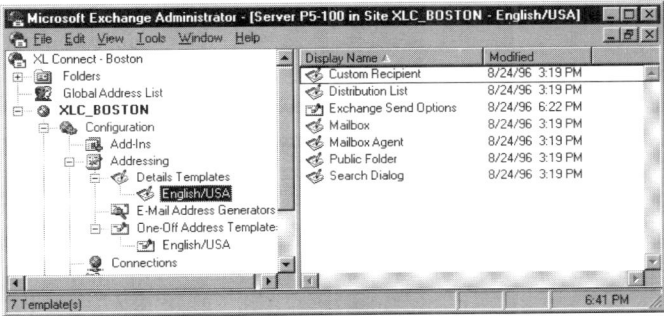

Figure 14.2: Modifying the Details Templates from the Administrator Program

tains no immediately useful properties for customization, but it does have a Template Help frame that will allow you to import an entirely new help file (in Windows Help File *.HLP 16-bit or 32-bit format) if you wish to rewrite the online help users receive from their Mailbox Properties pages. For quicker methods of customization, click on one of the Templates tabs.

There are actually two separate templates for every object—one for MS DOS–based clients and one for all other clients. The methods for altering either template are identical, and we'll review the Templates tab modifications rather than the MS-DOS Templates tab modifications, but bear in mind that templates for DOS-based clients must be edited separately.

When you click on the Templates tab, you will see the scripting information for each field visible on the Mailbox Properties page (Figure 14.3). Your first reaction will probably be "huh?" because this scripting is probably the least intuitive aspect of Exchange. The Templates tab consists of a Controls Properties text box with six columns. Each

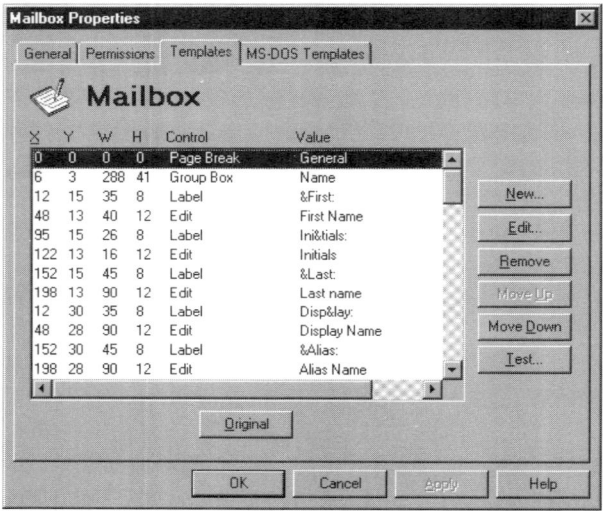

Figure 14.3: Editing the Mailbox Template

column contains a value that defines one of the following properties for the listed control:

1. **X**   The X coordinate (how far from the left side of the Properties page the control is)
2. **Y**   The Y coordinate (how far below the top of the Properties page the control is)
3. **W**   The width of the control
4. **H**   The height of the control
5. **Control**   The type of control
6. **Value**   The default text for a label or the database field for the control, depending on the control type

The control in question could be a label for another field, in which case the Value would represent the text of that label (e.g., the word "Name:"). The control might also be an entry or selection field, in which case it must be associated

Modifying Details Templates   289

with an available field in the Exchange database. The Value in this case would be the name of the database field being used to store the information. This association with existing database fields means that when creating new controls, you should associate the control with an unused database field, i.e., remove or edit an existing field such as "Custom Attribute 10" in order to make one available. The available control types, and a description of each, are as follows:

Control Type	Description
Label	A simple text label for another control or other text appearing on the tab.
Edit	A text entry field allowing data to be typed in.
Page Break	Creates a whole new tab upon which new controls can be placed.
Group Box	Creates an outlined box; can be used to group related controls visually. Has only cosmetic value.
Check Box	Creates a check box; to allow entry of yes/no or off/on settings for different options.
List Box	Creates a list box for selection of available options.
Multivalued List Box	Creates a list box with scroll bars for multiple simultaneous selection of available options.
Multivalued Drop Down	Creates a list box with a drop-down arrow for multiple simultaneous selection of available options.

Once you've created or edited a control (and the label for it as well), click on the **Test** button for a quick check of your craftsmanship. You may edit and re-edit controls without risk, since changes are not committed until you hit the **OK** or **Apply** button. If you are editing the default values, and not a custom template you've previously created, the **Original** button can be useful, restoring all settings to their installation defaults.

Once you've created a different-looking Properties page for the mailbox, any user can open the Address Book from the Exchange Client and see and use the production changes. If you open the Properties page of that mailbox in the Administrator program (from one of the Recipients containers), however, it will look like nothing has changed—the Details Templates affect only the way the information is viewed by the client. This means that it is possible to maintain information in the Mailbox Properties pages (such as home phone number or pager number) that is not visible from the Global Address List. To arrange to hide information, simply remove the field you wish to hide from the Details Template for that object.

The same procedure used to alter the Mailbox Details Template can be used on the other Details Templates as well, which include the Properties pages for distribution lists, Custom Recipients, even the search form used within the Global Address List. With a little bit of trial and error in Details Template modification, you can customize Microsoft Exchange to look as if it was written just for your company.

One-Off Address Templates

One-Off Address Templates are used to generate the forms Exchange Client users see when creating a "one-off," or

One-Off Address Templates 291

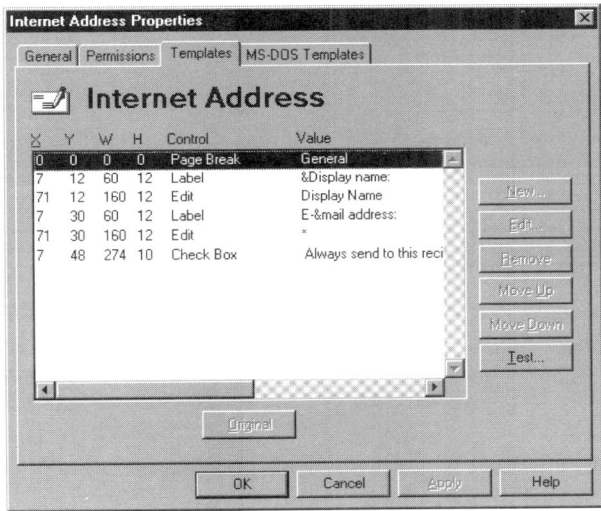

Figure 14.4: The Internet Address One-Off Template

manually entered address. To create such an address, and either address a one-time use message (hence the name) or store it in the user's Personal Address Book, the user creating the address must know the Address Type (e.g., Internet, MS Mail) and enter the address manually. The forms used to enter these addresses manually are not customizable through modification of the One-Off Address Templates. However, these templates are displayed just like Details Templates (pretty confusing—they look like they can be modified, but no dice!). They are located in the Administrator program directory structure within the appropriate language subdirectory (e.g., English/USA) of the One-Off Address Templates object in the Addressing container of the site's Configuration container. The location in directory path notation would be

```
ORGANIZATION\SITE\CONFIGURATION\ADDRESSING\
ONE OFF ADDRESS TEMPLATES\ENGLISH
```

The default One-Off Address Templates are very Spartan in presentation. The Internet Address One-Off template has only two fields. One field is for the display name to be used in the Address Book, and the other is for the e-mail address itself. It would be useful in most organizations to add some online help instructions for Exchange users on how to address Internet mail and enter those addresses in the Address Book, but it can't be done through the template. Instead, click on the General tab on the One-Off Address Template's Properties page to access the one item you can change—the online help.

Each One-Off Address Template (and Details Template as well) has its own Windows Help File (*HLP) format online help file. This file is automatically copied upon client request (hitting the **Help** button) from the server to the client machine's TEMP Directory. You may use any of the help-file authoring tools available on the market today to write your own help file, in either 16-bit or 32-bit format, and import it. You need to import a new help file twice— once for the 16-bit clients and once for the 32-bit clients.

When you import a new help file, you completely overwrite the help file used originally by Microsoft Exchange. Prior to doing so, you may wish to log on to Exchange using the Exchange Client and access the help file for One-Off Address creation. You may then copy the help file and use it to reimport the default settings later on. Once the new help file is imported, click on the **OK** button to finalize the change, and clients will download the new file from then on.

From Here

You've now seen some of the esoteric features of Exchange—Details Templates, online help file customization routines, even how to make everyone's mailbox properties pages have a "Favorite Cheese" Custom Attribute. Next we'll look at implementing Key Management Server to provide digital signatures and encryption for Exchange messages, and then on to our last chapter—Exchange's integration with Windows NT components.

Key Management Server: Digital Encryption Security

Microsoft Exchange comes with a sophisticated message encryption and digital signature system that can protect the integrity of all Exchange messages (Figure 15.1). This system, called Key Management Server, installs on an existing Exchange Server and runs as an NT Service (the Microsoft Exchange Key Manager). The Key Management Server uses public/private key technology and any of three administratively chosen top security algorithms, including DES.

Of course, tighter security comes not without a price. With Key Management Server that price is increased administration and increased hardware costs. The hardware cost increase comes from the overhead of running Key Management Server on a dedicated Exchange Server. Simply, for

296 Key Management Server

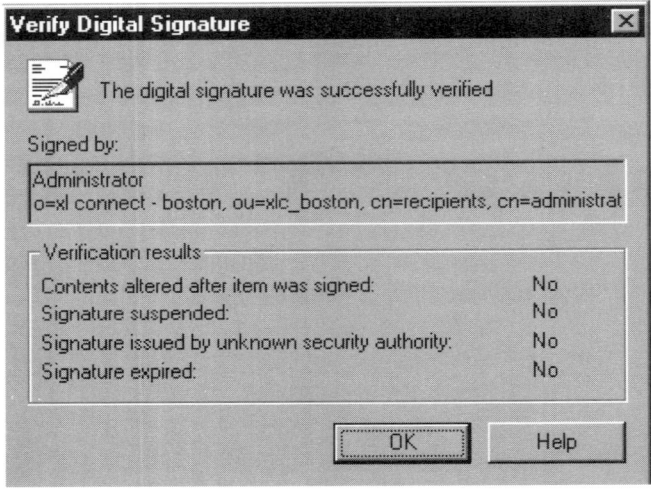

Figure 15.1: Verifying a Digital Signature

all but the smallest Exchange sites, a dedicated machine should be used for the Key Management Server—i.e., it should have no user mailboxes or Public Information Store. This is because only a single Key Management Server is used per site; this increases traffic to the Key Management Server because all users will need to access it every time they send or receive an encrypted message. Also, the Microsoft Exchange Key Manager Service itself consumes a fair amount of system resources and requires a properly configured machine for smooth operation.

The increased administrative cost is another issue to consider when deciding whether or not to implement Key Management Server. Administrators must input a startup parameter password, directly in the Control Panel or through use of a key disk, every time the service is started.

Each Exchange client mailbox must be enabled for security on the server, a temporary security token manually transmitted to each user, and then each client mailbox must be configured from the Exchange Client—and the process must be repeated when the security password is lost or forgotten. Let's not forget the actual client "administration" as well—each user must be responsible for encrypting messages when needed, or else encrypt all messages by default, and receive error messages when recipients are not security enabled. They must also enter a security password every time they send or receive an encrypted message, although they can set it so that they need do so only once for each time logged into Exchange.

Key Management Server is a sophisticated message encryption system—but it will probably not make sense to install it unless your site deals frequently with highly secure data or is backboning site connections over the Internet. In either case, the Exchange users who are enabled for security functions should be limited in order to minimize administrative tasks associated with Key Management Server operation.

Server Location and Hardware Configuration

You will want to choose high-quality hardware for your Key Management Server to ensure smooth operation for all members of your site. The requirements for Key Management Server hardware are the same as the requirements for Exchange—just don't try to "get away with" running Key

Management Server on the same machine used to host hundreds of mailboxes or a frequently accessed Public Information Store.

Don't think of Key Management Server as just an application, either. It uses an encrypted version of the Exchange database to store keys and certificates and runs as an NT Service while integrating with every Exchange Server in your site. Memory and disk access are still crucially important for performance, and the performance of the Key Management Server can affect the performance of every client in the site.

When choosing your hardware, give equal thought to the machine's location. Due to the nature of the Key Management Server's functionality, it would be wise to keep the machine under lock and key, or at least away from nonauthorized access. Remember that a master password must be used to start the service, entered directly or by use of a diskette. You will want to keep prying eyes away from the server, and take into account ventilation needs and media storage security as well. You want the box to be secure, but don't put the machine in a closet where it will overheat. Also, make certain you have a solution for secure media storage—the password diskette as well as full backup tapes of the Key Management Server should be kept safely away from other media.

Server Software Installation

By default, the Key Management Server is not installed along with the other Exchange Server files. It is, however,

Server Software Installation 299

easily found on the Exchange Server Installation CD in the SETUPI386EXCHKM directory (substitute "ALPHA" or "MIPS" for "I386" if using a non-Intel platform). Running the SETUP.EXE program in that directory will launch the Key Management Server Setup program (Figure 15.2). Key Management Server will not install unless the Exchange Server is running, so make certain that the Microsoft Exchange Directory Service is operating before beginning setup.

The setup program will ask you for a directory in which to install Key Management Server. Unlike the main Exchange Services, the Exchange Optimizer will not relocate Key Management Server database files for best performance, so be sure to install the Key Management Server on a fast drive with ample room for its database to grow.

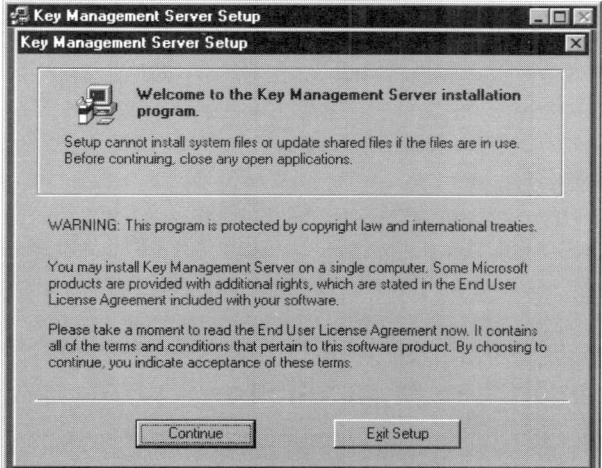

Figure 15.2: Key Management Server Setup

Once you have selected the install directory location, you will be presented with your choice of installation mode. Your choice is Typical mode or Typical mode (there are no other choices). Click on the **Typical** button to continue. You will next be prompted for the Service Account information. Enter the same Domain Administrator Service Account you created for your Exchange installation, and click on the **OK** button to continue.

The final step is to choose your country (it will use a simpler security algorithm due to export restrictions if being installed outside the United States), and then select whether or not to create a Key Management Server startup floppy disk. The disk creation option is checked by default—do not disable it unless you have a pen and pencil handy to write the startup password down, and you want to have to enter it by hand every time the service is started. Choose your country and click on the **OK** button to continue. You will be prompted for a blank formatted floppy on which the service startup password file will be created. After the disk is written, the software setup is complete. It's now time to configure the Key Management Server using the Administrator program.

Key Management Server creates two objects in the site's Configuration container—the CA object and the Encryption object. The CA (Certification Authority) object has no useful configurable properties and is present to provide a directory location that other servers can identify. If you install other Key Management Servers in different sites within your organization, as long as the CA object of the initial installation is visible from the site you're installing to (using the Administrator program to view it), then the new installation will recognize that a Key Management Server already exists and integrate with it.

The Encryption object's Properties page is where you can modify your encryption algorithm and add Security Administrators. To alter either, double-click on the Encryption object and click on the Security tab. The default security algorithm for the United States is CAST-64, but DES is available as well. You might also choose the non-U.S. default, CAST-40, if you were in an export-restricted country.

To add Security Administrators, click on the **Key Management Server Administrators** button (it's a big button). You will be prompted for a password. The default password is the word "password"—all lowercase. Type it in and also select the "Remember password for up to 5 minutes" option so you don't have to constantly re-enter it. Clicking on the **OK** button will open the Key Server Administrators window, which will allow you to add administrators from the Global Address List, assign them passwords, remove administrators, or change your own password. The default password for every administrator, until they log on and change it, is the word "password." Once you have completed adding people to the list of Security Administrators, click on the **OK** button to complete the update. All that remains is to set some recipients up for security.

Mailbox Security Properties

To enable an Exchange user to encrypt messages and use digital signatures, you must now alter their mailbox properties using the Administrator program, and then have them enable security on their client software. To define their mailbox security properties, use the Administrator program to locate the user's mailbox, double-click on the mailbox to open the Properties page for that mailbox, and then click on the Security tab (Figure 15.3).

The Security tab will initially have one enabled button, the **Enable Advanced Security** button. Click it to enable security for the user and generate a pop-up window with the new "temporary token" for that user. This token is a one-time password that the user must know in order to configure his or her client software to use Key Management Server. You must write down the token (it's supposed to be secure, so an automatic e-mail message wasn't generated) and then hand it to the user or call the

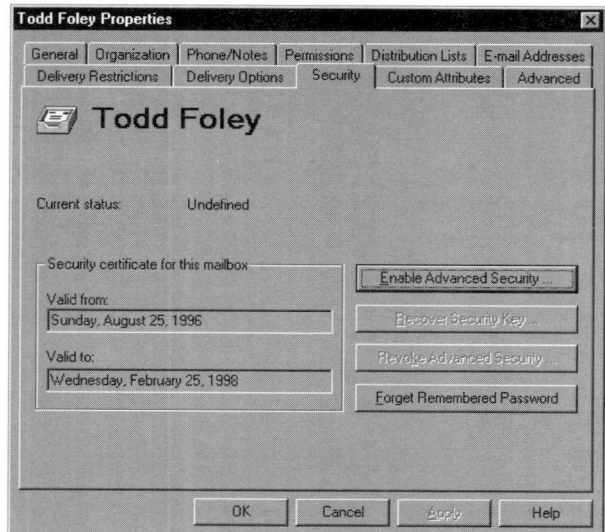

Figure 15.3: Mailbox Security Properties

user with the information. The user can then configure his or her client software to use Key Management Server.

Client Configuration

To enable Key Management Server from the client, have the user log on to Exchange and use the **TOOLS...OPTIONS** menu item to open the Options window. Click on the Security tab and then the **Set Up Advanced Security** button to start the process. The Setup Advanced Security window (Figure 15.4) will open,

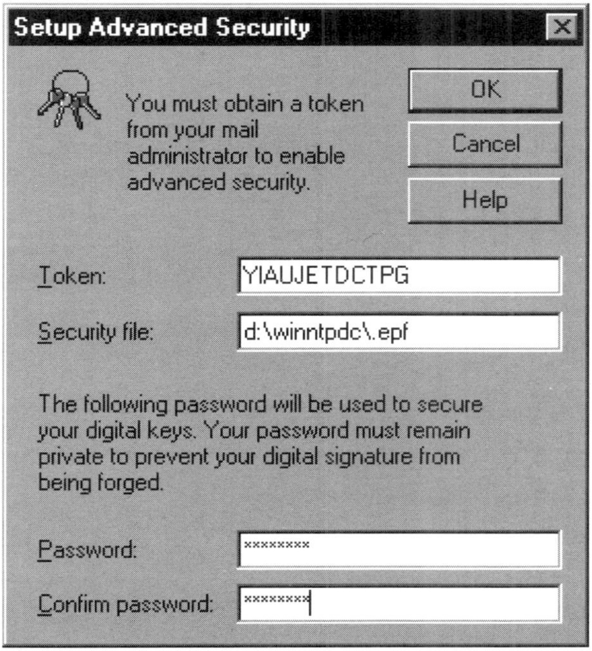

Figure 15.4: Client Configuration

prompting the user for the temporary token as well as a new password to be used whenever they use encryption. Once the information has been entered, clicking the **OK** button will send it via (encrypted) e-mail to the Key Management Server, which will reply within a minute or two with a pop-up message requiring an additional confirmation of the new password. While waiting, you could set the default message to be encrypted and use a digital signature, or you could hit the **OK** button on the Setup Advanced Security window and exit. The use of digital signatures and message encryption can be toggled from the Security tab of each new message's Properties page (accessed using the **FILE...PROPERTIES** menu option when composing a message).

When the confirmation message from the Key Management Server arrives, users will be required to re-enter the new password they selected for confirmation. This password is written to a local *.EFP file on the user's hard drive after receiving server confirmation. After it is accepted, users are security enabled and may encrypt messages and use and verify digital signatures to their heart's content—provided the recipients of their messages are also security enabled.

Using the Bulk Security Token Generator

Generating temporary tokens one by one for every user in an organization can be a mind-numbing process. To help alleviate this burden, Microsoft provides a utility that does

Using the Bulk Security Token Generator 305

bulk generation of tokens. This utility will enable security for recipient mailboxes and write out tokens for each mailbox to an SRESULTS.TXT file in the SECURITYBIN directory with the Key Management Server Executables.

To run this utility and create the SRESULTS.TXT file full of tokens (which you should still hand out directly to the user), run the SIMPORT.EXE file, also located in the SECURITYBIN directory, from a command line (Figure 15.5). You will be prompted for the following information:

- The name of the Exchange site
- The name of the home Exchange Server for the mailboxes for which you're generating tokens
- The Key Management Server administrator's password (your password, not the service boot code)
- The server name of the Key Management Server

Once the final information is entered, the utility will enable security for all mailboxes on that server and will write the generated tokens out to the SRESULTS.TXT file. Sure beats enabling Advanced Security on hundreds of Properties pages!

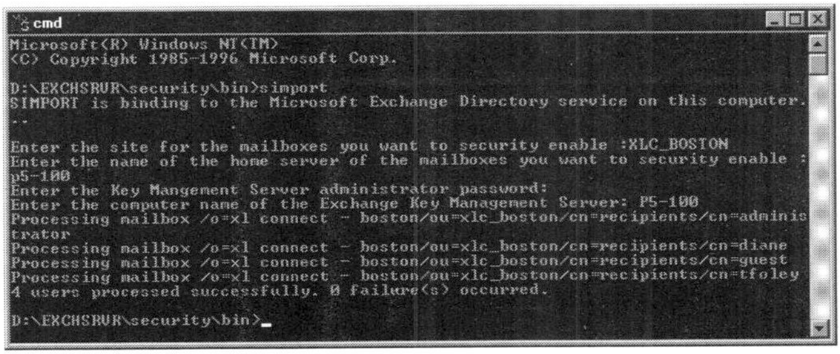

Figure 15.5: Running the SIMPORT.EXE Utility

From Here

You've seen all that Exchange has to offer on its own—next we'll look at what Exchange has to offer with Windows NT. You've seen all of the features of Exchange and most of the tricks to administering it. The final piece of the puzzle (and our last chapter) deals with how to take advantage of Exchange's special integration with the basic tools of NT administration to better administer Exchange. It's the final piece to becoming an Exchange administration wizard—so hang in there!

Windows NT's Interaction with Exchange

Microsoft Exchange not only runs on Windows NT, it runs with Windows NT. During installation, Microsoft Exchange installs new versions of or modifies the basic applications used in Windows NT Administration: the Control Panel, the User Manager for Domains, NT Backup, NT Performance Monitor, and the Event Viewer. These tools become very powerful ones for use with Exchange—not just with Windows NT. Even if you are very familiar with the basic NT applications, you will find some new and different features created by Exchange.

Services Control Panel

Microsoft Exchange runs as a series of Windows NT services, each of which can be controlled directly from the Windows NT Control Panel's Services window. The fact that Exchange runs as NT services is the basis for its tight integration with NT. Services, as opposed to stand-alone applications, automatically run whenever the system is powered on, even if no user is logged in, and can much more easily write to the Windows NT System Log, as well as interact with all of the other Windows NT tools.

The Control Panel's Services window allows you to check on the current status of all aspects of Exchange operation. It is the first place to look when troubleshooting, since it will tell you at a glance whether or not you are down and, if

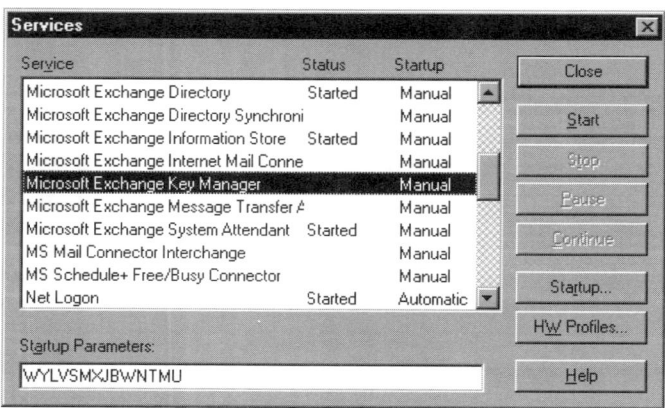

Figure 16.1: Exchange Control Panel Services

so, on what component service. It is also the place to resolve issues. The quickest way to fix most Exchange problems is to stop and restart the affected service.

The Exchange services each can be configured to start automatically upon power-on of the server, or manually when desired (useful for testing new connectors before placing them into production), using the Services Startup window options. It is in this startup window that you can directly edit the UserID and password of the Exchanges Services Account, under which all of the Exchange services run. This is important to remember in the event that the Service Account password ever needs to be changed—besides changing the password itself, each Exchange service must be adjusted in the Services Startup window to reflect the change.

The Control Panel Services window also offers the only method of starting the Key Management Server Service, if used, without having to use a floppy diskette. The password may be entered directly into the System Parameters field of the Services window and the service started without needing the key diskette in the drive.

Sometimes it is necessary to stop all Exchange services without bringing down the NT Server itself. Exchange allows you to quickly stop all Exchange services by simply stopping the System Attendant Service in the Control Panel Services window. Highlight the System Attendant Service, click on the **Stop** button, and all services will be stopped in turn. When restarting services, starting the Microsoft Exchange Information Store first will also automatically start the other two core services, the Microsoft Exchange System Attendant and the Microsoft Exchange Directory; starting any of the installed connectors will also start the Microsoft Exchange Message Transfer Agent.

The Exchange services (if installed) visible in the Services window are as follows:

1. Microsoft Exchange Directory Synchronization
2. MS Schedule+ Free/Busy Connector
3. MS Mail Connector Interchange
4. Microsoft Exchange Internet Mail Connector
5. Microsoft Exchange Message Transfer Agent
6. Microsoft Exchange Key Manager
7. Microsoft Exchange Information Store
8. Microsoft Exchange Directory
9. Microsoft Exchange System Attendant

The Control Panel Services icon provides the most direct way to start and stop the above Exchange component services, as well as acting as the repository for the Service Account information used by Exchange to interact with the NT domain.

Windows NT Backup

Installing Microsoft Exchange actually installs a new version of the normal Windows NT Backup program (Figure 16.2). This version is identical to the normal NT Backup program, except that it is completely integrated with Exchange, allowing for full online backups of the Exchange Server's Information Store and Directory— either locally or over the network.

Using NT Backup to back up Microsoft Exchange files is nearly identical to the process used to back up files and directories normally. The new NT Backup has an additional FILE...MICROSOFT EXCHANGE menu option that will

Windows NT Backup

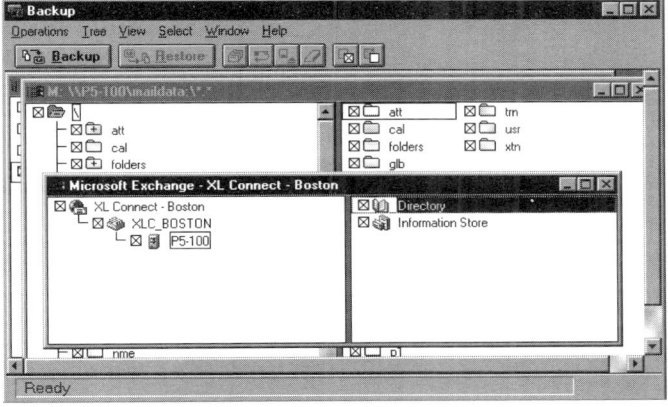

Figure 16.2: Windows NT Backup

allow you to connect to any Exchange Server, start the Information Store or Directory Services if they are down, and then choose the Directory or Information Store for backup. The Directory and Information Store are available for separate backup. This is because it is not as crucial to back up the Directory daily as it is the Information Store, since other servers can restore Directory information through replication.

In addition to backing up the Exchange Information Store and Directory while online, NT Backup can be used to back up all of the Key Management Server data, located in the SECURITYMGRENT directory. This is important because backing up the Information Store does not include Key Management Server data, and loss of that data would result in all encrypted messages becoming unreadable. Of course, NT Backup can still be used to back up system and application files, as well as the Windows NT Registry, in case of catastrophic failure.

NT Backup can be used to make full backups of Exchange data, as well as incremental or differential backups. The ability to make differential or incremental backups is disabled, however, when Microsoft Exchange's Database Circular Logging is enabled on the server being backed up. Simply put, Circular Logging is a setting that allows the Exchange database to overwrite its transaction log files when they reach a certain size (5 MB). This option is enabled by default, since archiving of logs, the alternative to circular logging, quickly chokes disk space unless the old logs are routinely moved to tape. There is no built-in tool or process that removes archived logs from the drive. Unless you are prepared to write one, or to routinely and manually offload old logs, leave Circular Logging enabled and make do with full nightly backups—they are much safer and quicker to restore in any case. If the backup process is too lengthy on your hardware, and you wish to use incremental backups as part of your recovery planning, you may remove Circular Logging from the Information Store or the Directory. This is done within the Administrator program on the Advanced tab of the individual Server's Properties page.

The User Manager for Domains

One of the most productive features of the tight integration of Windows NT and Exchange is the seamless tie-in with the Windows NT User Manager for domains. Whenever a new user is created on the NT domain, an Exchange mailbox can be automatically created. Whenever a user is deleted, the mailbox is deleted as well. In many ways, this integration means that, administratively, an NT domain

The User Manager for Domains 313

user account *is* an Exchange mailbox and vice versa. It represents a marked advantage Exchange has over other messaging systems that require monolithic user databases, resulting in twice the administrative overhead.

You need to configure reciprocal configuration properties in both Microsoft Exchange and the User Manager for domains in order to gain full integration. In the User Manager for domains, use the **EXCHANGE...OPTIONS** menu option to open the Options window (Figure 16.3) that allows you to set the default Exchange Server for new mailbox creation, the default Recipients container (if different from the server Recipients container), as well as

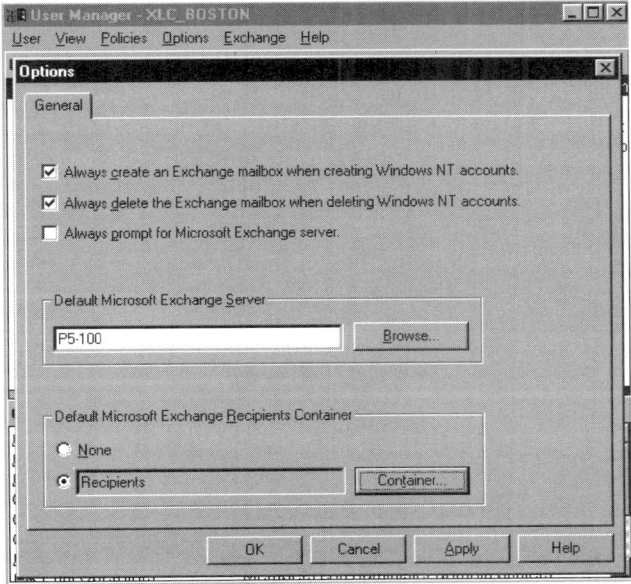

Figure 16.3: Setting Exchange Options in the User Manager

whether or not to automatically create or delete Exchange mailboxes when doing the same to an NT account. For full integration, specify a default Exchange Server and select both the "Always create an Exchange mailbox when creating Windows NT accounts" option, and the "Always delete the Exchange mailbox when deleting Windows NT accounts" option.

To configure integration with the User Manager for domains from the Exchange side of things, launch the Administrator program and use the **TOOLS...OPTIONS** menu option to open the Options window. Click on the Permissions tab to select the default Windows NT domain, as well as selecting whether or not to try to find an NT account when creating a new mailbox or delete an NT account when deleting an Exchange Mailbox. For full integration, select both options and click on the **OK** button to commit the settings.

Once both the Exchange and NT components are integrated, administration can be done simply from either the User Manager for domains or the Exchange Administrator program—and it need be done only once, in either place.

Windows NT Event Viewer

The Windows NT Event Viewer (Figure 16.4) logs all application, system, and security events for Windows NT components and applications. Microsoft Exchange uses the Event Viewer to log all operational events and errors. If the first place to look when troubleshooting is at the

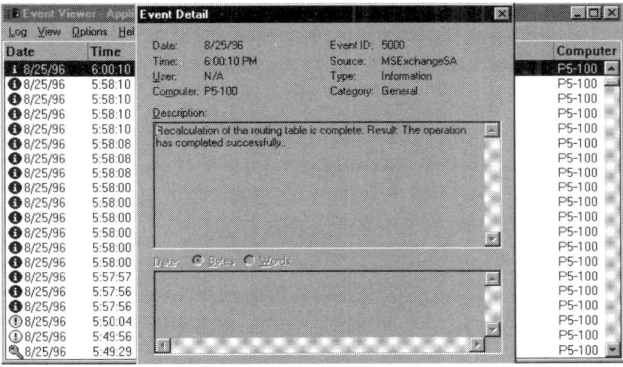

Figure 16.4: The Windows NT Event Viewer

Service window in the Control Panel, the second place is definitely the Event Viewer. Every Exchange Service stoppage, startup, or failure is logged in either the System Log (for failures) or the Application Log (for starts, stops, and errors). In fact, routine monitoring of the Event Viewer is the quickest way to detect potential Exchange problems. Some of the common Exchange Service events visible in the NT Event Viewer are as follows:

Service	Event
Microsoft Exchange Message Transfer Agent	Connecting to another Exchange Server, or failing to do so
Microsoft Exchange System Attendant	Routing table recalculation, succcess or failure
Microsoft Exchange Information Store	Alerts of "orphaned" Public Folders, folders without an owner due to mailbox deletion

Windows NT's Interaction with Exchange

Microsoft Exchange Information Store	Startup of the Public Information Store and successful startup of replication
Microsoft Exchange Directory	Directory import or export using the Administrator program
Key Management Server	Startup and successful Administrator logon

Other Event Viewer events can be generated depending on server conditions, logging levels, and any security audits configured. The large amount of data that Exchange can potentially write to the Event Viewer makes reconfiguring the Event Viewer settings to increase log space or allow overwriting of full logs a good idea. If not set adequately, the Event Viewer logs will fill to their limit and generate persistent pop-up error messages. Use the **LOG...LOG SETTINGS** menu option to allow overwriting of log files when full, or increase their maximum size and reduce their log wrapping interval in order to allow all Exchange event logging to be recorded without saturating the allowable log space.

Windows NT Performance Monitor

The Windows NT Performance Monitor (Figure 16.5) is the most useful monitoring and troubleshooting utility for Windows NT and, once Exchange Server is installed, for Exchange as well. Exchange adds several Exchange-specific objects to the collection of objects that Performance

Windows NT Performance Monitor 317

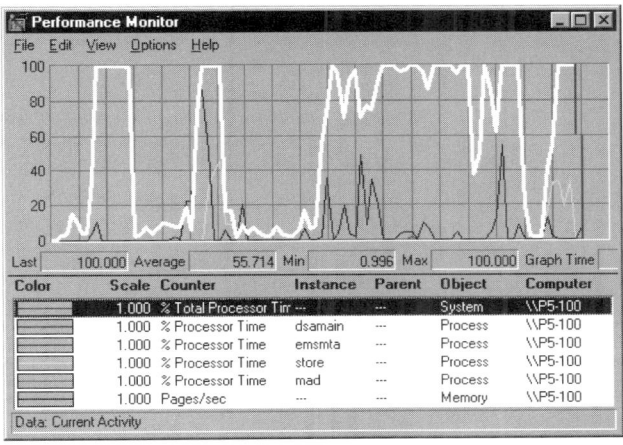

Figure 16.5: Windows NT Performance Monitor

Monitor can use to analyze system performance. It also installs several preconfigured Performance Monitor Charts designed to provide quick Exchange System Information for administrators without having to build Performance Monitor Charts item by item. Descriptions of some of these preconfigured charts' components and functions, any of which can be customized by the administrator, are as follows:

Microsoft Exchange Performance Monitor Templates

Title	Components	Function
Microsoft Exchange Server Health	Total Percent of Processor Time Used, Percent of Processor Time for each core Exchange Service, and Pages/Sec	Checks for processor and memory bottlenecks.

318 Windows NT's Interaction with Exchange

Microsoft Exchange Server History	Exchange Message Counts, Exchange User Count, and Pages/Sec	Checks server traffic and looks for memory bottlenecks. Uses a minute-long refresh rate, hence the "History" title. Good for a quick look at traffic trends over several hours.
Microsoft Exchange Server Load	Replication load, Address Book Access, MTA traffic, RPC calls, Message submit and receive rates, etc.	Monitors the overall activity on the Exchange Server.
Microsoft Exchange Server Queues	MTA Work Queue Length, Send Queue Size and Receive Queue Size for the Public and Private Information Stores	Monitors message flow by checking Queue contents.

The normal uses of the Windows NT Performance Monitor in locating server bottlenecks and monitoring system operation still apply—even more so than usual due to the demands Exchange places upon the server hardware. Be sure to enable physical disk monitoring (an important Exchange item—watch for excessive I/O) by running the **DISKPERF** command with the **-Y E** switches from the command line. If you utilize the Performance Monitor properly, you will be able to detect and resolve Exchange issues before they become serious end-user problems.

In Conclusion

Microsoft Exchange is a complex system that does much more than traditional messaging. It can make complicated groupware interactivity and functionality easy to use for thousands of connected users. Despite tremendous benefits gained from its integration with NT and its GUI-driven administration, its sophistication requires a matching sophistication on the part of Exchange planners and administrators in order to streamline administrative overhead and make Exchange as accessible as possible to end users.

This guide has hopefully helped you to reach the level where you feel comfortable working with Microsoft Exchange. Every effort has been made to anticipate the common, practical issues facing users and administrators in the real world. After you review this guide and become comfortable with its contents, it should serve as a handy reference for all of the changes and modifications that a production Exchange system can undergo as it becomes the messaging backbone of your company or organization.

If you are just about to embark on an Exchange installation—have fun. You are at the cutting edge of group communication and interaction—even if your server's disk drives fail during an Exchange Pilot Program Demonstration. Enjoy!

Index

A

Address Book, 5, 32–33, 65–80
　setting default book used, 113
addressee properties, 8, 33, 70–72
addressing, 65–80
　default Site addresses, 223–224
　on New Message form, 30
　to multiple recipients, 31
Administrative Monitors, 259–263
alignment of text, 45
Associations, 54, 56, 125
attachments, 6
　creating, 52–56
AutoAssistants, 15, 92–99
AutoReply, 99
AutoSignature, 8–9, 60–61

B

BCC: "blind carbon copy" addressing,,57–58, 119
bullets, 46–47

C

CC: "carbon copy" addressing, 14, 30–31, 57–58
CD–ROM, 175
centering text, 45
Check Names feature, 30
checking spelling, 58–59, 114
Client Installation Point, 203
client/server, 158
color of text, 47, 109–110
columns, 87–88

copying
 drag & drop, 51
cursor, 30
custom addresses, 75–76
Custom Attributes, 216–217, 284–286
custom recipients, 69–70
customizing
 changing Viewer defaults 108–120

D

default values
 changing Viewer defaults, 48, 108–120
Delegate Access, 16, 100–104
Deleted Items folder, 9, 113
delivery receipts, 111
deleting
 messages, 40–41
 text, 52
Details Templates, 286–290
dialog boxes, 24
directory objects, 212
Directory Service, 160
 checking consistency, 257
Directory Service Site Configuration, 215–217
 custom attributes, 217
Directory Synchronization Service, 162
distribution lists, 3, 69, 76, 186
drag & drop, 51
 copying, 51
 programming, 142–145

E

EDBUTIL, 254–257
EFD (see Microsoft Exchange Forms Designer)
e-mail, 2
embedding objects, 52–56, 132

Exchange Client, 1–7
 toolbar, 29

F

fault tolerance and redundancy, 170–171
Favorites, 129–130
Filters, 3, 85–86
file associations, 54, 56, 125
Find, 13
 in the Address Book, 33, 67–69
 within a message, 49–50,82–84
folder contents list, 5
Folder Design Cue Cards, 135–137
folder group, 5
folder list, 5
folders
 designing, 134–137
 owners, 133
 posting, 6, 38
 properties, 133
 remote access, 139
fonts
 changing, 44–48, 109–110
formatting text, 44
Forms, 29, 141–156
 fields, 29
 templates, 146–147
Form Template Wizard, 143
forwarding, 39–40

G

garbage collection, 216
GIGO, 267
Global Address List, 8, 66
Global Forms Registry (see Organization Forms Library)
grouping messages, 88–89

H

Help, 24–25

HotKeys, 24

I

importing users, 183
Inbox Assistant, 15, 92–97
indenting, 46
Information Store Service, 160, 167
   configuration, 217–219
   offline maintenance, 254
   maintenance, 252–259
inserting
   objects, 52–56
installing Clients from the Network, 202–205
installation (server), 172–186
   creating the service account, 173
   granting initial permissions, 180
   how to configure disk drives, 166–168
   requirements, 165
   setting up additional servers, 187, 193–194
   setting up the server administrator's group, 174
Internet
   addressing messages, 75–78
   audio and video clips, 56
   default Site SMTP address, 224
   shortcuts to Web pages, 133
   URLs, 133
Internet Mail Connector, 161, 242–249
ISDN, 197
italics, 44

K

Key Management Server, 162, 295–305
   Bulk Token Generator, 304
   client configuration, 303
   digital encryption, 300
   digital signatures, 296
   hardware configuration, 297–298
   installation, 298–300
   server location, 298
keywords, 128

L

laptop use (*see* remote access)
Link Monitor, 259–261
links
   folders, 130
   inserting, 55
Load Simulator, 265–281
   distribution lists, 270
   test topology, 268–269
   user initialization, 272–275

M

Macintosh addresses, 75
mail alerts, 112
mailbox, 9, 66
   adding folders, 104–105
   creating, 183
   granting multiple access, 17
   importing, 183
   moving to another server, 191
   permissions, 101–102
   security and key management, 301–302
   setting properties on Server, 228–230
   subfolders, 9
mailing lists (*see* distribution lists)
message
   creation, 28
   deleting, 40
   forwarding, 39
   grouping, 88–89
   headers, 18
   importance, 63, 90
   printing, 40
   properties, 63
   reading, 35–36
   receipts, 111

replying, 37–38
saving, 34, 61–63
sending, 34
sorting, 86–87
templates, 62
tracking, 220–221
message priority, 6
Message Transfer Agent Service, 161, 221–223
messaging backbone, 3
Microsoft Exchange
   Administrator Program, 181, 211–232
   definition, 1
   Forms Designer, 141–156
   hierarchy, 162–163
   Load Simulator, 265–281
   Migration Wizard, 207–208
   NT Services 160–162
   Performance Optimizer, 163, 166, 178–179
   planning, 187–191
   RPC Ping utility, 214–215
   Server distribution, 190–191
   Services, 138
   setting up the first Server, 162–185
   Setup Editor, 205
   starting the Client, 18–21
Microsoft Mail
   Addresses, 75, 223
Microsoft Mail Connector, 161, 236–240
Microsoft Visual Basic, 155
migrating from other systems, 207–209
mirroring, 171
MTA Transport Stack, 199

N

network logon, 19
NetWare, 206–207
NT (*see* Windows NT)

O

offline access (*see* remote access)
Offline Address Book 183–185, 216
One-off Address Templates, 290
Organization Forms Library, 153–155, 185
Out of Office Assistant, 16, 97–99
Outbox, 9

P

page faults, 164
paging files, 167
Personal Address Book, 8, 72–79
personal distribution list, 76
Personal Folders, 12–13, 137–140
   remote access, 139
   saving, 137
polling, 158
posting, 122
printing, 40
Private Information Store, 191
Profiles, 19
   using from multiple computers, 20
program groups, 23
Public Folders ,11–12, 17, 121–137
   affinity, 192
   applications, 122
   in the Global Address List, 70
   navigation, 123–125
   posting, 122, 125–126
   replying, 127
   restricting access, 12, 219
   using for memos, 11
Public Information Store, 191, 226–228

R

RAS transport stack, 197
read receipts, 112
receipts, 111–112
remote access, 12, 18

Index   325

to folders, 139
replacing text, 50
Reply options, 37–38, 127–128
Rich Text Format, 44, 62
Roles, 100, 181
Rules, 16, 83–84, 94–96

S

Sample Applications, 148–151
saving
   messages as templates, 62
Schedule + Free/Busy Connector, 161
screen elements, 119
searching (see Find)
secretary access (see Delegate Access)
Send on Behalf of Permission, 16, 102–103
Sent Items folder, 9
server hardware configuration 164–170
Server Monitor, 261–263
services, 138
Setup
   Exchange Client, 20
sharing information, 17, 125–126
shortcuts, 131
Sites, 163
   creating a Site , 177, 193
   joining a Site, 177, 193
   required connectivity, 163
   setting up additional Sites, 194–201
Site Connectors, 194–201
   dynamic RAS connector, 196–198
   RPC support, 195
   target servers, 195
   WAN connectivity, 196
   X.400, 198–202
SMTP (see Internet), 76–77
sorting messages 86–87
spelling, 58–59, 114
storage limits, 219
subfolders, 105, 124
synchronization, 139

System Attendant Service, 160

T

TCP/IP, 242–249
telephone message form, 151–153
thrashing, 164
threading messages, 89
tombstones, 216
toolbars, 38, 115–119
transport (messaging), 3

U

underlining, 45
Undo, 52

V

Viewer, 4–7
Views, 3,14, 90–92
   Personal View, 14, 91
   Folder View, 14, 91

W

Windows, 22–24
Windows NT , 307– 318
   Control Panel, 308
   Event Viewer, 314–316
   NT Backup 310–312
   Performance Monitor, 316–318
   Server service configuration, 171–172
   Service Packs, 175
   services, 160–162
   User Manager, 312–314
workflow processes, 141, 145
WYSIWYG, 40

X

X.400
   Address Space, 196
   addresses, 76
   Connector, 161, 234–236